Storming Little Round Top

Storming Little Round Top

The 15th Alabama and Their Fight for the High Ground, July 2, 1863

Phillip Thomas Tucker

DA CAPO PRESS
A Member of the Perseus Books Group

Published by Da Capo Press
A Member of the Perseus Books Group
http://www.dacapopress.com

Typeset and designed by K & P Publishing

Cataloging-in-Publication data for this book is available from the
Library of Congress.

ISBN 0-306-81146-4

Da Capo Press books are available at special discounts for bulk
purchases in the U.S. by corporations, institutions, and other
organizations. For more information, please contact the Special Markets
Department at the Perseus Books Group, 11 Cambridge Center,
Cambridge, MA 02142, or call (800) 255-1514 or (617) 252-5298, or
e-mail j.mccrary@perseusbooks.com.

First edition, first printing.

1 2 3 4 5 6 7 8 9—05 04 03 02

Printed and Bound in the United States of America.

Contents

Introduction

One of the enduring Gettysburg controversies has been the debate about which Confederates at Gettysburg made the deepest penetration in the Union lines—which Southern troops could rightfully claim to having reached the "High Water Mark of the Confederacy." Many believe the rightful claim belongs not to the men of Pickett's Charge but to the men of the 15th Alabama, since, in the words of Colonel Strong Vincent, for the Army of the Potomac to "lose Round Top would [have been] fatal."

And in striking contrast to the doomed and ill-fated Pickett's Charge, the offensive effort of Colonel Oates's 15th Alabama up the southern and eastern slopes of Little Round Top to turn the left flank of the Army of the Potomac had a better chance for success. The 15th Alabama's story at Little Round Top involves one of the great lost opportunities of the war for if they had been properly supported and reinforced, Colonel Oates's offensive effort might well have achieved a decisive Southern victory at Gettysburg.

Thus, one of the best remaining untold stories of the Civil War is the forgotten struggle for Little Round Top from the 15th Alabama's perspective. This negligence of the 15th Alabama's story is especially ironic as the tenacious struggle which raged for hours between the 15th Alabama and the 20th Maine was possibly the most important and recently most publicized small-unit action of the Civil War.

Ironically much like the fate of the performance of the 83rd Pennsylvania Volunteer Infantry which fought next to the 20th Maine, the distinguished role that the 15th Alabama played during the bitter struggle for possession of Little Round Top has been minimized by generations of historians, while the 20th Maine's role has been magnified and embellished to reach legendary if not mythological proportions. The glorification and romanticization of the story of Little Round Top from the Union perspective represents one of the best examples of what results when history is rewritten after the war by the winners.

Striking the vulnerable left flank of the Army of the Potomac at a key moment, a few hundred Alabama Rebels suddenly found themselves poised on the threshold of achieving significant gains for the Confederacy. Indeed, Colonel Oates's Alabamians not only briefly turned the Union army's left flank but also threatened the Army of the Potomac's vulnerable rear. There, the ammunition, ordnance, and supply train of the Army of the Potomac stood for the taking.

However, neither a stately monument or memorial dedicated to either the 15th Alabama or Colonel Oates can be found today at Gettysburg. This glaring absence of recognition for the Alabamians's distinguished role is most ironic, especially on the most generously monument-covered battlefield in the nation. In popular films and paintings that focus on the struggle for Little Round Top, Colonel Oates and his Alabama soldiers serve as little more than bit players. Even in books that analyze Gettysburg and the fight for Little Round Top, the Alabamians serve as backdrops with obscure, shadowy support roles for Union heroics—anonymous and forgotten.

With the resurgence of interest during the early 1990s, Civil War historiography has finally shifted toward taking a closer look at what exactly happened at Little Round Top on July 2, 1863. But ironically this new emphasis on the importance of the struggle there has again not focused on the Alabamians's role. Instead, these elite Alabama soldiers have become modern-day casualties—literally "missing in action." Colonel Oates and his Alabama

Rebels remain men without faces, motivations, and identities. Sadly, in this instance Americans could learn more valuable lessons from defeat rather than victory.

Even during the war years, the 15th Alabama received little recognition in relation to its key role at Gettysburg. Along with his men Colonel Oates gained neither the promotion nor fame he deserved for his losing but valiant effort, though in truth, Colonel Oates and his soldiers fought harder, longer, and against greater odds than the 20th Maine on July 2, 1863.

Such historical regression based on romanticism and glorification and the evolution of fact to fiction first began with the extensive postwar writings of Colonel Chamberlain himself. As explained by Civil War historian William C. Davis in early 1998, Chamberlain's "own stirring memoirs always made him a favorite with longtime scholars and buffs [and he has become] so glorified . . . that a backlash has already started, with less flattering sides of his personality and character being emphasized now in order to leaven the portrait of a man who was still, by any measure, remarkable."

The enduring and growing historical legacy established by the skilled pen of Chamberlain was destined to be even further embellished by modern scholars. Consequently, Chamberlain's version of what happened at Little Round Top has been accepted as fact. The reality that Chamberlain's own versions of Gettysburg were self-serving and exaggerated has been conveniently overlooked and ignored by most of today's historians.

Not the least of the Little Round Top fictions was that the 20th Maine faced odds of ten to one. In reality, it was the Alabama soldiers who were outnumbered on July 2. The story that Colonel Chamberlain led his regiment to victory with a brilliant, innovative, and preconceived plan of action—the famous wheeling movement by the left half of the 20th Maine rolling down Little Round Top to align with the regiment's right half—is, in fact, also popular fiction. Indeed, the 20th Maine's surge downhill was a spontaneous advance to regain lost ground and recover wounded which turned into a general attack only *after* the 15th Alabama had been ordered by Colonel Oates to withdraw because of heavy losses and lack of support and ammunition.

On July 2 the 15th Alabama soldiers actually out-performed the 20th Maine—marched farther to reach Gettysburg; fought longer against the odds; encountered rougher terrain during a more lengthy advance; fought on their own longer without support, assistance, or specific orders; exhibited more command initiative; suffered heavier losses; and faced greater obstacles for a longer period and more often and with less chances for success.

The dramatic showdown between the 15th Alabama and the 20th Maine on that bloody afternoon in Adams County, Pennsylvania, was the second fight of the day for Colonel Oates's Alabamians. The 15th Alabama's earlier fight at the base of Big Round Top plays an important role in understanding the later battle and in determining the final outcome of the struggle for possession of Little Round Top. During this contest with Colonel Hiram Berdan's 2nd United States Sharpshooters, a number of key Alabama soldiers, both officers and enlisted men, were lost—long before Colonel Oates and his regiment reached Little Round Top and met the 20th Maine. In contrast, the 20th Maine only fought one battle at Gettysburg on the bloody second day.

But worst of all for the Alabama Rebels, the struggle for possession of Little Round Top was a Fredericksburg in reverse. On July 2, Colonel Oates and his soldiers repeatedly charged an impregnable defensive position which was all but impossible to capture: a formidable high-ground position manned by hardened and relatively fresh veterans who fought from behind rocks, logs, and trees—a naturally fortified line on dominant terrain—with modern weaponry and the added psychological factor of defending Northern soil.

General Lee's adjutant, Colonel Walter Herron Taylor, penned without exaggeration in a letter immediately after the battle how the Army of the Potomac's left flank was "protected by two insurmountable, impracticable rocky mountains. It was out of the question to turn them. We reached the very base of the stronghold only to find almost perpendicular walls of rock [and] there was no opportunity whatever for a successful flank movement . . ." But despite facing this formidable objective in assaulting a high-ground defensive position held by veterans, Colonel Oates's Alabamians did succeed in briefly turning Chamberlain's left flank at the zenith of their bloody attack. If support and reinforcements had been forthcoming, then the 15th Alabama's gains could have been exploited to perhaps achieve a decisive success.

But fixated with the romance and glamour of Pickett's Charge, both the public and historians quickly forgot the Alabamians's role on Little Round Top in the years immediately following the battle. An increasingly angry and frustrated Oates made a determined attempt to have a 15th Alabama monument placed on Little Round Top beyond the present-day designated lines of the 20th Maine, where his regiment fought. But like the futile effort to win the Confederacy's independence decades earlier, Colonel Oates's dream would never be realized. As on July 2 on Little Round Top, Colonel Oates lost his battle for the second time after the war.

But like the 20th Maine's performance at Little Round Top, Colonel Oates and his Alabama soldiers' role was also most distinguished. Colonel Oates's five assaults against a heavily defended high-ground position against the odds—the forgotten story of the 15th Alabama's achievements on July 2—needs to be told in detail for the first time.

CHAPTER I

Rallying of the 15th Alabama

" . . . I don't believe that a better army ever trod the earth than the one which followed General Lee to Gettysburg. . . It was certainly the grandest army, although they were poorly clad and provisions scarce. Still they had a courage, determination and patriotism that is a credit to the whole of the American people . . ."

—soldier in the 15th Alabama

With high hopes and soaring ambitions during the summer of 1863, General Robert E. Lee led his three corps of almost forty battle-hardened brigades of the Army of Northern Virginia north toward Pennsylvania with the confidence that another Chancellorsville-like victory lay north of the Potomac. This was the Confederate army's first invasion of the North after its ill-fated thrust into Maryland during the late summer and fall of 1862. General Lee's invasion of Pennsylvania would be the last such bid to win a decisive victory north of the Mason-Dixon Line during the war. Lee was determined to exploit his Virginia victories and win greater successes, such as capturing Harrisburg and Philadelphia in the Keystone State and then perhaps even Washington, D.C.

A host of tactical, logistical, political, and strategic reasons had drawn the Army of Northern Virginia north and toward Pennsylvania like a magnet. Among them it was hoped a demonstration north of the Potomac would relieve fortress Vicksburg and war-torn Virginia. In addition, General Lee's starving army would be able to draw upon the resources in a rich "land of milk and honey" that could not be obtained in Virginia.[1]

At the time of the march north, Colonel William Calvin Oates's 15th Alabama Infantry, C.S.A., were among the battle-hardened troops of General Lee's best combat division under the command of an aggressive leader of promise, young John Bell Hood. Colonel Oates was also a young and aggressive commander who liked and knew how to fight. He was also independent-minded, free-thinking, and unorthodox.

Marching north with the Army of Northern Virginia, Colonel Oates's Alabama Rebels could look with pride upon a lengthy list of battlefield and campaign accomplishments that included seven pitched battles, dozens of lesser engagements, and hundreds of skirmishes. They had marched across the Shenandoah Valley and won brilliant successes as part of General Stonewall Jackson's famed "Foot-Cavalry" of General Isaac Trimble's hard-fighting brigade; had battled Pennsylvania "Bucktails" during Jackson's Valley campaign; clashed with the tough Wisconsin soldiers of the Iron Brigade and defended the railroad embarkment for two bloody days against attacking Union waves of infantry at Second Manassas; helped to lay siege to Harpers Ferry; charged with bayonets, using them effectively in the heat of hand-to-hand combat; fought in western Maryland at Antietam on the bloodiest day of the war; and shot Federal attack formations to pieces on battlefields from Virginia to Maryland.

Establishing an early reputation for reliability and combat prowess, the highly disciplined 15th Alabama served as shock troops. They could meet any battlefield challenge, with the entire regiment often skillfully maneuvering and fighting either as skirmishers before the main army or covering brigade and division withdrawals. But never before had the soldiers of the 15th

Alabama Infantry been so far north or so far from home as when they finally reached Pennsylvania soil on Wednesday, July 1, 1863.

The long march north toward the bounty and promise of the Keystone State had begun in mid-June when General John Bell Hood's Division had pushed out of its sprawling encampments around Culpeper, Virginia. On June 15 to disguise the Confederate thrust northward, the fighting men from southeast Alabama first swung west to march along the eastern edge of the Blue Ridge Mountains, which served as a screen against reconnoitering Union cavalry. Then, the lengthy columns of Rebels eased up through the rich farms lands of the Shenandoah Valley, with Colonel Oates's veterans trudging through quaint valley towns like Front Royal and Winchester, Virginia, which Stonewall Jackson had made famous during his 1862 Valley campaign.

Along the way, the intense heat and swirling dust which rose from the narrow roads tormented the hard-marching Confederates. Colonel Oates later recalled that, "the weather was very warm when we marched from Culpepper [sic], and so continued until the day we crossed the river [the Potomac], when there was a very heavy cold rain, which drenched us to the skin . . . the 15th Alabama had 600 men in ranks and 42 officers when we started on that march, and during its progress lost four men by desertion and over fifty by heat and sickness." But confident of success on Northern soil, General Hood's jaunty troops crossed the shallow waters of the Potomac River at Williamsport, Maryland, with rifles and cartridge boxes held high. On June 26, the Alabama Rebels of Colonel Oates's command struggled through the cold, swift-flowing waters, while the brass bands of General Lee's army played "Dixie" and the ragged soldiers in gray and butternut cheered. One member of General Law's Alabama Brigade stated that many Alabama Rebels "marched in four states [Virginia, Maryland, and Pennsylvania] that day, the fourth in a state of intoxication."

However, twenty-six-year-old Private William C. Jordan, future colorbearer of the 15th Alabama and "one of the best soldiers in the regiment," according to Colonel Oates, viewed the long march north into Pennsylvania in a different perspective. He described the many hardships of the march, writing how "more men fainted and fell out of rank the day we left Culpepper [sic] than I ever saw before or since."[2]

In terms of the distance covered on the long march into Pennsylvania after passing through Hagerstown, Maryland, the 15th Alabama performed as expected of General Stonewall Jackson's famous "foot-cavalry." The twice-wounded Captain Noah Baxter Feagin, a teenager commanding the "Midway Southern Guards" of Company B from Barbour County and the brother of Colonel Oates's "right arm," Lieutenant Colonel Isaac Feagin, and Assistant Quartermaster Samuel J. Feagin, described in an early 1863 letter the Alabamians's confidence as the result of serving under Stonewall Jackson: they "think they are better, tougher, braver than any other soldiers, can stand more hardships, march faster and farther, go barefooted oftener on [the] move and wade the deepest stream than any other soldier, can out flank, out fight, whip oftener, get whipped less, retreat faster and farther, capture more and get captured less, tear up more railroad and ride on it less, burn more commissaries and quarter master's stores . . . than any other soldiers" in the Confederacy.

Describing the march northward into Pennsylvania, Private Jordan, an inspirational member of Company B of the "Midway Southern Guards," explained how, "it is wonderful that a man in my condition never straggled on the long march. I have thought of it frequently and have never been able to express in a way to give anything like a true idea of what I endured. Can simply say that it was terrible." Nevertheless, Colonel Oates's soldiers continued to push ever northward, through the choking dust and deeper into Northern territory with the determination to "conquer a peace" in the promised land of Pennsylvania.[3]

To these Rebels from the dense forests and untamed lands of southeast Alabama, Pennsylvania was an incredibly rich and bountiful land beyond anything that they had seen before. Never before had the Alabama boys beheld such a rich expanse of well-cultivated country. Orchards, broad wheat and cornfields, sprawling meadows, and lush pastures spread to the horizon in every direction as far as the eye could see. And the richness of Pennsylvania caused some invaders in gray and butternut to question the merit of the institution of slavery.[4]

One of General Lee's veterans, for instance, wrote with amazement to his family: "Since I have seen how well people live without [slaves] I am tempted to wish I never had one. I seen something of private life in a free State while in Penn." During the early summer of 1863, the prosperity of Pennsylvania served as a stark contrast with the South and its less efficient "King Cotton" society and economy. Admiring the bounty of the richest state they had ever seen, Colonel Oates's Alabamians noted the many contrasts between their broad valley of the Chattahoochee and the rich lands of southern Pennsylvania.

Some 15th Alabama soldiers were haunted by other concerns during the push northward in pursuit of Southern dreams. In a letter from his wife, for instance, Private Jordan had learned on the march northward that his two-year-old son had died. While trudging through the dust and heat of Pennsylvania, Jordan took the news hard, for "I never had been so shocked in all my life up to that time . . . it completely unhinged and wilted me . . . it was a great trial indeed." Nevertheless, he somehow kept moving forward in the 15th Alabama ranks, ignoring the pain and anguish of this personal tragedy.[5]

Other Alabama soldiers worried about what the Yankees were doing in Alabama. Like General Lee's determination to protect Virginia and Richmond by pushing north of the Potomac, one of the primary reasons Colonel Oates's soldiers marched north into Pennsylvania was to win the decisive victory that would save their Alabama homeland from invasion. In the past, the Union forces were known to burn and pillage, such as in Huntsville, Alabama, and this fact was on the minds of the Alabama Rebels as they pushed northward with muskets on shoulders and high hopes for future success.[6]

The physical exertion of the hard march plagued Colonel Oates's soldiers throughout the push into Pennsylvania. By this time, a number of barefoot Alabamians hobbled onward with blistered, cut, and bruised feet, thanks in part to the crossing of the Potomac. However, like disciplined soldiers, most would catch up with the regiment at the night's encampment, limping into camp and complaining of the march's rapid pace. Private Jordan described how, "on our way to Gettysburg we passed through Winchester and crossed the Potomac at Williamsport. We had to wade through. It had a very rough, rocky bottom, which wrecked havoc on barefeet." And as it turned out the shallow Potomac was also a river of no return for many Confederate dreams and lives—one-third of Lee's Army of Northern Virginia would never return to Virginia soil.[7]

But at this time, General Lee's followers could not imagine the full extent of the terrible carnage and nightmarish fighting which lay ahead at Gettysburg. The hardy veterans from southeast Alabama were optimistic and as confident of success as their cocky commander. One of Colonel Oates's soldiers described with pride how, " . . . I don't believe that a better army ever trod the earth than the one which followed General Lee to Gettysburg as they were immune to service, had gone through the hardening process, were well disciplined, were in good spirits and in the main were well officered. It was certainly the grandest army, although they were poorly clad and provisions scarce. Still they had a courage, determination and patriotism that is a credit to the whole of the American people . . ."[8]

Few Rebel soldiers understood the amount of risk involved in General Lee's desperate gamble to win victory on Northern soil. If General Lee's bid to relieve the Mississippi River fortress of Vicksburg by sending the Army of Northern Virginia into Pennsylvania failed, then the strategic citadel in Mississippi would be doomed. And if Confederate defeat resulted in Pennsylvania, then twin reversals in both the East and the West would ensure the eventual fall of Richmond and the Confederacy's early demise. And as fate would have it, these twin reversals during early July 1863, did guarantee the end of the Confederate experiment in nationhood.

But the bold Northern invasion hardly seemed like a glorious push into a promised land of Confederate dreams to the Alabama soldiers marching into Pennsylvania in the high humidity of that sweltering summer. The hot, steamy weather made life miserable while locusts played their mournful choruses as the dropping sun hovered over the sprawling grain fields. Even the blazing red sun lowering on the western horizon failed to ease the intense heat of late June. Sweat rolled down the necks and shirts of Colonel Oates's men, while the gaunt, lanky Alabamians swung along the dirt roads of southern Pennsylvania which they hoped would lead them to the ever-elusive decisive victory on Northern soil.

With tin cups and canteens clanging against bayonet scabbards and Enfield rifles on shoulders, the 15th Alabama soldiers continued to push deeper into the Commonwealth. Their weapons had been run through the Federal blockade, taken off the bodies of Yankee dead, and captured from Harpers Ferry. On the night of June 26, General Hood's soldiers encamped on the rolling hills south of Greencastle, Pennsylvania, and just north of the Pennsylvania border. By the evening of June 27 they reached Chambersburg, where a dirt road called the Chambersburg Pike by the locals led eastward toward a small town named Gettysburg. After pushing through Chambersburg, the worn Alabamians continued to march a short distance east down the pike and then turned south toward New Guilford. Immediately west of the small mountain village of New Guilford Courthouse and southeast of Chambersburg, the 15th Alabama soldiers finally rested after seemingly countless days of marching ever northward.

The second great invasion of the North by the Army of Northern Virginia was more demanding in terms of logistics and manpower requirements than the army's ill-fated first Northern invasion into Maryland during September 1862. And much like the Maryland invasion, General Lee's second and most ambitious thrust north of the Potomac possessed little chance of decisive success.[9]

But the Alabama Rebels had made good time and endured the fatigue better than many of General Lee's troops during the seemingly endless days of hard marching. Who were these hard-fighting Rebels who served with distinction in the 15th Alabama Infantry, C.S.A.? What made these young men and boys from southeast Alabama march away from the Wiregrass country and the Chattahoochee Valley with such lofty idealism and high hopes? What factors motivated these 15th Alabama soldiers to march hundreds of miles in tattered rags, without shoes, and with empty haversacks to fight so far from home north of the Mason-Dixon line in Pennsylvania?[10]

Representing a relatively little-known section of the Deep South, the soldiers of Colonel Oates's regiment hailed from seven Alabama counties of the Wiregrass and the Chattahoochee River Valley country of the Coastal Plain in southeast Alabama. Corporal "Gus" McClendon, Company G, wrote that the 15th Alabama was "composed mostly of farmers' boys, a hale, hearty set of young fellows, and in a skirmish [or battle] with the 'Yanks' they found us tough stuff, and hard to drive." From the beginning, these young men from southeast Alabama, wrote one soldier, had "needed no practice or instructions as to how to give the 'Rebel Yell,' a yell that became famous, and which so often caused terror and dismay in the ranks of the Yankees, and on several occasions that which we failed to do with our guns, we would accomplish with the rebel yell."[11]

The vast majority of these men were farmers who made their living from the soil in the tradition of their forefathers. Few of Colonel Oates's officers or enlisted men were among the class of wealthy cotton planters whose power, money, and prestige dominated the political life of the Chattahoochee River country. These common men of the yeomen class tilled the soil, primarily raising enough food for their families and gaining some small profits from surplus crops. Few of the 15th Alabama's soldiers called white-columned and Greek Revival mansions home. A large percentage of these soldiers were too young to own African Americans themselves but lived with their parents who did. One slave-owner of the 15th Alabama was twenty-nine-year-old Private Casper W. Boyd, who was mortally wounded at the battle of Cross Keys during Jackson's Valley campaign. Private Boyd, of Company I, often ended his letters to his family with references that partly indicated the paternalistic bond between whites and blacks even under the obvious horrors of the institution of slavery: "Tell the servants howdy for me" and "My kind regards to the servants."

Issues of race and ethnicity had been features of southeast Alabama life from the beginning, and this region was a melting pot of various ethnic groups. Like Colonel Oates, many young Alabamians in gray possessed a dark complexion. This look not only reflected a French and Spanish heritage but also the widespread racial mixing on the Alabama frontier between whites and Native Americans. In fact, Alabama was an Indian word for a tribe known as the Alabamas. Life on the early Alabama frontier had seen an intermingling of the two peoples to a degree not seen elsewhere in the South.

Most important, a liberal political heritage and republican tradition were also historical legacies of Colonel Oates's Alabamians, fueling motivation in their own struggle for independence which they saw as the Second American Revolution. A strong and vibrant sense of Southern nationalism and the righteous sense that they were defending their homeland of southeast Alabama—one of the state's most militant and secessionist regions—were key factors to explain "why they fought" on a rocky hill in south central Pennsylvania called Little Round Top. Ironically, this feeling was quite unlike that of the Unionist hill country of north Alabama which was so anti-secessionist in the war's early days that Alabamians had "actually feared civil war within Alabama between its factions . . ." People across much of Alabama opposed secession at the secession convention at Montgomery, including the future commander of the 47th Alabama, Colonel Michael Jefferson Bulger. He faced a hostile mob in standing firm to his political and philosophical beliefs.

Seeing the war as not primarily over the issue of slavery, Colonel Oates wrote that "for slavery alone, or the money values of the slaves, two-thirds, and probably three-fourths, of the Confederate soldiers would not have risked their lives and fought as they did." This was seen as a war for a new nation's independence.

One southeast Alabama soldier summarized how "the spirit of devotion to our Southland bound us together as comrades in a holy cause." This young Rebel from the Chattahoochee River country also explained how the Union's war against the South was nothing more than a case of the Northern people's aggressive attempt "to destroy our nationality," which had to be protected at all costs.

And twenty-eight-year-old Private Samuel D. Lary, a Texas-born soldier of Company B, 15th Alabama, from Union Springs, Alabama, where he was a newspaper editor, described how in the war's beginning the "enthusiastic southerons [sic] were flocking to the new ensign of liberty, the banner of the 'lone star' which arose undimmed in the cloud of the world's despotism [and] Heaven set it bravely before us." Indeed, such a revolutionary Alabama banner, decorated with an armed goddess of Liberty and the words, "Independent Now and Forever," early waved from the dome of the state capitol in Montgomery, Alabama.

But perhaps Colonel Oates explained it best in emphasizing how the overwhelming urge of these southeast Alabama Rebels to go to war was much like "the enthusiasm of the religionists to enlist in the crusades [against] the infidels [and] they believed it was to be a fight for their homes and the inalienable and ancient right of local self-government [and] they felt that they were going to fight for home and its sacred precincts." Clearly, a host of historical, philosophical, societal, psychological, and cultural legacies were primary factors to explain motivation. For instance, Corporal McClendon explained the cultural and historical influence on the young Alabama soldiers, emphasizing how when "in my teens . . . all my relatives were strong Southern people and politically were democrats, and ardent secessionists." During the excitement-filled spring of 1861, McClendon and his southeast Alabama comrades had marched to war from Abbeville, Alabama, "with a step to the martial music of Dixie and the 'Bonnie Blue Flag' . . . to resent an insult offered to the South by her enemies."

In the early days of the war, young Private Jordan explained his decision to follow the destiny of his state "although a Whig and a Union man after my state seceded I felt it as much my duty to serve in the Southern cause as if I had been a secessionist." However, by the summer of 1861, Private Jordan and other Barbour County men had been transformed into "regular fire eater[s]" by events beyond their control.

Representative of the many ideological and political influences of the American Revolution, Corporal McClendon and other young Abbeville volunteers had rallied with enthusiasm around a "Liberty Pole"—a historical legacy of the American Revolution. Another revolutionary influence was evident among the Henry County Rebels who wore secession cockades like the revolutionaries of the French Revolution who espoused "Liberty, Equality, and Fraternity." Other Alabama Rebels rejoiced in singing the revolutionary lyrics of "The Southern Marseillaise."

One history-minded Alabama soldier described "how trifling were the wrongs complained of by our Revolutionary forefathers, in comparison with ours! If the mere imposition of a tax could raise such a tumult what should be the result of the terrible system of oppression instituted by the Yankees?" In a letter written after his capture at Gettysburg, another Alabama Rebel scribbled with obvious pride how he and his comrades were struggling for "the same principles which fired the hearts of our ancestors in the revolutionary struggle."

Even by the time of Gettysburg, idealism and revolutionary idealogy remained strong from the colonel down to the most humble private in the ranks. In one letter, Private Sam Lary emphasized how the Alabamians fought to "drive back the invader and trample on laws that would have made [us] slaves [for the] votaries of freedom and constitutional equality [had] rall[ied] around the standard of our rights [and] the great question . . . to be decided [was] whether we should be slaves or free men, whether we should be branded with the stigma of rebellion, or handed down to posterity as a free and independent people."

Without exaggeration, another Alabama soldier was resolved

to fight to the bitter end, penning how, "I am willing to fall for the cause of Liberty and Independence." Embracing a hatred for the invaders of his homeland, Corporal McClendon felt no pity for any Federal soldier "who lost his life in trying to subdue a people who asked for nothing more than 'Equality in the Union, or Independence out of it'." In idealistic terms, one Alabama soldier summarized the South's defiance, declaring how "the Confederates were standing for their inalienable rights of property, country, and home."[12]

Another Alabama officer penned how, "we should be proud of [the] noble name" of Rebel because "George Washington . . . Thomas Jefferson, Patrick Henry, and 'Light Horse' Harry Lee [Robert E. Lee's father] . . . were all Rebels . . . Our martyred Saviour [Jesus Christ] was called seditious." Like Colonel Oates, many 15th Alabama boys hailed from Henry County, which appropriately had been named for Patrick Henry. As these 15th Alabama soldiers realized, the Virginia country lawyer and revolutionary had cried "Give me Liberty or Give me Death" in defiance to the infamous Stamp Act of King George III. And now, like their forefathers before them in the first American Revolution, the Alabamians in gray embraced this same defiant attitude toward President Abraham Lincoln in fighting for their nation's self-determination in what they considered the Second American Revolution.[13]

A cockade-wearing Corporal McClendon recalled how throughout the town of Abbeville "all prided themselves in wearing a badge of 'Red, White and Blue'." For Corporal McClendon, Private Jordan, and other 15th Alabama soldiers, the Stars and Bars banner flying across southeast Alabama in the war's early days was suddenly "the colors of my first love," after taking the place of "Old Glory."[14]

Colonel Oates, who was likewise inspired by the revolutionary spirit and sight of the "Liberty Pole" in Abbeville and identified closely with the many historical analogies between the South's struggle and the American Revolution, explained some of the other key motivating factors of his Alabama Rebels. Besides years of sectional tension and hostility, Colonel Oates described how the threat of slave revolt in the Wiregrass country of the Chattahoochee Valley played a key role in laying a foundation for the rationale for secession. Southeast Alabama men like Colonel Oates saw the Republican Party as controlled by the abolitionists who they feared would promote slave revolts. Consequently, by 1861, this party seemingly posed the greatest threat and danger to the people of the South. Most of all, these Alabamians feared slave insurrections from the potential black revolutionaries in their midst, resulting in the destruction of Southern society. Not surprising, fears of slave revolt around Montgomery immediately before the state secession convention had helped to hasten Alabama's departure from the Union.

With some bitterness at those who he felt had sparked this fratricidal conflict, Colonel Oates penned how "bands of [Northern] fanatics [came] to believe that they were inspired by Heaven to light the torch of revolution in Southern, to invade a Southern state for the purpose of inciting the slaves to insurrection, arson, and indiscriminate murder of the white people . . ." Consequently, going to war for the volunteers of southeastern Alabama was a case of only doing what was necessary to protect their homes and families. As Corporal McClendon explained upon crossing the Chattahoochee River on the way to the war in Virginia, the 15th Alabama soldiers realized they were saying "farewell to Alabama, we are going in your defense." Continuing to explain the popular ideology among the 15th Alabama, Corporal McClendon, an Irishman who was a popular and natural leader in the enlisted ranks, summarized how this "fine looking body of young Alabamians [were eager] to fight the invaders of their homes."[15]

Spiritual and religious faith would also play a leading role in fueling the fighting spirit of the 15th Alabama Rebels, especially as the war became more bloody. In late 1862, the first spiritual revivals swept through the encampment of the 15th Alabama and General Trimble's brigade, and then continued to consume General Jackson's Corps and the rest of the Army of Northern Virginia. A good many of Colonel Oates's soldiers laid down their rifles to be baptised while so far from home.

Many, if not most, of the personal letters from 15th Alabama soldiers were filled with repeated references to God and the moral righteousness of their struggle. For instance, Private Sam Lary rationalized the transformation process that turned peaceful United States citizens to revolutionaries as one which had been made "under the blessing of God . . ." And Private Casper Boyd, a yeoman of Company I, 15th Alabama, recorded in one letter [containing many misspellings] the importance of religion in the daily life of the average soldier of Colonel Oates's regiment: "The greates pleasur that I have is when I am reading my bible and praying to my Creater my Heavenly Father for his care a lon do I feel safe [and] I som time tad my bible on the sabath and go to som grove where I have no one to desterbe me there I try to worship God in my umble way . . . "

Other Private Boyd letters likewise contained numerous references to God and the redeeming qualities of religious faith that comforted the 15th Alabama soldiers: "My trust is still in God, who will take care of those who love, and serve Him—and should we not meet again my dear mother in this world I have assurance we will in another & better [world], where all is love, peace, & happiness . . . I hope to see [you] when this dreadful war is over [and] May God spare us until we meet." Destined to be fatally cut down in battle, young Private Boyd would find a permanent home in the Virginia soil far from Alabama.[16]

Private Lary described the importance of the key role played by the regimental chaplains of the 15th Alabama, especially after the war became more murderous. He wrote in a letter how one of these devoted chaplains in gray was "a good man [whose] ambition . . . is to do good to his fellow man. To this all the energies of his mind and heart are directed [and] where disease or sorrow exists there is he found, nor are his attentions confined to particular friends or companies—it is enough for him to know that pain and suffering exists to draw him to its home . . . the effects of his teachings are apparent—universal respect and esteem awaits him whenever he approaches . . ." Indeed, one reason why the spiritual revival had first begun in General Trimble's brigade and the

15th Alabama was because of these zealous and devout men of God in Colonel Oates's regiment.

Employing an appropriate analogy between religion and nationalism in this righteous struggle, Private Lary also emphasized how the deaths of 15th Alabama soldiers across Virginia and Maryland to the ravages of disease and Yankee shells and bullets was a "sacrifice upon the altar of their country for their country's salvation."[17]

Thus for Colonel Oates and his men of the Wiregrass country, the secession of Alabama on January 11, 1861, became the only recourse in defense of the South. South Carolina's "sister state in secession," Alabama followed the example of South Carolina which led the way in initiating the Southern experiment in rebellion. After the departure of South Carolina and despite the relatively slim margin of sixty-one to thirty-nine among convention delegates' votes, Alabama was the first Deep South state to leave what secessionist-minded Southerners now considered to be an obsolete and hostile Union. Not surprisingly, 15th Alabama soldiers often sang a popular song while in camp and on the march and no doubt during the long trek to Gettysburg: "We honor, yes, honor bold South Carolina, Who cast her brave bark alone on the deep."[18]

Private Sam Lary described in a wartime letter how "the plow of destiny had upturned a furrow in which were sown the seed of a future republic [and] the election of Abraham Lincoln upon the principles of avowed hostility to the 'peculiar institution' of the South culminated an antagonism of feeling which no pacification could ally . . . unwilling to remain in the Union which no longer promised her protection and true to the prestige of her fair name," the South left the Union in behalf of her own interests and in self-defense: the same formula that had resulted in the thirteen colonies successfully breaking away from Great Britain during the American Revolution.[19]

Ironically at the beginning of the conflict the greatest concern of the 15th Alabama soldiers was that the war would not last long enough and that they would miss a good fight and glory. As seventeen-year-old Corporal McClendon explained, "hearing of so many victories for the South, and only a few getting killed, I began to think that the war would soon end and that I wouldn't get to smell gunpowder much less burn any." And a much wiser Private Lary in a letter later in the war described the naive mindset at the war's beginning before innocence was destroyed by Yankee bullets and shells: "Hitherto we had regarded wars as a pastime. We knew none of its severities—none of its horrors."

The romance of war for Company G, 15th Alabama, began when Captain Oates organized his company in Abbeville during the summer of 1861. A new silk battle flag was presented to the "Henry Pioneers." This colorful banner had been sown by the ladies of Abbeville, including wives, mothers, sisters, aunts, and grandmothers of the young men and boys in the ranks. Handsome Captain Oates "in his eloquent and patriotic style accepted it for his company, accepting the flag with promises by himself and company which he and [his] company faithfully kept." Ironically, Corporal McClendon described this battle flag of the "Henry Pioneers" as "our little flag of Red, White and Blue." Thereafter, the 15th Alabama Rebels cherished this symbolic emblem of their Wiregrass country homeland—"as the Southern breeze unfurled its folds, [while] the boys looked upon it with pride and as a reminder of those they had left behind."

When they marched away from their southeast Alabama homeland for the first time during the summer of 1861, the yeomen of Captain Oates's company went to war in red flannel shirts with grey pants . . ." Consequently, these Henry County soldiers were also widely known as the "Red Shirted boys from Henry." As the war lengthened and the combat prowess of these soldiers was repeatedly demonstrated on battlefields across the South, the company letters of "H.P." for the "Henry Pioneers" which were painted and stenciled on their equipment, were said to indicate the "Hell Pelters." Before departing Abbeville for the Virginia theater, Corporal McClendon's father, overcome with emotion upon watching his son march off to war, made one last appeal to the commander of the "Henry Pioneers": "Capt. Oates, take care of my boy." And Oates would do just that, looking out for the welfare of his boys from the beginning to the end of the war.[20]

A number of Colonel Oates's men desired more than simply to kill Yankees who were in truth little different from themselves. A local Abbeville blacksmith, an African American of Henry County named Ned, at the war's beginning made "them some large knives [which] were similar to the Spanish matchetta [and] many were the vain boastings of some of these men who carried them strapped to their side before they had smelt gun-powder [and] some went so far as to say they were going to cut Abe Lincoln's head off . . ."[21]

After volunteer companies from the Wiregrass country of southeast Alabama banded together in their crusade, the Chattahoochee Valley men of the 15th Alabama were organized at Fort Mitchell, in Russell County, Alabama, located across the Chattahoochee River from Columbus, Georgia, on July 3, 1861. Then, the zealous volunteers of the 15th Alabama departed Alabama for the Virginia theater in early August 1861. By the time of the Gettysburg campaign, the 15th Alabama consisted of eleven companies. Company A, the Cantry Rifles, hailed from Russell County; Company B, the Midway Southern Guards, from Barbour County; Company C came from Macon County; Company D, the Fort Browder Roughs, from Barbour County; Company E, the Beauregards, from Dale County; Company F, the Brundidge Guards, from Pike County; Company G, the Henry Pioneers, from Henry County; Company H, the Glennville Guards, from Barbour and Dale Counties; Company I, the Quitman Guards, from Pike County; Company K, the Eufaula City Guards, from Barbour County; and Company L, the Pike Sharpshooters, from Pike County.[22]

Three of these counties bordered the Chattahoochee River, lying opposite, or west of, Columbus, Georgia, and extending south to the far southeast corner of the state—Russell, Barbour, and Henry Counties. Immediately adjacent to, or west of, these three adjoining river counties, were the counties, from north to south, of Macon, Pike, and Dale. This was a fertile land upon which bountiful crops grew in the light and sandy soil. There, in this land that was once a bone of contention between early settlers and Indians, the yeoman farmers had thrived for generations, after winning the land from both nature and the Creek Indians. Corn, wheat, oats, and potato fields and small patches of cotton dotted the lush lands along the bottoms that bordered the wide Chattahoochee, providing support for middle-class families in the wilderness.

The great waterway of the Chattahoochee River was the vital highway of the region, defining its history, culture, and character for generations. Colonel Oates's men also hailed from the region around the primary tributary of the Chattahoochee, the muddy Choctawhatchee, which also cut through the Wiregrass country. This unique name for this distinctive region derived from the durable and tough natural grasses which covered the plains of southeast Alabama like a blanket beside stretches of open woodlands of pine, hickory, and oak. These vast expanses of heavy forests later made this area of southeast Alabama a rich timber belt.[23]

The names of the 15th Alabama's soldiery reflected primarily an Anglo-Saxon heritage which was dominated by the Scotch-Irish who had settled the Wiregrass country. But the names of Colonel Oates's men also indicated the widespread impact of political and revolutionary ideologies of the past as the influence of the American Revolution was evident. This can be seen in the names of the first elected officers of the 15th Alabama. Thomas Jefferson Nuckolls served as the third lieutenant in Company A; Benjamin Franklin Coleman fought as a second lieutenant in Company B; Benjamin Franklin Lloyd served as third lieutenant in Company C; and Benjamin Franklin Lewis acted as captain of Company F. This psychological and inspirational legacy of the American Revolution—the dominate historical influence of the Civil War generation—was prevalent in the names of the common soldiers in the 15th Alabama as well. The most common first and middle names of Colonel Oates's soldiers that reflected this revolutionary heritage were George Washington and Thomas Jefferson.[24]

For the most part, the men of the 15th Alabama were young and in the prime of life. One of these boy-soldiers was slightly cross-eyed and diminutive Private Thomas D. Wright, a handsome boy of sixteen who had yet to shave. Thomas was the brother of twenty-two-year-old Captain Richard "Dick" E. Wright, who would be severely wounded at Second Manassas. After fighting at Gettysburg, Private Wright of Barbour County would be killed in the dark forests of the "River of Death" at Chickamauga. Of the four Wright brothers of Company B, one was killed in battle, and one fell victim of disease—Private Robert Q. Wright, age twenty-three, who died in October 1862.[25]

The drummer boys of the 15th Alabama were even younger. Whenever the regiment was facing a crisis on the battlefield, these young drummer boys would lay down their drums and pick up muskets to fight in the ranks. This was very much a boy's war and a brothers' war in more ways than one, and the 15th Alabama was no exception.[26]

But more than simply the young served in the ranks of the 15th Alabama because the entire community responded to the call to arms. Northern-born Private Edmond Sheppard, a physican, was age seventy. And despite being "too old for soldiering," in Colonel Oates's estimation, Private Jefferson F. Beecher served at age sixty-one.[27]

Every class was represented in the ranks of the 15th Alabama, but the men were united by bonds of comradeship and sacrifice which helped to ease social tensions and distinctions. Private Lary described how the 15th Alabama Rebels had "volunteered irrespective of class and regardless of position [because] there was a common interest in the common cause." Colonel Oates gave a good representative view of the entire regiment by summarizing how his Company G of Henry County soldiers was "composed mainly of young men and boys from sixteen to thirty years of age, sons of farmers." Impressed by the physical athleticism of his comrades, Corporal McClendon wrote how the 15th Alabama men consisted of " . . . crack jumpers, crack wrestlers, crack runners, crack dancers, and crack athletes." These resilient soldiers of the

15th Alabama were "basically [Chattahoochee Valley] area farmers [who] planned to plant their crops, grab their guns and settle this little squabble in time to come back and help the women gather the crops." These hardy common soldiers in the ranks believed that decisive success was inevitable in this war: an illusion soon shattered forever by the grim realities of the most horrible war in American history and the climatic showdown at Gettysburg.[28]

CHAPTER II

The Officers and Men
of the 15th Alabama

*They "think they are better, tougher, braver than any other soldiers,
can stand more hardships, march faster and farther, go barefooted
oftener on [the] move and wade the deepest stream than any other
soldier, can out flank, out fight, whip oftener, get whipped less,
retreat faster and farther, capture more and get captured less, tear
up more railroad and ride on it less, burn more commissaries and
quarter master's stores . . . than any other soldiers."*

—Captain Noah Baxter Feagin, 15th Alabama, Company B,
describing his regiment in early 1863

As could be expected from a community response to the war that
resulted in widespread enlistment, a number of Alabama blue-
bloods were in the 15th Alabama's ranks. One such societal and
community leader was Robert J. Reynolds. He was the privileged
son of a wealthy court judge, member of the legislature, and aristocratic planter. At the age of twelve, Robert had learned how to
act like an aristocratic member of a "superior" race while serving
as an overseer on his father's plantation. There, he managed a
large number of slaves in the planter tradition, grooming himself
for the day when he would own his own plantation and slaves.

33

Most highest-ranking regimental officers in the 15th came from the upper class of the Wiregrass country. In general, these community leaders owned more slaves than the average yeoman farmers of the enlisted ranks. Like other officers, Captain William N. Richardson of Company H had his African-American slave, Dick, beside him during active campaigning. Some of the Alabama officers brought their servants with them to Gettysburg, where African American slaves then served on Northern soil.[1]

Ironically, the social and political elites of the wealthy upper class of local communities dominated the officer corps of the 15th Alabama because of the votes of the men in the ranks. At the beginning of the war, they had elected these officers, reinforcing the belief in the social obligations of the upper class and its leadership role in Southern society. Ironically, this complex relationship was sometimes almost as paternalistic as that of master to slave.

Many of the field and staff officers of the 15th Alabama were leading citizens not of Alabama but of Georgia because the regiment represented the Wiregrass country as much as the state of Alabama. For example, some 15th Alabama leaders hailed from the thriving port town of Columbus, Georgia, which was the major city of the Chattahoochee Valley. Leading societal members of Columbus in the 15th Alabama's ranks included regimental surgeon Dr. Frank A. Stanford, a thirty-three-year-old Georgia native and bachelor; James Vernoy, assistant commissary; Sergeant Major Van Marcus, who had enough intimate knowledge of the temperamental nature of the tricky Chattahoochee River to eventually become a steamboat captain on that major waterway; forty-two-year-old Quartermaster Sergeant Henry D. Doney, who would not survive the war; and towering Color Sergeant Charles V. Smith, who could be relied upon to carry the regimental battle flag amid the hottest fire.

Many 15th Alabama officers possessed extensive political and social connections to the top levels of antebellum life in southeast Alabama and in the Chattahoochee River region. Georgia-born Charles Carter Hay was the nephew of the mayor of Columbus, Georgia. Hay had first trained and drilled in the color company of the 45th Alabama Infantry. He then served in the Russell County troops of the Glennville Guards, 15th Alabama. Hay helped to stabilize Company H with his steady influence, then became a member of the unit. Hay knew intimately of the "brothers' war" as his own brother served as a United States naval officer. This fact no doubt was a source of considerable embarrassment for Hay, fueling his martial efforts to wipe the stain from the family name.

A member of the upper class from the noncommissioned officers' ranks of the 15th Alabama was Sergeant Major Robert Cicero Norris. The son of Colonel William Hutchinson Norris, he had received his education at Fulton Academy. This was one of the finest Alabama institutions of higher learning before the war. In addition, Norris had studied to become an attorney, acquiring sufficient legal knowledge to practice law in Alabama. Then, as if hungry for another challenge, he had embarked upon a new career, studying medicine at the Mobile Medical College. Norris laid down his medical books to take up arms, participating in the capture of the United States Navy Yard at Pensacola, Florida. In the 15th Alabama, this versatile and talented intellectual, who would be wounded three times in the war, served in a variety of roles, including sergeant major, regimental adjutant, and scout.[2]

The 15th Alabama's surgeon, Dr. Harvey Oliver Milton of Selma, Alabama, could boast of a splendid education. The South Carolina-born Milton had received his medical education at one of the best medical schools in the North, the Jefferson Medical College in Philadelphia. At the beginning of the war, Dr. Milton never realized that the southeast Alabama boys would march into Pennsylvania and designate Philadelphia as a primary target during their summer of 1863. Major John W. Daniel, Barbour County, was an active member of the Alabama secession convention in Montgomery which followed the state's leading fire-eater, William L. Yancey, and voted for secession. He became the captain of Company B, 15th Alabama, the Midway Guards from Barbour County.[3]

Another blueblood in Colonel Oates's ranks was the commander of Company H at the time of the battle of Gettysburg, Captain William N. Richardson, age thirty-five. He was a wealthy planter who owned a large tract of acreage and many slaves who worked his cotton fields. He enjoyed drink and high living, relishing his wealth and upper-class status as a leading planter of the Chattahoochee Valley. In regard to his close bond with whiskey, Colonel Oates described how Captain Richardson "was fond of it and [occasionally] got full" of his favorite brand.

It was universally agreed that Captain Richardson was an unusual character. He "was indeed an eccentric man [and] was an educated farmer of wealth and position; and a great many amusing stories are told of him during the war, and in the main they were correct," recalled Colonel Oates. For instance, Captain Richardson "never had his company in marching order until a few minutes later than the order required us to move." At the battle of Fredericksburg in December 1862, a laughing Captain Richardson was known to have yelled to his men amid one of the heaviest cannonades of the war, "Is this not a hell of a way for a man to celebrate his birthday; it has just occurred to me that I am thirty-seven years old this day." Captain Richardson's eccentricity was more than a seemingly endless series of odd habits stemming from a strange personality. Upon losing his wealth, many of his 15th Alabama comrades, and his dream of Southern nationhood, insanity would become the eventual fate of this most unusual captain.[4]

Despite the common bonds and motivations, some friction persisted in the 15th Alabama partly because of the socio-economic and class differences between officers and enlisted men. However, such clashes were minimal. This was largely because societal leaders of antebellum Southern society were expected to naturally lead their "less elevated" fellow Alabamians both in war and peace. Class distinctions between the common yeomen and upper-class elements in the 15th Alabama's ranks did surface though in the words of aristocratic Lieutenant James M. Ellison. He was a Georgia-born slaveowner who lived on a large plantation at Creek Stand in the southeast corner of Macon County below Tuskegee. Related to a leading Baltimore, Maryland, family, the Keys, Ellison's wife possessed a good deal of money and political and social connections. One influential relative was Francis Scott Key of Fort McHenry and national anthem fame, who once had been sent to Alabama on a diplomatic mission by President Andrew Jackson. In his letters to his wife, Camilla Searcy Key, Lieutenant Ellison often referred to the less educated and uncultured privates of the 15th Alabama as "little dirt eating fellows," "little Devels [sic]," and even "Crackers."[5]

Contrary to the stereotype of a typical Deep South regiment, the 15th Alabama was hardly a culturally homogeneous unit. Colonel Oates's regiment was flavored with a distinctive ethnic composition lacking in most Confederate regiments. Clearly, the most colorful company of the 15th Alabama was Company K, which consisted of the Irishmen of the "Eufaula City Guards," hailing from the bustling port town of the Chattahoochee River. Celtic traditions and legacies thrived in the hearts and minds of these Irish Rebels. More than any other company besides his old Company G, Colonel Oates was proud of this unique ethnic unit not only because of its fighting prowess and iron discipline but also because he was partly of Irish heritage.

Most Irish immigrants of Company K had first reached United States soil by way of the Gulf of Mexico port of Mobile, Alabama. Then, to find abundant economic opportunities and a better life not attainable in impoverished Ireland, these Sons of Erin had continued their migration northward up the Chattahoochee to Eufaula, Alabama, which had been named for a Creek Indian village. Other Irish then continued north upriver to the major Chattahoochee River port of Columbus, Georgia. Branching out from Columbus to search for their share of the American dream, these Celts had found many opportunities in the thriving Chattahoochee Valley. Common laborers were in demand to develop the new land on the southeast Alabama frontier, and for manual labor in the bustling port towns along the sluggish river.

Company K was organized at the small but busy community of Eufaula and consisted of ninety high-spirited Irishmen from Henry, Dale, and Barbour Counties. This was one of the original companies of the 15th Alabama because the Irish had flocked to the Confederate banner as quickly, if not quicker, than most Southerners. When the Emerald Isle unit was first formed during the early days of the war, they elected Henry C. Hart as captain; George A. Robert as first lieutenant; Alexander R. Baugh as second lieutenant; and William J. Bethune as third lieutenant. These elite Irish Confederates bragged in their thick Irish brogues how any one of them could kill ten Yankees in the first fight.[6]

During the long march north and toward Gettysburg, the fun-loving and light-hearted Irishmen of Company K kept spirits high in the regiment. It seemed as if whenever the 15th Alabama's soldiers were the most leg-weary, thirsty, and exhausted, it was the Irish Rebels who always lifted spirits with cheery songs, jokes, or wisecracks. Like Colonel Oates's other companies, the Celtic officers' ranks of Company K had been severely culled by the time of the Gettysburg campaign. In early July 1863, this steady attrition—an effective process that tempered the unit's combat capabilities—had left a hardened cadre of the most dedicated and experienced officers.

Thirty-one-year-old Captain Hart, a pampered merchant, had been simply too "accustomed to indoor work and high living, and the rudeness of a soldier's life went rather hard with him," critiqued Colonel Oates. After the terrible bloodletting of the Seven Days, Captain Hart was "absent sick" before finally resigning, having sickened of the war. Lieutenant Roberts, age thirty-five, likewise resigned because of poor health and diminished enthusiasm for fighting Yankees who now battled as determinedly, especially when defending Northern soil, as any Rebels could have possibly imagined back in the optimistic spring of 1861. Sick of conflict and the mindless killing, Lieutenant Roberts retired with a medical disability in late 1861.[7]

War-weariness and the ceaseless bloodletting had also affected other leaders of Company K as well. For instance, Lieutenant Baugh, age twenty-two, had shot himself in the hand with his revolver, while skulking behind a tree during a raging battle. Colonel Oates bitterly complained how Lieutenant Baugh "was a coward and shot himself to get out of the service." Lieutenant

Baugh left the service in 1862 to return to Alabama, making the regiment a better unit with his departure.

Clearly, the horror of the war and the high casualties were too much to bear for some of these young Alabama officers, who had learned only too well of the brutal realities of this fratricidal conflict during the first two years. By the time of the Gettysburg campaign, other 15th Alabama companies had been culled by the exodus of more fainthearted soldiers, leaving tried and tested veterans, including the best Celtic officers of Company K.[8]

With the brutal attrition which seemed to have no end during the campaigns across Virginia, Lieutenant William J. Bethune, a fine officer of promise, now led the troublesome and spunky Irishmen of Company K. Like his fellow Emerald Islers, Lieutenant Bethune was a hard-fighting and resilient Irishman, serving as a capable leader of the tough Celts. Because of his age, this Celtic officer of much promise was determined to do his best, and succeeded in winning the respect of his men. In fact, Lieutenant Bethune accomplished what older and senior officers of Company K had been unable to do—instill some much-needed discipline upon his independent-minded and rowdy troops. Lieutenant Bethune's iron discipline made him unpopular but he was respected for his relentless efforts to turn Company K into the regiment's best company.

Colonel Oates bestowed high compliments upon the young lieutenant writing, "though not very popular among his men on account of the rigidity of his discipline, he was brave, and never absent," especially when a battle was imminent. As Lieutenant Bethune and Colonel Oates realized, such discipline would most of all be needed for a severe battlefield challenge such as they were about to meet at Gettysburg.[9]

On that fateful July 2 at Gettysburg, Lieutenant Bethune would have a trusted lieutenant by his side, twenty-four-year-old Lieutenant Fred M. Porter. He had been badly wounded in August 1862 at Second Manassas, falling in defense of the bloody railroad cut. Porter had recuperated during the second winter of the war and by the time of the Gettysburg campaign the young lieutenant was once more serving beside Lieutenant Bethune. Though he would survive Gettysburg, Lieutenant Porter was destined to be killed before the summer's end at Chickamauga.[10]

With the great clash at Gettysburg on the horizon, Lieutenant Bethune felt comfort in also being able to rely on high quality leadership from the experienced noncommissioned officers in Company K's ranks. One such dependable Celtic warrior in gray was Sergeant James H. Gray, age twenty-six. He was "a fine soldier," evaluated Colonel Oates, who knew a good fighting man when he saw one. Sergeant Gray's leadership qualities would earn him a lieutenant's rank and a battlefield death before the end of 1863.[11]

But most of all, it would be the Irish Rebels in Company K's enlisted ranks who would rise to the fore during the upcoming struggle at Gettysburg including Privates Burrell V. McKlevane, another teenage warrior, Cicero Madden, James Henry Murdock, and John Nelson, a hot-headed Irishman who loved to use his fists at seemingly every opportunity. But the hardest fighting and most inspirational Irish Rebel of Company K was Sergeant Patrick O'Conner. In the view of both officers and men, Sergeant O'Conner was considered the finest and most dependable soldier of Company K. According to Colonel Oates's evaluation, "O'Conner was . . . one of the bravest" of the 15th Alabama. The sergeant served as a natural and inspirational leader for not only Company K but also the entire regiment. He was "always at his post, and never missed a battle." For his bravery soon to be displayed at Gettysburg, he would win promotion to lieutenant before the end of 1863. But like so many of the Irish Confederates of Company K, Sergeant O'Conner would be killed on a Virginia battlefield, receiving his death stroke on June 1, 1864: "a loss to his company and the regiment that could not be replaced."[12]

Private William Hall Harrell, age twenty-seven, "was a very sound, stout man, never sick, and fought well until along in the summer of 1862, when he had seen so many good men killed and wounded that it slightly demoralized him and made him dodge, and he did not fight as a brave man should, but he struck to it," and would serve in Company K's ranks at Gettysburg.

By the time of the Gettysburg campaign, though, it was inevitable that some war-weariness had crept into the culled ranks of Company K, like other 15th Alabama companies, after the nightmarish fighting across Virginia and the bloodiest day of the war at Antietam. One Irish Confederate of Company K, Private John Nelson, "would go into every battle, and then at the first opportunity would run out of it." Nevertheless, like Private Harrell, Private Nelson would soon march toward the cruel fate which awaited him and so many of his 15th Alabama comrades at Gettysburg. Many of Oates's men were haunted by the memories of past slaughters on the battlefields of Virginia and Maryland. Lieutenant James M. Ellison wrote in a letter to his wife of the war's horrors at Antietam which repeatedly disrupted his sleep and flooded his memories with nightmares: "I do not think the like of killed and wounded was never seen as was killed in the MD [Maryland]." But what Colonel Oates and his other men of the 15th Alabama never forgot was the most distinctive characteristics of the Irish soldiers in gray—their utter fearlessness, tenacity, and bravery in the heat of combat.[13]

Besides the rowdy Celtic warriors of Company K, other Irishmen were scattered throughout the 15th Alabama's ranks. One of these was twenty-five-year-old Michael Murray of Company A, a native of Ireland. At the beginning of the war, he had been detailed to serve as a body servant to the aristocratic Colonel James Cantry, the regiment's first commander, and care for his horses. As could be expected, the high-spirited Irishman did not relish the demeaning assignment of serving a Southern master anymore than an English master in Ireland. Nevertheless, he faithfully carried out his duties, serving as directed. But by early 1863, wrote Colonel Oates, a thankful Murray was freed his "bondage" and "returned and went to duty in the ranks, and so continued until the close of the war. He was a jolly, good-hearted Irishman, a true man [and] he loved a drink and his friends."[14]

Besides the Irish, the second largest ethnic group in the 15th Alabama were those men of French heritage. Reflecting the early settlement period when Alabama was a French territory from 1720 to 1763, these Rebels of French descent gave the 15th Alabama an added measure of ethnic diversity. In Company A's ranks alone, for example, the distinctive French names of J. L. Gulifer, Joseph Potee, and Calvin Sulivant reflected the rich French cultural heritage and legacy of Alabama's Gulf coast.

Other "foreigners" in gray likewise served with distinction in the 15th Alabama. A well-educated Englishman with a law background and who was good with numbers, Joseph R. Breare was "a bright, intelligent little man; genial, sociable, and full of good humor." He was in his twenties, and would shortly leave the regimental commissary position for the opportunity to fight at Gettysburg. There, he would be captured in the upcoming struggle for Little Round Top.

Also in the 15th Alabama's ranks was Daniel McLellan, a Scotsman with a thick accent and plenty of fighting spirit in the Celtic tradition. Lewis Coleman served with distinction in the 15th Alabama while retaining pride in his distinctive Jewish heritage and religion. And in Company K, James R. Watts, age twenty-eight, was a soft-spoken soldier of Italian descent. Much to his comrades' amusement, the Italian in gray lisped, and somehow served in harmony with the troublesome Celts who were not usually known for their tolerance of other nationalities.

In addition, some Northerners served in the 15th Alabama as well. One such individual was the regimental commissary officer, forty-four-year-old Captain Cornelius V. Morris. He was a New Yorker, like his brother James R., also of Company G and from the Franklin community. Colonel Oates described Morris as "though a New Yorker by birth and education, he was an ardent Confederate . . ."[15]

Serving beside Colonel Oates to provide emotional support in times of crisis for the young Abbeville colonel was his younger brother, Lieutenant John Alva Oates, and also a number of boyhood friends. Oates's brother-in-law, Private George Washington Linton, who was married to his youngest sister and "a very fair soldier" in the colonel's estimation which betrayed no favoritism, served in Company I. Among Oates's long-term friends were

Private Jeff Hussey and twenty-eight-year-old Private M. E. Meredith, who would fall severely wounded at Gettysburg. Entire familial clans also served in many companies, these men having enlisted together to represent not only their communities but also their family names as well.[16]

Toughened by the frontier experience and the struggle for survival in a rural environment and past campaigns across Virginia and Maryland, the 15th Alabama Rebels were physically, mentally, and psychologically tough by the time of Gettysburg. These "Cotton State" soldiers were superior to the Virginians in terms of combat prowess in the opinion of some of the top officers in the Army of Northern Virginia. Naturally, Colonel Oates shared this opinion.

And last but not least, another key factor to explain the battle-field prowess, iron discipline, and resiliency of the 15th Alabama was its quality and experienced leadership at the top—its aggressive young commander by the time of Gettysburg, Colonel William Calvin Oates. By this time, Colonel Oates was more responsible for turning the 15th Alabama into a crack regiment than any other officer.

William Calvin Oates

CHAPTER III

William Calvin Oates

"[Oates] is a fine disciplinarian, controlling his men with the greatest ease in camp and on the march. He is cool and collected in action, and has again and again showed that infallible test of a good commander, the ability to maintain a perfect ascendancy and control over his men amidst the excitement and danger of battle [and] the extraordinary skill & gallantry he has displayed on every battlefield."

—General William Perry

*L*ike the 20th Maine, the 15th Alabama had a slow start in its transformation into one of the most dependable and hard-fighting regiments of the Army of Northern Virginia. Ironically, the original regimental commander, Colonel James Cantry of Russell County, contributed little in terms of the regiment's development into an elite fighting machine. An aristocratic attorney and gentleman planter who could command slaves with more skill than Rebels, Colonel Cantry was a political commander. Consequently, he had done more harm than good when leading the 15th Alabama. A fossilized relic of the Mexican War without imagination or flexibility, Cantry's ineffective leadership resulted in the exodus of many fine officers, who transferred out of the regiment to escape Cantry's

45

wrath and incompetence. Like other capable young officers, William Calvin Oates became one of Colonel Cantry's victims, being denied recognition and promotion. In consequence, Oates had almost departed the 15th Alabama during these darkest days for his ambitions.

As an energetic captain obsessed with the singleminded purpose of molding his soldiers into crack troops, Oates had early transformed Company G into one of the best units of the 15th Alabama. Company G consisted of soldiers from the "north end of Henry County, about Abbeville, and the eastern part of Dale County," explained the colonel of his first command. Lieutenant Barnett Hardeman Cody, then a Company G private of the "Henry Pioneers," penned in a letter how, " . . . we have the finest looking company in the Regiment, and have the praise of being the best drill company in the manual of arms . . ." As events on Little Round Top would shortly demonstrate, Lieutenant Cody was not guilty of exaggeration in regard to Company G's quality.

By the time of the Gettysburg campaign, Colonel Oates was a reliable and aggressive young colonel of promise in a successful and confident army in which such officers were on the rise. These young warriors were replacing the older officers of less merit, moving up to take higher command at the brigade and division level.

But much like his troubled youth, Colonel Oates's rise had not been easy. In fact, his appointment to lead the 15th Alabama was under investigation, after Major Alexander A. Lowther—the second regimental commander to have replaced Colonel Cantry after Gaines's Mill—returned to the regiment after a long absence on June 1, 1863, and found Oates in charge and Isaac Feagin second in command. An infuriated Lowther filed a protest because he considered Oates and Feagin junior officers who had been promoted by General Evander McIver Law over him. At the time of the battle of Gettysburg the case was caught up in the red tape and bureaucratic tangles of Richmond.

An animosity had existed between Lowther and Oates from the beginning with Oates despising the autocratic and aristocratic Lowther. Oates believed that an election should have been held for regimental commander when replacing Cantry which would have usually been the case. And he felt that he was more entitled to that position than the less-experienced Lowther by way of ability and battlefield experience, including the shedding of his own blood in a skirmish along the Rapidan River. The ever-popular Oates, of course, would have easily won the election, which was not held, because Lowther was an old crony of Colonel Cantry.

Besides his leadership abilities and tactical flexibility demonstrated on numerous battlefields, one secret of Colonel Oates's success as a commander was his unrivaled popularity among the enlisted ranks. This close relationship between Oates and his men developed early as a result of the colonel's homespun ways, sense of fairness, and unpretentious nature. He treated everyone with equal respect from the humblest private to the highest-ranking general. Oates early understood that in order to get the best battlefield performances from his men, he would have to first earn not only their respect but also their friendship with balanced measures of compassion, fairness, and understanding but without sacrificing firmness. Such a combined approach allowed Colonel Oates to more easily instill the iron discipline necessary for the creation of crack troops.

Many examples can be found of Colonel Oates's humanitarian spirit and almost excessive concern for his soldiers' welfare. The colonel explained that he was the type of commander who always "gave his men as good care and attention as any captain" of the regiment. And he "always contended strenuously and doggedly for their rights" against either state or Confederate authorities.

At one point when orders were issued to transport the 15th Alabama's sick from the regiment and segregate them without adequate care in a separate facility, for instance, Oates exploded in anger. As he described his hot reaction: "I regarded this as a criminally foolish order and determined to disobey to the extent of sending a good faithful, well man to take care of the sick from my company." Colonel Oates decision was a wise one, resulting in "very few of my sick men died, while the number of deaths in other companies was appalling."

Repeatedly, Colonel Oates's careful attention to the welfare of his soldiers rose to the fore. When stricken with a bad case of "the Mumps," Private Cody wrote in a September 1861 letter how "I had the attention given me by My Capt [Oates] and Leut [sic] [Henry C.] Brainard and by my mess [of Company G, which included the colonel's brother Lieutenant Oates] that could be given to me. Capt Oats [sic] will not let me do duty yet for several day[s], he makes me stay in my tent for fear that I will catch cold. Sister he is very kind to me. Sister you know your self that there is and was a great deal of prejudice against Capt Oats and his Company [G]. There was some in Abbeyville that thought he would be a tyrant to his men, but he is not. While I was sick he got any thing that I could eat, and gave it to me. Capt Oats is liked more by the Regiment than any other Captain. There are a great deal of men here that wants to be under him."

Many years after the war Corporal McClendon recalled that when "measles broke out on one of our boys, and on account of friendship existing between his father and Captain Oates, and in fulfillment of his promise that he would take care of the boys, Capt. Oates lost no time in procuring a place at a private residence [and] detailing our 1st Corporal J. F. Melvin . . . to nurse him until he recovered. This was only one of the many kind acts of Capt. Oates to his men whenever an opportunity presented itself . . ."

Oates demonstrated a strong sense of loyalty not only to his men but his commanders. When the 15th Alabama was ordered from Stonewall Jackson's command to a new Alabama brigade under General Law in January 1863 as part of General Lee's decision to reorganize brigades into same-state commands, Oates and other independent-minded Alabamians like Captain Noah Baxter Feagin opposed the decision, for the hard-fighting Stonewall brought success.

Clearly a defiant nature was yet another personal quality of Oates which endeared him to his soldiers. Oates often boldly confronted the Confederate bureaucracy to make sure that his men received what they needed. He made considerable efforts to obtain provisions and supplies, especially shoes for his barefoot soldiers.

At Fredericksburg during the bitter cold of December 1862, the pragmatic leader directed his barefoot men to strip the Yankee dead of their shoes, and these highly disciplined soldiers readily obeyed the unorthodox order. The close familiarity between Oates and his enlisted men was evident on cold winter nights when soldiers, wrote Corporal "Gus" McClendon, were "packing up like a bundle of cigars around Capt. Oates to keep warm."[1]

By any measure and despite his neverending concern for his soldiers' welfare, Oates was also "a strict disciplinarian when on duty, but otherwise allowed his men the largest liberty consistent with proper discipline and the good of the service. He gave his men as good care and attention as any captain in the service possibly could. He always contended strenuously and doggedly for their rights. In this connection [as a captain] once flatly refused to obey an order of the lieutenant-colonel, for which [he] might have been court-martialed . . ." But such defiance, free-thinking, and unorthodox ways slowed Oates's advancement. Colonel James Cantry, evidently envious of his young rival for regimental command, refused to back his advancement.[2]

Unlike some of his officers of inherited wealth and social status, Oates was a self-made man from a poor family of the soil in the Wiregrass country of the Chattahoohee River Valley. As indicated by his easy-going manner, outlook, and behavior, he was a product of the middle-class yeomanry of southeast Alabama. But life had not been easy for William Calvin Oates. Forced to fight for his rights and struggle for survival at an early age, this natural rebel had been born into a dysfunctional family with an alcoholic and sometimes abusive father. But despite the early adversity and setbacks of a hard life, he managed to escape his humbling beginning to create a better life for himself by hard work, determination, ability, and sheer willpower. Despite his advancement in life, Oates knew as little about the privileged world of white-pillared Greek Revival mansions and gangs of slaves in the cottonfields as his humble privates whom he led into battle.

William Calvin Oates had been born in a rustic log cabin to lower middle-class parents on November 30, 1833. Hardworking but not prosperous, his parents were North Carolina-born William Oates and Sarah Sellers. Independent-minded and strong-willed, Oates's mother was ten years older than her husband.

Saddled with much responsibility at an early age as the senior sibling of a large, debt-ridden, and hard-luck family which merely struggled to survive in the Wiregrass country, William Calvin grew into a rough-and-tumble, and optimistic youth despite experiencing more than his fair share of adversity. He took his darkly handsome good looks from his attractive mother. Oates was proud of his unique mixture of Irish, Welsh, and French heritage. His mother's family had migrated southwest from the piney woodlands of North Carolina to Alabama in 1830, searching for the promised and more fertile lands which lay across the mountains. Oates's father had been born in Moore County, North Carolina, and was of Welsh descent. His mother could claim a distinctive mixture of French and Irish heritage. One of Colonel Oates's South Carolina ancestors on his mother's side fought beside the elusive "Swamp Fox," Francis Marion, during the American Revolution.

The Oates clan of the Baptist faith thrived in numbers but not prosperity around a small Pike County settlement known as Oates's Crossroads. There, in the Wiregrass country, the people labored on small plots of land, scratching out a living as best they could under difficult and demanding circumstances.

This was a conservative land, with relatively few slaves and a middle-class populace that was more hardworking and religious-minded than prosperous. However, his mother's deeply religious nature and the fiery spirit of Deep South and backwoods revivalism had little effect on the youthful Oates, who early learned that rural life in untamed southeast Alabama often came down to a simple equation which he also saw in the natural world around him: the hard law of survival of the fittest. Hence, young Oates learned early to forcefully stand up and fight for what he believed to be right and to defend himself out of necessity.

Becoming a leader of the Henry County Rebels in the spring of 1861 only followed a lifelong trend of rebelliousness for Oates. He first began fighting in defense of himself, his younger brothers and sisters, and his own opinions at an early age. And later in life, Oates's hot and sometimes uncontrollable temper guaranteed a good many fistfights and brawls even with larger and stronger opponents.

Not surprisingly, with the difficulties at home he basked in the carefree wanderings of a wild youth, first running away from home at age sixteen after his father unfairly whipped him for not completing farm chores, evidently because of his greater interest in reading than plowing. Oates's relationship with his father was never the same after this beating, which evidently was quite severe. He headed for south Alabama, surviving on his own as a common laborer for several weeks.

By this time, he was bored with farm life and unhappy with his home situation, wanting more out of life than years of mindless drudgery behind a plow and hoping to do little more than feed his own family. Regular attendence at school was denied him because his father needed William in the fields, helping to provide for the family. Oates only attended school for several months out of the year because his father informed him "that he was too poor and had so many children he could not afford me or them any better advantages than the schools [around Oates's Crossroads and] I would not leave him but stuck to my plough daily until the crop was made." For Oates to obtain an education, he earned money by working on nearby farms—for $10.00 per month. He learned enough to become a local teacher of youngsters in the area, indicating an early love of books and knowledge which came primarily from his mother. However, the rougher side came from his father. After Oates was thrashed by a larger school bully who yet "did not whip me," Oates attempted unsuccessfully to secure a firearm to shoot his antagonist. Thereafter, young Oates, who was not the type to forget and forgive, "had it in me for years afterwards to kill him" and carried a pistol for that purpose.

Frustrated with farm work and the lack of educational opportunities, a restlessness took a firm hold of young Oates and at age seventeen he again ran off, this time to the panhandle of Florida after he incorrectly believed that he had killed another man in a violent confrontation in Alabama. This incident that radically changed the course of his life began when a fraudulent spiritual reader came to Oates's Crossroads in June 1851. When the ever-skeptical Oates discovered she was a hoax during a session with the spiritualist, her father, brandishing a board, took out after Oates to protect his investment from the young man's talk. Instead of being intimidated and cowed into silence or run off, Oates turned and faced the father after grabbing a shovel for self-protection. With the father swinging his board, Oates swung his shovel in self-defense, catching the father with "a glancing lick which fractured his skull [and] knocked him unconscious, inflicting a terrible wound," wrote Oates of the incident that caused him to hastily depart Oates's Crossroads.

After fleeing Pike County with only fifty dollars in his pocket and a duffel bag over his broad shoulder, Oates encountered numerous brushes with the law thanks to a hot temper, exaggerated sense of pride, and his own recklessness, while roving across the southwest Southern frontier and through the Gulf states from the early summer of 1851 to the start of 1854. Oates discovered a penchant for getting himself into deep trouble. Like something from an exciting novel, he lived an action-filled and adventurous life which he deliberately kept vague in later years and for good reason, for many of his actions were indeed criminal and immoral: he ran with criminals and desperadoes; gambled at cards as a riverboat gambler for fun and money; fought with his fists with toughs and drunks in saloons and dusty streets outside bordellos; bashed heads, hurled whiskey bottles, gouged eyes, and kicked downed opponents during drunken brawls; survived a nasty bout with yellow fever at Pensacola; acquired three arrest warrants in three different states; discovered to his delight the many seductive charms of French- and Spanish-speaking, dark-eyed, and sultry mulatto women of Louisiana; learned of the seedy aspects of life in cosmopolitan Mobile, New Orleans, and Shreveport; became friends and companions to African Americans, both men and women, of the lowest social standing; fell in love with a Port Lavaca, Texas, girl who broke his heart by infidelity; and thus survived by his wits and natural instincts for year after year on his own. He made a living by selling cigars from a small rented stand on the streets; constructing and painting houses and doing other carpentry work (shingle-maker); serving as a deck hand on a Gulf of Mexico schooner; and working as a common laborer. This was a hard existence, but Oates could not return to Pike County after learning from friends that a warrant for his arrest had been issued.

But living by his wits, cunning, and brute strength laid the foundation for a flexible, experienced and natural leader of Alabama Rebels. In the process of out-smarting and over-matching both the law and lawbreakers across the frontier as well as young women who wanted to marry the reckless wanderer from Alabama, Oates's many adventures and brushes with the law served as a training ground for a free-thinking and resourceful Confederate regimental commander.

However, Oates suddenly tired of his wild lifestyle and returned to his love of books and education at a school in Marshall. He changed the deadend course of his life permanently, gaining wisdom, stability, and maturity by way of his varied experiences. For the first time since he left home, Oates began thinking about and preparing for the future. Most of all, he thought about Oates's Crossroads, missing his family and friends whom he now appreciated more than ever.

Unable to return to Pike County, Alabama, a world-wise, hardened, and cynical Oates settled down in nearby Henry County. There, just southeast of Pike County, Oates embraced a newfound maturity during the early part of 1854, becoming a changed man at the age of twenty. He was determined to start a new life there in the Wiregrass country of the Chattahoochee Valley.

Thanks in no small part to a number of close calls, he transformed his life's values, priorities, and goals, devoting his efforts toward self-improvement and enhancing his position in life. The ever-ambitious Oates redirected his considerable energies into positive pursuits. Even in these efforts, he possessed a talent, meeting with considerable success in everything he did. In many ways, Oates merely embraced former values. Indeed, even as a youth, he had attempted to convince his father that he needed more schooling, but farmwork remained the top priority in the Wiregrass country.

Oates now turned toward the God that he had been rebelling against in almost every possible way, no doubt thanks to his mother's pious influence. Young Oates's sudden transformation from hellraiser to one embracing the Puritan ethic came as a result of a religious experience. Forsaking his sinful ways, he soon developed into a hardworking individual who demonstrated a surprising degree of maturity and responsibility for one of his age. In fact by this time, Oates and his younger brother, John, contemplated devoting their lives to the ministry to spread the word of God.

Savoring his new beginning and fresh start, Oates began teaching school at the small southeast Alabama community of Cottonwood, Houston County. There, near the Alabama–Florida border in the far southeast corner of Alabama on the Chattahoochee, he taught at a one-room school for children and adolescents from 1854–1855 while also continuing to earn money as a carpenter, house builder, farmhand, and house painter to make ends meet.

Wise and worldly beyond his years, Oates was also a student during this formative period, learning as much as he could while teaching in order to grasp the promise of the future. More than ever before, he now realized that education was the key to his future advancement and started saving money for a higher level of education.

By 1855 after about a year of teaching at Cottonwood, Oates was ready to accept the challenge. Determined to succeed, he applied for admission at the Lawrenceville Academy in nearby Lawrenceville, Alabama. There Oates learned what he had missed in his early days, working hard to achieve his goal. In his own words, Oates recorded with pride how he "made most rapid progress." He excelled and surpassed the toughest academic standards of the academy where he became proficient in Latin and composition and joined the debating society. In addition, he became a master of six books of geometry.

After the end of the six month session at Lawrenceville and with a high standing in his class, Oates was forced to secure more permanent employment to pay for the next year's tuition. He traveled to Houston County for the opportunity to teach school at the Rocky Creek Camp Ground near the small town of Woodville [now Gordon and immediately northeast of Cottonwood] on the Chattahoochee. For the first time, he became a player in community life and was presented with the opportunity to climb the social ladder by joining the Masonic Order.

But Oates possessed ambitions that soon took him away from Woodville, and he returned to Lawrenceville to complete his education. As a full-time student, Oates eagerly embarked upon more difficult courses, which forced him to cease his part-time work as a farmhand. Oates was, in his own words, "one of the best debaters in the school [and] was apt in composition . . ." More important, Oates developed an interest in political matters, especially the issue of states' rights and Southern nationalism.

Having felt a sense of community in Woodville where he was respected by people of all standing, and unable to return to Oates's Crossroads, the young man returned to Houston County near the Florida border. There he resumed teaching once again. But more important, he became an active participant in the community and political life of Woodville. Even while being wanted by the law of Pike County, Oates was so respected in Woodville that he became an arbitrator of conflict, serving as the unofficial justice of the peace and judge for the community. In 1858, Oates headed north and upriver to the thriving commercial and trading center of Eufaula in Barbour County on the Chattahoochee, where opportunity beckoned as never before. Compared to Oates's Crossroads, Cottonwood, Lawrenceville, and Woodville, Eufaula was the New Orleans of the Chattahoochee River Country of the Wiregrass.

Continuing to be a player in the society that he had so often rebelled against, Oates entered into the study of law at the established and respected law firm of Pugh, Bullock, and Buford in Eufaula during the spring of 1858, serving as a clerk for the powerful law firm. Thus began Oates's legal education, which often consisted of studying sixteen hours each day under Jefferson Bullock's guidance. By October 1858, the fast-learning and intelligent Oates felt confident enough to attempt to pass the bar, which he did after what a judge—one of the oral examiners—deemed was "the best examination I ever witnessed." By any measure, the young man had come a long way from the hardscrabble farm at Oates's Crossroads and the unruly life on the wild frontier.

As the youngest member of this influencial law firm, Oates early demonstrated the skills of a successful lawyer, showing flashes of legal brilliance and clear and precise reasoning in the courtroom. He quickly established a reputation for a shrewd mind and a work ethic second to none. After serving on the hard-hitting legal team for several months, Oates was determined to begin his own law practice, striking out on his own as so often in the past. On December 1, 1858, after departing Eufaula, Oates established himself as an attorney in Abbeville, southwest of Eufaula in neighboring Henry County, after passing the Georgia bar in the same year as gaining his admission to the Alabama bar. It was a meager beginning, with Oates renting out a small shop and setting up his practice after purchasing a few law books.

The ambitious Oates also pursued another line of work to compliment his thriving law practice, buying a small newspaper in Abbeville. He became the outspoken editor of the leading Democratic newspaper, a weekly which he proudly named *The Abbeville Banner*. Oates reached his intellectual zenith during this period, gaining a free reign to fully expound his views and ideas on a wide variety of subjects. As could be expected from his past, Oates often took controversial positions based more upon sound reason and logic rather than popular appeal. In this sense, Oates remained yet the rebel, challenging the status quo as in the past. To ensure a longlife for *The Abbeville Banner*, he sold stock to enterpreneural Henry County planters, merchants, and businessmen, guaranteeing a secure voice in Abbeville and the Chattahoochee Valley.

With the pragmatic legal sense of a smart lawyer and as a political moderate who sought solution in compromise rather than a clash of arms, Oates opposed secession unlike the majority of southeast Alabama residents and a rival Abbeville newspaper, *The New South*. Most of all, he was a Southern nationalist, believing that wise statesmenship, diplomacy, and compromise could avert the horror of civil war. He boldly penned front-page editorials which were anti-secessionist, running counter to the popular sentiment of his community and region.

Busy with legal disputes and newspaper work, Oates had no time to choose a wife and remained a confirmed bachelor despite his success in life and his Gallic good looks and engaging personality. He possessed a handsome appearance with dark eyes and hair. He stood straight and tall with a well-developed physique. But Oates's past frolicking in bedrooms, meadows, and wagons left him with few, if any, romantic illusions about love and romance even though yet a young man.

By 1861, Oates could proudly look back upon a successful life despite its hard beginning. By the start of the war he was an esteemed and respected member of the community of Abbeville and Henry County. "His advantages in the struggle for a foothold in life were very poor [having] never obtained anything in life worth having except by his own exertions. He relied on his natural energy, indomitable courage and strict integrity for his success in life."

In a letter to the author, a relative of an Abbeville community leader of the day described Oates as an "extremely intelligent [man and] he could be very cool, calculating and shrewd, but on the other hand, he could be kind and gentle and loving and generous." But Colonel Oates's most important traits had been forged during the antebellum period—resourcefulness and determination.[3]

★ ★ ★

Thus when the call went up in 1861, Oates helped raise a company of men for his beloved South from northern Henry County and the eastern half of Dale County—the Henry Pioneers, or Company G, 15th Alabama. With his men wearing the brown floppy hats that identified them on the battlefield, he led "Oates's Tigers" skillfully in the Virginia battles of Front Royal, Winchester, and Cross Keys during Stonewall's Valley campaign. Then he demonstrated more leadership ability on the eve of the Maryland invasion until falling wounded at Chantilly, Virginia, on September 1, 1862, just after General Lee's dramatic victory at Second Manassas.

Like everything else he achieved in life, Oates's rise in the Confederate army was the result of hard work, natural ability, and applied skills, including leadership abilities, tactical judgment, and aggressiveness. As demonstrated on battlefields across the South, he was a natural soldier and leader of men. In fact, Oates served capably as the acting commander of the 15th Alabama at various times after Antietam in the absence of both Colonel James Fletcher Treutlen, the regiment's second commander after Cantry, and Major Lowther throughout most of 1862, including at Fredericksburg after Lieutenant Colonel Isaac Ball Feagin fell wounded at Boteler's Mill.

After Colonel Treutlen resigned in late April 1863 and with Major Lowther, who was to have replaced him by right of senority, remaining absent, Oates took command of the regiment in time for the Gettysburg campaign. Lieutenant Colonel Feagin waived his right to take command—a compliment to Oates's skill and leadership ability.

Lieutenant Colonel Oates came close to receiving a full colonel's rank when he was promoted to colonel on May 12, 1863, but that rank was not yet confirmed by the Confederate Congress. This well-deserved rank was never officially approved by Congress, with the commission becoming entangled in political intrigue and controversy.

In mid-August 1864 outside Petersburg near Fussell's Mills and while leading the 48th Alabama Infantry, Colonel Oates would lose his right arm to a minie ball. Oates's tragic loss was not surprising as his aggressiveness on the battlefield bordered on recklessness. But not until February 1865 would Congress *officially* bestow Oates with his long-deserved rank of lieutenant colonel.

But despite never officially earning the full rank of colonel, he considered himself a colonel and claimed that rank for himself in typical Oates style.

A previously unrecognized factor may partly explain why Oates would perform so well during the war and especially on July 2, 1863, at Gettysburg. This factor might also explain Oates's sudden, if not miraculous, transformation from a wild, undisciplined life on the run as a fugitive from the law to his rapid rise up the social ladder. Some new evidence indicates that this hard-fighting "citizen-soldier" from southeast Alabama might have possessed a formal military background. Indeed, the name of a "Wm C. Oates" from the state of Alabama was listed on the original cadet roster of the Weston Military Institute, Nashville, Tennessee, for the year 1854. Based on this evidence, Oates might well have attended the Weston Military Institute during the 1855 academic year. If so, then such military training would partly explain not only Oates's rise in antebellum society but also his performance at Little Round Top.

In any event, by the time of the Gettysburg campaign, "Colonel" Oates would be well-suited for the challenge of Little Round Top. He was aggressive and hard as nails with a widespread reputation as a promising young officer of ability. Tactically flexible and open-minded unlike many respected West Pointers of the Army of Northern Virginia, Oates led by example, going into combat at the head of his Alabama soldiers.[4]

Oates had been forced out of necessity to early rely upon his own abilities and instincts both as a means of survival and in order to build a decent life for himself. Most of all, he was a survivor who had struggled through tough times by strength of character. And in the upcoming clash for possession of Little Round Top at Gettysburg, Colonel Oates would be forced into a familiar position of once again relying upon his own abilities and instincts to face the stiff challenge that lay before him and overcome the odds as so often in the past.[5]

CHAPTER IV

Deadly Roads to Gettysburg

"The practice in all the Confederate armies was to charge the Union troops in strong positions and to charge and capture batteries of artillery. They thus displayed reckless gallantry and many men were unnecessarily sacrificed."

—Colonel William C. Oates

*I*n many ways, the final outcome of the 15th Alabama's effort to capture Little Round Top would be determined by the complex relationship between General Robert E. Lee and his top lieutenant after Stonewall Jackson's fall at Chancellorsville, General James Longstreet, and their divergent tactical views at Gettysburg. The primary reason the 15th Alabama soldiers would be fated to attack an all but impregnable position without support and with little chance for success on July 2 was because General Lee continued to place too much faith in the wisdom of the tactical offensive, while overestimating the offensive capabilities of his army and underestimating his opponent.

In opposition to General Lee's views, General Longstreet

placed his faith in the tactical defensive during the Pennsylvania invasion. Ironically, however, it would be Longstreet's troops who would be ordered by Lee to launch the offensive thrust in an effort to roll up the left flank of the Army of the Potomac on July 2. During the three bloody days of destiny in early July 1863 in south-central Pennsylvania, this difference in tactical thought between Lee and Longstreet would come to the fore.

The fate of General Lee's army during its second invasion of the North ironically had already been largely determined by the new realities of modern warfare, with modern weaponry far out-pacing traditional tactics, and General Lee's uncritical faith placed upon the supremacy of the tactical offensive. Indeed, the excessively high cost of the past battlefield performances of the Army of Northern Virginia as a result of the over-reliance on the tactical offensive already could largely predict the almost inevitable outcome of the three-day struggle at Gettysburg. Colonel Oates would long lament how, "the practice in all the Confederate armies was to charge the Union troops in strong positions and to charge and capture batteries of artillery. They thus displayed reckless gallantry and many men were unnecessarily sacrificed."

General Lee's adjutant, Colonel Walter Herron Taylor, described in a May 1863 letter how, "the operations of this army under Genl Lee during that time will compare favorably with the most brilliant engagements ever recorded. When I consider our numerical weakness, our limited resources and the great strength & equipments of the enemy, I am astonished at the result. Surely the hand of God was on our side."

But, in terms of paving the way to decisive victory, it must have been a Yankee God who was granting "the most brilliant engagements ever recorded" in 1862–63, while the Army of Northern Virginia was slowly being destroyed by a gradual attrition of its best men and officers. And it was this fatal attrition which was leading the Union ever closer to decisive victory with each passing month, while sabotaging the Army of Northern Virginia's chances for a successful Northern invasion.[1]

The most recent example of this ill-fated equation for Rebel fortunes at Gettysburg was one of the greatest of Southern victories to date, Chancellorsville. There, in May 1863, the dynamic leadership team of Generals Stonewall Jackson and Robert E. Lee performed at their best. The Army of Northern Virginia reached its zenith by once again defeating the Army of the Potomac on Virginia soil, releasing it for the march north into Pennsylvania. But, ironically, this dazzling success had brought neither decisive results, independence, or foreign recognition, which the South now needed most of all to survive. And in the process, General Lee's invaluable "right-arm," Stonewall Jackson, had been mortally wounded after being hit by the bullets of a panicky group of North Carolina soldiers. But worst of all for Southern fortunes, to achieve this success the Army of Northern Virginia had once again been severely punished during the brutal fighting west of Fredericksburg. The Chancellorsville victory cost the lives of thousands of hardened veterans who General Lee simply could not afford to lose. The conflict had turned into a brutal war of attrition, and one that the manpower-short and resource-short Confederacy could not possibly win given the horrendous losses with each barren victory. Consequently, despite beating the Army of the Potomac again and again, time was already running out on the Army of Northern Virginia by the summer of 1863.

Captain Ham Chamberlayne emphasized the frightful cost among General Lee's crippled officer corps during the largely futile victories across Virginia, writing in a letter how "our loss in officers was unparalleled." Amid the springtime fields and forests of Spotsylvania County around Chancellorsville, five of General Lee's colonels were killed, and almost seventeen hundred hardened veterans of the Army of Northern Virginia were fatally cut down amid the carnage. In total, more than thirteen thousand Confederate officers and men, who could not be replaced in Lee's depleted ranks unlike the Army of the Potomac, out of an army of barely sixty thousand were lost at Chancellorsville. General Lee had lost 22 percent of his strength while the Army of the Potomac lost only 13 percent of its strength. This disproportionate loss resulting from General Lee's dramatic "victory" at Chancellorsville shortly before the Pennsylvania invasion bode ill tidings for Southern fortunes in regard to the outcome of the decisive clash at Gettysburg.

Some of the best units—regiments, brigades, and divisions— had been reduced to dangerously low numbers by the grim harvest up to the time of the Pennsylvania invasion. Even General Jackson's famous II Corps, now under the eccentric General Richard Ewell, was "crippled" after the bloodletting at Chancellorsville. And by the midpoint of the war, it was becoming more difficult, if not impossible, for General Lee to replace the thousands of killed and wounded officers with men of equal caliber. By July 1863, many of the best and brightest of the Army of Northern Virginia were lying in shallow graves across Virginia and Maryland.[2]

Blinded by optimism, Colonel Taylor, General Lee's faithful adjutant, wrote in a hopeful letter from Chambersburg, Pennsylvania, on June 29, 1863, "We have progressed swimmingly thus far and find the country a pleasant one . . . with God's help we expect to take a step or two towards an honorable peace." But the burning desire to capture Pennsylvania's capital of Harrisburg and other Northern cities to "conquer a peace" had taken Lee's army too far north with too little. Yet the Confederates marching into south-central Pennsylvania continued to envision lofty dreams of future success in the North and Generals Ambrose Powell Hill's and James Longstreet's corps were concentrated around Chambersburg, Pennsylvania, by the end of June.[3]

By the time of the Gettysburg campaign, the 15th Alabama was serving in General Law's Alabama Brigade of Hood's Division in Longstreet's I Corps. And because General Lee would decide against Longstreet's defensive tactics at Gettysburg, it would be the common soldiers like Colonel Oates's Alabama Rebels who would pay the high price for the folly of the heavy reliance upon offensive tactics to bring decisive victory. This self-defeating policy would once again result in devastating losses, working to the advantage of a more powerful opponent—the Army of the Potomac. And the high losses from overly aggressive tactics in the past on the eve of the greatest battle about to be fought on Northern soil would be a fatal combination for Confederate fortunes. The army's soaring spirits resulting from a string of past victories caused these Rebels, including General Lee, to largely overlook their army's limitations and deficiencies. The past victories of the Seven Days, Second Manassas, Fredericksburg, and Chancellorsville had not only limited the chances for future success in Pennsylvania but had also fostered a dangerous overconfidence which now helped to set the stage for a decisive Confederate defeat in Pennsylvania. While pushing through the rich farmlands of southern Pennsylvania, this confidence had only continued to swell through General Lee's ranks. Ironically, the Confederate faith in inevitable success in Pennsylvania that summer caused General Lee to bet everything on winning decisive victory there.

The folly of Northern invasion and the many limitations of the Army of Northern Virginia to wage a successful invasion north of the Potomac was evident in the words of some of the army's high-ranking leaders. As General Lee's adjutant wrote in a September 21, 1862, letter: "Give us the men & then talk about invading Penn. Our present army is not equal to the task in my opinion."

Likewise having a realistic assessment of the army's ever diminishing capabilities, General Pender scribbled in a September 22, 1862, letter that "our Army has shown itself incapable of invasion and we had better stick to the defensive." But now these not openly acknowledged truths about the Confederate army's serious limitations and lack of offensive capabilities continued to be ignored, minimized, and overlooked by the top levels of Confederate leadership. General Lee had proposed the Pennsylvania invasion and President Jefferson Davis had accepted it.[4]

Despite the serious manpower, supply, and logistical limitations, General Lee was gambling everything on one toss of the dice in Pennsylvania in part because his army was in such bad shape. Thanks to bureaucratic incompetence in Richmond and logistical and transportation limitations across the Confederacy, the common soldiers in the Army of Northern Virginia's ranks continued to fight without many bare essentials, and this only increased during the campaign north of the Potomac.

Back in 1862, for instance, Oates had thanked the ladies of the Soldiers' Aid Society for donating clothing to the 15th Alabama, appreciating the timely arrival of the "large quantity of clothing . . . Shirts, Drawers, Socks, etc, which I have distributed among the most needy members of my company. The clothing arrived most opportunely, being very much needed by many of the men." And supplies had dwindled as the war lengthened until the Alabamians subsisted upon what they took from the bodies of dead Yankees.[5]

During the lengthy march into Pennsylvania, General Lee could count only around 75,000 in the Army of Northern Virginia to defeat the Army of the Potomac, capture Harrisburg, subdue thousands of other Northern troops and militia, and then turn east to march upon and conquer the most heavily fortified city on the North American continent, Washington, D.C.[6]

During the 1862 battles across Virginia and Maryland, the 15th Alabama had suffered proportionately, losing some of its best soldiers during the bloody culling that seemed to have no end. The officer corps of the 15th Alabama was "badly depleted in the fighting of 1861 and 1862" alone. One of the lucky ones who would survive to endure the ultimate humiliation at Appomattox Court House in April 1865, Corporal McClendon wrote of the terrible slaughter during General Lee's first invasion of the North in western Maryland at Antietam. Shocked by the 15th Alabama's decimation, the young 15th Alabama soldier described how "all our brigade and nearly all of the regimental field officers were either killed or wounded in the engagements over at Manassas, and we were without a brigade commander [and during the Maryland campaign] our regiment was ably commanded by Captain J. B. Feagin of Co. 'B' afterwards Colonel Feagin."[7]

Besides Federal bullets and shells and the epidemics of disease and an increase in desertions, the mere physical demands of hard campaigning throughout 1862 had also reduced the Southern army's capabilities. And the cost of earning the reputation of

Stonewall's "Foot-Cavalry" after months of arduous marching likewise had not come cheaply for the 15th Alabama. Many 15th Alabama soldiers had been broken down in body and spirit after months of hard marching and the demands of vigorous campaigning. One such victim to fall out of the ranks of Colonel Oates's command was William J. Hillard. Along with many comrades, Hillard's "health succumbed to the fatigues of the rapid marches and exhausting work by which Jackson's 'foot-cavalry' succeeded in defeating the enemy . . ."

These affects of hard campaigning were evident in the 15th Alabama in the deaths of two young brothers of Company H. The unfortunate victims were Robert Byrd, age twenty-six, and Ira Byrd, age twenty-four, who died in January 1863 and November 1862, respectively. Exhaustion and weakness from months of arduous campaigning throughout 1862 caused widespread disease, taking many 15th Alabama soldiers from the ranks.

In a letter to his mother, then Private Barnett Hardeman Cody scribbled how " . . . it takes a person with an iron Constitution to stand [Stonewall Jackson's] marches. I have often marched day and night without a thing to eat. When we march we march from fifteen to twenty five miles a day. If all of our Generals was like Jackson this war would not last long." And Lieutenant James M. Ellison penned in a July 1862 letter to his wife Camilla at their Alabama plantation how "nearly all the officers of our Regt. are in town sick & used up" by the rigors of hard campaigning.[8]

After marching and fighting month after month, Private Lary was disillusioned and war-weary from his exertions and the loss of so many comrades before the end of 1862. Private Lary recorded in a bitter letter the tragedy of the 15th Alabama's service in Virginia: "Tis here the reaper commenced the harvest of death which had already gathered and still continues to reap the choicest heads in the regiment . . . beneath the soil of Prince William [County, Virginia], now slumber in quiet repose, secure from summer's heat and winter's cold, from the cares of life and shock of strife, the noblest and best of the regiment [and] in less than six weeks over one hundred of the regiment were buried—sleeping the death sleep—from which no sound can ever disturb them until the great awaking morn . . ." Then later, while the 15th Alabama was encamped near Haymarket, Virginia, he described in another letter how "pneumonia, rheumatism, jaundice and the thousand other ills . . . have killed or temporarily disabled two-thirds of the command."[9]

By any measure, the devastating losses from disease and battle had reduced the 15th Alabama's ranks fearfully by the time of the Gettysburg campaign. And as cruel fate would have it, the 15th Alabama would suffer the highest losses of any regiment in General Law's Alabama Brigade during the four years of war, with nearly 260 either killed or wounded in battles and another 438 who died from disease, while another 136 of Colonel Oates's soldiers were captured.

But the awful devastation from the battles in Virginia and Maryland and the ravages of disease left behind a seasoned and well-honed cadre of hardened veterans. What was now left of the decimated 15th Alabama was an elite group of crack veterans who believed themselves to be "better, tougher, [and] braver than any other soldiers" in the army, wrote Captain Noah Baxter Feagin, who commanded the "Midway Southern Guards" from Barbour County. Such high-spirited soldiers would soon rise to the challenge of the struggle for Little Round Top.

By this time, Colonel Oates was also convinced that he commanded some of the finest infantry of the Army of Northern Virginia, and he believed that they fought better than the Virginia boys and other eastern troops from the South. But he understood that his men never received the credit and recognition due in an army dominated by Virginians. During the war and long afterward, Oates lamented the only too common injustice of Virginia troops continuously gaining the lion's share of recognition and credit for battlefield performances.

Later Colonel Oates would attempt to ascertain why Rebels from the Deep South and the West generally fought better than the Virginians. In Colonel Oates's analysis, "without the least prejudice I do believe now and thought so all along through the war, that the men from the Cotton States (and the farther west the more so) were better soldiers and harder fighters than those from the Border States [which can be] attributed . . . to the difference between the frontiersman and the citizen of more refined and regular habits of the older States." The stirring drama which was about to be played out on the stage of Little Round Top on July 2 would soon prove Colonel Oates's analysis to be largely correct.[10]

CHAPTER V

Destiny Calls

*"Certainly there was no premonition that the next morning
[July 1, 1863] was to open the great battle of the campaign."*

—Col. E. P. Alexander on the accident
of the battle of Gettysburg

Like many great battles throughout the course of history, the battle of Gettysburg began by accident. On a scorching July 1, the
advance units of both armies suddenly collided in the rolling fields
and ridges northwest of the small town of Gettysburg, a tiny agricultural community of strategic importance, with a host of dusty
roads converging from every direction like the spokes of a wagon.

General Lee's army was on the march toward the state capital
of Harrisburg and was scattered across southern Pennsylvania
unprepared for a decisive showdown. In fact, General Ewell was
closing in on the state capital of Harrisburg when recalled to concentrate at Gettysburg, infuriating "Old Baldy," who was thus
denied the opportunity of being the first Confederate to capture a
state capital north of the Potomac.

The fighting began when Confederate soldiers of the division of General Henry Heth, a West Pointer and Mexican War veteran of A. P. Hill's corps, marched for Gettysburg in search of supplies, especially shoes. Instead, Hill's Rebels met Union cavalry on the ridges of the northwestern outskirts of the small town of 2,400, which was nestled in a shallow valley. The fighting intensified, roaring to levels that warned the advancing troops on both sides that a large battle was brewing at Gettysburg.[1]

With the fighting starting to rage out-of-control, General Lee recalled his widely scattered units as rapidly as possible to concentrate them before the entire Army of the Potomac arrived. This was a formidable objective, especially in the intense heat of early July with his units widely scattered and divided by miles. Undertaking the army's longest return march was General Ewell in advance at Harrisburg. In the army's rear with the supply and munition wagons and serving as the Army of Northern Virginia's guardians in enemy country, General Longstreet's veterans were encamped in the lush fields and shady woodlots of summer among the rolling hills along the western edge of South Mountain around Chambersburg when the great storm erupted.

Before the end of July 1, General Lee's forces had mauled the two advance corps of the Army of the Potomac after savage fighting from morning to evening. A victorious tide of Southerners hurled the XI Corps through the body-strewn woodlands and grain fields north of Gettysburg. Unleashing the "Rebel Yell," the victorious Confederates pushed the I Corps off the high ground of Seminary Ridge and through Gettysburg in panic. Before the onrushing waves of howling Rebels, the defeated Yankees fell back east of town. There the shattered blue units regrouped to take defensive positions on the high ground of Cemetery Ridge.

Meanwhile, just west of New Guilford Courthouse, Colonel Oates's men heard the rumble of cannon booming like distant thunder to the southeast during the sweltering afternoon of July 1. But at first no one was particularly alarmed by the sound of fighting off in the distance. If a serious fight was brewing, they would have been ordered forward to that point, and so far no word was forthcoming from headquarters. Some of the Alabamians spent the evening of July 1 around their campfires along the crest of a ridge near New Guilford, writing letters, smoking pipes, and thinking of home, while others remained on "picket duty at or near a place called New Guilford . . . the men were tired and hungry," wrote Private Jordan. There, encamped along the dusty Chambersburg Pike leading east to Gettysburg, General Law's Alabama Brigade lay in the army's rear on detached service from Hood's Division. Because of the scorching hot weather, Colonel Oates's soldiers enjoyed the respite far behind General Lee's advance units, resting and gaining strength for the challenges that they knew loomed ahead somewhere down the pike.

Situated far east of the main army, the Alabama soldiers served as the army's guardians. Indeed, Jeb Stuart and his cavalry were absent, because Lee's foremost Virginia cavalier "had decided to do what he wanted"—raiding and winning more personal acclaim as in the past—rather than what General Lee expected which was to serve as the "eyes and ears" of his army on the march deep in enemy territory. But if a threat in the Army of Northern Virginia's rear suddenly developed, then these Alabama veterans would be in position to parry the threat. Oates and his men felt honored by their role in providing the protective service usually assigned to General Lee's vigilant cavalrymen.[2]

Enjoying a comfortable bivouac amid the broad grain fields and grassy meadows west of Guilford Courthouse, the Alabama boys rested beside their lengthy rows of stacked muskets in the descending July 1 darkness shrouding the quiet, dark valley of the Cumberland. The soldiers' legs were weary, with feet blistered and sore, after marching from the depths of Virginia. But there would not be enough time for Oates's men to fully recuperate from the fatigues of the hot summer weather and the past two weeks of hard marching through the valleys and hills of Virginia, Maryland, and Pennsylvania.

Some ragged Alabama Rebels literally lived "high on the hog," killing and butchering a few fat Chester White hogs for dinner around smoking campfires. Despite Lee's General Orders No. 27

forbidding such actions that meant the destruction of private property of the people of the Commonwealth of Pennsylvania, Colonel Oates felt that his boys should have decent food whenever possible, which was not often. Therefore, he decided to ignore Lee's General Orders No. 27. Already he had been amused by his farm boys in gray expertly working cows' utters with well-honed skill to fill canteens with milk at a farm near Greencastle and had said nothing to them. Now outside New Guilford, he allowed twenty-six-year-old Captain William A. Edwards, who led the Dale County Beauregards of Company E, to head a hog-killing detail. A natural forager as well as a hard fighter, Captain Edwards was a good choice for the assignment because, as Colonel Oates explained, "he was a good man [a future Methodist minister], but became so excited in battle that he scarcely knew what he was doing." As indicated by his directive that went against General Lee's orders, the young Alabama colonel instinctively seemed to know that his soldiers would need all their strength during the next few days. Now among the last remaining infantrymen in the Army of Northern Virginia's rear, the 15th Alabama soldiers hoped that no nightmarish fighting such as that witnessed at Antietam was imminent but the booming cannon around Gettysburg earlier seemed to indicate otherwise.

Finally, not surprised to receive a new set of marching orders, Colonel Oates was suddenly placed on the alert. "About dark we received an order to be ready to move at any moment. Subsequently we were ordered to cook rations and to be ready to move at three o'clock A.M.," penned the colonel of the inevitable directives that he had known were headed his way. Indeed, a courier from General Longstreet arrived with orders for General Law's brigade to link with General Hood's division and rejoin the I Corps at Gettysburg.

General Hood's other three brigades of his division had already begun marching southeastward for Gettysburg during the previous night. Now the Alabamians's spirits rose upon receiving the orders releasing them from their boring rear-guard assignment. General George Pickett's division reached Chambersburg to take over guarding the supply and munition wagons in the army's rear along with General John D. Imboden's cavalry, which garnered the same assignment. General Law's Alabama Brigade was free to march southeast for Gettysburg.[3]

With Enfield rifles on shoulders, the westernmost Alabama soldiers formed in column in the blackness and hurriedly departed their bivouac area west of Guilford Courthouse as early as "about 2 o'clock in the night in the evening of July 2," wrote Private Jordan.

However it was some two hours later before the entire 487 soldiers of the 15th Alabama and General Law's Brigade swung out of their New Guilford encampment in high spirits, knowing that they would soon meet the Yankees. Colonel Oates described how "it was near 4 o'clock when the brigade was put in motion" and the march began. In the darkness yet warm and humid, after pushing northeastward to regain the Chambersburg Pike, the men from southeast Alabama in ragged and sun-faded uniforms swung down the narrow, dirt road toward Gettysburg, about twenty-five miles to the southeast.

Colonel Oates's Alabama soldiers moved off at a brisk pace after gobbling down only a few mouthfuls of breakfast. At this time of early morning only the sharp cry of the whippoorwill or circling night hawk could be heard echoing out of the darkness from the direction of the black mountain range to the east. These nocturnal sounds of the forest no doubt reminded Colonel Oates's farmers, woodsmen, and hunters of their Chattahoochee River Valley homeland, which was now farther away than ever before.

Meanwhile, General Lee's army remained widely scattered. Generals Pickett and Law's brigades were at one end of the Army of Northern Virginia, General Ewell's division was at the other, and Jeb Stuart's absent cavalry was roving the Maryland countryside on the outskirts of Washington, D.C. far away from Gettysburg where it was now needed for General Lee to ascertain the Union army's strength and position.[4]

For hours in the dark of the sultry Pennsylvania night, the Alabama Rebels in Colonel Oates's command marched rapidly toward the southeast, racing the sunrise to link with the main army at Gettysburg before it was too late. These hardened Alabama veterans moved swiftly through the inky darkness, almost as if sensing that they would play an important role in the upcoming contest. Certainly, General Law sensed as much, hurrying his Alabama regiments forward without a break and with no stops to rest as usual.

Finally, the blazing sun of July 2 inched up through the heat-hazed skies of early morning, promising another hot and humid summer day in south-central Pennsylvania. These Deep South soldiers knew that they would soon begin to feel a blistering early summer heat that they had once believed was only possible in the Chattahoochee Valley. All the while, they kept pushing rapidly onward at a rate that they had never equaled even as General Stonewall's famous "foot-cavalry."

The blood-red sun rising in a cloudless sky only caused the 15th Alabama men to march faster before the intense heat increased to take its inevitable toll on their legs and bodies. Hour after hour they pushed forward, swinging relentlessly through the agricultural county of Franklin and into Adams, where Gettysburg was the county seat.

It was not easy marching for the ill-shod Alabamians, especially upon crossing the imposing range of mountains looming just west of Gettysburg, the South Mountain Range about halfway between Chambersburg and Gettysburg. However, the distant boom of cannon echoing to the southeast around Gettysburg kept the Alabama boys in a tight column and moving swiftly.

Seemingly becoming heavier with each passing mile, the rifled muskets on shoulders made muscles ache, and the march's grueling pace caused increasing numbers of Colonel Oates's soldiers to hobble on blistered and sore feet. Consequently, some Alabama soldiers began to fall out of column never to rejoin the regiment during its most important engagement on this day of destiny. The intensifying heat and the swirling dust which rose like a cloud parched the throats and lips of those who remained in column.

All the while, a cloud of dust covered the uniforms of the marching men like a dirty blanket, giving Oates's boys the look of dirty scarecrows from the nearby cornfields. The constant rattle of clattering gear echoed down the long column stretched out for miles along the dirt road. Canteens, bayonets scabbards, and tin cups clanged in a steady rhythm in the humid July morning air, while the lengthy formations of General Law's Alabama brigade trudged past the green and yellow fields of Pennsylvania, which lined the dusty Chambersburg road leading to Gettysburg.

During this grueling march to reach the gathering Army of Northern Virginia at Gettysburg, the 15th Alabama Rebels could be identified by the brass company letters and regimental numbers on their slough hats and kepis. By the time of the Gettysburg campaign, Colonel Oates's soldiers wore this distinctive identification for good reason. As captain of Company G, Oates had ordered his men to do so because far too many of his close friends and neighbors from the Wiregrass country had been buried in graves marked "Unknown" across Virginia and Maryland. Oates explained that "to avoid just such contingencies, and that the men of the company might be identified, I procured and placed on their caps Co. G, 15th Alabama." The soldiers of other 15th Alabama companies followed suit, placing brass letters of A through K on hats. Also some of the more states-rights-minded of Colonel Oates's Rebels placed the letters "AL" or "ALA" on their hats to designate the home state they now believed they were fighting to save in Pennsylvania.

For the 15th Alabama Rebels, "veterans ruddy and brown, with the health and hardness that outdoor living creates," the march of July 2 to reach Gettysburg to join the fight was the most arduous and demanding of the war because of the hot weather, clouds of choking dust, and orders forbidding a halt. Having a longer distance to cover than most of General Lee's soldiers, additional numbers of the 15th Alabama's men fell out of the column to never reach Gettysburg. After falling by the roadside in exhaustion or with injured feet and legs, some worn Alabamians slumped in fence corners, and under trees or in the dusty ditches lining the road. And some 15th Alabama men left the column for different reasons on this day. For instance, "a good soldier," Allen W.

Sholen, and James W. Calloway, age nineteen and "always healthy and active," fell out of line with permission to fill canteens with spring water. But the two Rebels never rejoined the column for some unknown reason. Fearing the worst, Colonel Oates could only lament how since "they were in the enemy's country and none of their Southern friends have ever heard a word of either since, it may be that they were killed by bushwhackers."

The rapid march to reach Gettysburg to join the main army was costly for the 15th Alabama. A good percentage of the Alabama regiment that had crossed the Potomac River would not reach Gettysburg to join the struggle. Of the almost six hundred 15th Alabama soldiers who originally marched into Pennsylvania with supreme confidence and the 487 who departed the New Guilford encampment, only around 450 remained with the regiment as it finally neared Gettysburg.[5]

All the while, General Law's Alabama Brigade moved ever southeastward at a rapid pace, crossing small creeks and pushing for Gettysburg along the dust-shrouded Chambersburg Pike. The hardened warriors in gray and butternut of the 4th, 15th, 44th, 47th, and 48th Alabama Infantry continued onward with the belief that another Second Manassas or Chancellorsville victory awaited them. And having enlisted at the war's beginning, the men of the 15th Alabama considered themselves vastly superior to the soldiers of the less experienced "Fortykins," or the 44th, 47th, and 48th Alabama which entered the war relatively late in 1862.

Finally just before noon on July 2, the weary Alabama boys, sweaty and covered in dust, crossed the clear waters of Marsh Creek about four miles west of Gettysburg. All the while, the summer heat grew more intense as the sun inched higher in a blazing sky and the fate of the beleaguered Southern nation hung in the balance during the most decisive clash between the Army of Northern Virginia and the Army of the Potomac to date. Nearing the small agricultural community of Gettysburg on the double, these hard-marching Alabama Rebels braced for the serious work ahead after having listened to the steady roar of cannon and musketry growing closer hour after hour.

The dull thudding of the cannon now kept the column closed-up and straggling ceased as Colonel Oates's soldiers finally neared Gettysburg. Indeed, the Alabamians understood that there could be no more straggling today when everyone would be needed for their next meeting with the enemy. As so often in the past, these Alabama soldiers were eager to once again engage the boys in blue. Indicating the serious work which lay ahead, the Alabamians were presented with the grisly sight of the aftermath of the bitter fighting that had already taken place. As Colonel Oates explained: "For two or three miles before we arrived [at Gettysburg] we saw many field hospitals—wounded men and thousands of prisoners, evidencing the bloody engagement of the previous evening."[6]

In record time, the 15th Alabama had surpassed even the legendary standards of Stonewall's "foot-cavalry," especially during summer weather. Colonel Oates's soldiers trekked more than twenty grueling miles to reach Gettysburg and rejoin the nearly 7,500 Deep South Rebels of Hood's Division near Herr's Tavern on the Chambersburg Road. Even General Longstreet, who rarely bestowed compliments, wrote how the nonstop march of more than twenty miles in eight hours by the 15th Alabama was "the best marching done in either army to reach the field of Gettysburg." General "Old Pete" Longstreet also described the 15th Alabama's marching to and on the field of Gettysburg as "the most unprecedented march in history."

Even more impressed than General Longstreet by his soldiers' endurance and marching ability during the hot summer weather, Colonel Oates penned how, " . . . after a rapid and fatiguing march, [and after] passing the smoking ruins of Thad Stevens's property [and iron works, the 15th Alabama] arrived on the field within sight of Gettysburg at about 2 o'clock P.M., having marched twenty-five miles." But after the record-setting march across Franklin and Adams Counties, Colonel Oates's exhausted Alabamians were in poor shape, especially for offensive operations. Private Jordan described how the Alabama soldiers were "hungry and very much fatigued." One amused Federal never forgot his first close look at General Stonewall's famed "foot-cavalry." He described how these legendary Rebel soldiers looked like a "mongrel, barefooted crew who follow his fortunes . . . such a looking crowd! Ireland in her worst straits could present no parallel, and yet they glory in their shame." The Irish of Company K, 15th Alabama, would certainly have found amusement in this Yankee's ethnic analogy. But reunited once more after the late arrival of General Law's Alabama Brigade, Hood's Division was finally intact and aligned on the high ground of Herr Ridge west of Gettysburg by the early afternoon of July 2, with the Alabamians on the division's right.[7]

But General Longstreet's 15,000-man I Corps was not yet intact. "Old Pete" could now only count two of his three divisions at hand. General Pickett's division was still serving as the army's most rearward unit to the west on the open road leading from Chambersburg to Gettysburg. However, there was no longer time for General Longstreet to wait for General Pickett's arrival as General Longstreet had already awaited the arrival of General Law's Alabama Brigade before unleashing the I Corps's offensive effort that Lee hoped would deliver a killing blow like at Second Manassas.

Not long after reaching the field, Colonel Oates carefully surveyed the area with the eye of an experienced regimental commander. He soon noted the nearby conference of the army's top commanders. There, the leading strategists of the Army of Northern Virginia discussed what tactics would be formulated to determine the destiny of a nation. Colonel Oates described how "Generals Lee and Longstreet were together on an eminance [sic] in our front, and appeared to be inspecting, with field glasses, the position of the Federals." Now with General Longstreet's I Corps up at last, General Lee unfolded his grand strategy which was as bold as it was offensive-oriented. "It was determined to make the principal attack upon the enemy's left, and endeavor to gain a position from which it was thought that our artillery could be brought to bear with effect. Longstreet was directed to place the divisions of McLaws and Hood on the right of [A.P.] Hill, partially enveloping the enemy's left, which he was to drive in."

Besides a late morning start in implementing General Lee's offensive tactics, the lengthy delay of the defensive-minded General Longstreet in awaiting the arrival of General Law's Alabama Brigade, so that he would have all of Hood's Division available, was indicative of an early breakdown in communication and cooperation between Lee and Longstreet. Indeed, General Longstreet was indicating his displeasure and subtle resistance to Lee's orders which ran counter to his vision of how this battle and campaign should be conducted. The commander in chief's orders were for Longstreet to take the tactical offensive against a strong defensive position, and "Old Pete" was not in agreement with such aggressive "attack and die" tactics. General Lee's plan to drive the Army of the Potomac from its strong defensive positions and off the high ground of Cemetery Ridge seemed like folly to the sensible Longstreet. He only too well understood the high cost of launching frontal assaults against well-defended positions on elevated terrain against thousands of hardened veterans in blue.

Nonetheless, though hardly able to put one foot before the other, the worn soldiers of General Law's Alabama Brigade rejoined Longstreet's corps on the wooded high ground of Herr Ridge in the early afternoon. Then General Longstreet began to make preparations to march south in obedience to General Lee's orders to strike and turn the Federal left. During the respite, General Longstreet had held Generals McLaw's and Hood's Divisions idle in position on Herr Ridge for hours, while quietly awaiting General Law's arrival, as if time was of no great concern. But most of all, the fate of the most decisive battle to date hinged upon timing and which side would make the best use of it on July 2. So far on the second day of the battle, the Army of Northern Virginia was accomplishing little more than wasting that precious time. While Longstreet had waited under the shade of the trees, an additional corps of the Army of the Potomac had continued to push rapidly toward Gettysburg, diminishing the chances for the successful implementation of General Lee's battle plan of getting Longstreet's corps in position to strike Cemetery Ridge at its lowest point north of the Round Tops in order to turn the Army of the Potomac's left from the south.[8]

To exploit his gains of July 1 after Gettysburg had been overrun and two beaten Federal corps were hurled through town, General Lee was now relying upon the offensive capabilities of Longstreet and his hard-hitting I Corps to inflict a mortal wound upon the Army of the Potomac. By this time, General Longstreet's was perhaps the best corps of the Army of Northern Virginia, and Lee's "Old Warhorse" seemed an ideal choice for the mission. Indeed, Longstreet's fine corps had earned a hard-won reputation as "a rock" because of its dependabilty and combat prowess.

To turn the Federal left, Lee had decided to shift his reliable I Corps to the far right of the Confederate battleline. According to plan and after marching southward to get in position to roll up the Federals's left flank, General Longstreet would deploy his brigades southward down the length of Seminary Ridge southwest of town.[9]

Including Colonel Oates and the 15th Alabama, the Rebels of Hood's Division were confident and cocky. By this time, these hardened veterans in gray believed that "no army on earth can whip these men. They may be cut to pieces and killed, but routed and whipped, never!" Colonel Oates firmly believed, with good reason, that his boys were "terribly in earnest." With the 15th Alabama and the remainder of Law's Alabama Brigade now reunited with the other three brigades of Hood's Division, one of Hood's Texas soldiers wrote how, "coming over the mountains, moving along the valleys, deploying on the plains with flying banners and glittering arms, music calling from every crest and hilltop an echo to swell the chorus, was the grand pageant of gathering armies." As he had delivered the knock-out blow that garnered victory at Second Manassas, General Longstreet now needed to repeat the performance of Stonewall Jackson's II Corps in successfully completing a lengthy flank march to smash and roll-up the Army of the Potomac's right to ensure the dramatic victory at Chancellorsville, the apex of the Army of Northern Virginia's fortunes.[10]

After much delay, General Longstreet's I Corps finally began its long flank march southward to extend Lee's right below Gettysburg. While screened by the elevation and woodlands of Herr Ridge west of Seminary Ridge, which ran southward directly west of Gettysburg and parallel to Cemetery Ridge, General Longstreet's battle-hardened troops pushed southward to accomplish great things. Concealment was vital for a successful flank march because the I Corps was slipping southward to gain a position from which to catch the Union army's left by surprise and then crush it with an overpowering blow.

Colonel Oates described how after the grueling march to Gettysburg, the 15th Alabama soldiers "were allowed but a few minutes rest, when the divisions of McLaws and Hood were moved in line by the right flank around to the south . . ." Without adequate rest and with no time to refill nearly dry canteens, the veterans of the 15th Alabama once again moved out, embarking upon a new assignment as the already hot day grew hotter.

Leading the way southward, McLaw's Division was followed by Hood's Division. And as fate would have it, General Law's worn brigade led the advance of the better-rested brigades of Hood's Division. Envisioning a flank march that would bring decisive success, both divisions pushed southwestward along Herr Ridge, a little more than a mile west of Seminary Ridge, following a road that eased along the west side of Herr Ridge.

With high hopes, General Longstreet's Confederates surged southward with the objective of first gaining the dirt road which followed March Creek and led to the Black Horse Tavern. This stately two-story stone structure, built in 1812 and soon to become a hospital for Longstreet's corps, stood on the Fairfield Road, where it crossed the clear waters of Marsh Creek.

However, a grassy knoll of open high ground immediately east of the stately rock tavern, just beyond the Fairfield (or Hagerstown) Road, which the Confederates would have to march over in column created consternation among Southern leaders at the formation's head. Sunlight reflecting off a number of Union muskets on the barren slope of Little Round Top, almost two and a half miles to the southeast and on the other side of Plum Run, caused a concerned General McLaws to halt his column at the base of the ridge before attempting to pass over the knoll. Not wanting to take any chances with so much at stake, McLaws now feared that the Yankees would ascertain the Confederate flank march southward if they crossed over the knoll.

If so, the unexpected sight of thousands of Rebels pushing south would immediately warn the Federals of Lee's flanking strategy. Shortly, "Old Pete" Longstreet was also atop the knoll with McLaws to ascertain the tactical situation as best he could. Knowing that marching over the knoll would reveal General Lee's battle plan to the Union army's new commander, General George Meade, Longstreet declared in no uncertain terms, "Why, this won't do." Consequently, an alternate route that promised concealment from prying Yankee eyes was chosen.

However, this sudden change of plan required a return to Herr Ridge, a lengthy countermarch of an additional eight miles over rough terrain. Worst of all, reversing course meant wasting more valuable time, additional precious hours that could never be regained. In fact, the countermarch to avoid detection would double the march's length when time was crucial for success.

General Longstreet's agreement to alter such time-consuming tactics as proposed by General McLaws continued to indicate the I Corps commander's subtle reluctance—perhaps subconscious—to adhere to General Lee's offensive tactics. A reluctant Longstreet was demonstrating a passive resistance to accept General Lee's aggressive tactical plan.

Nevertheless, concealment for the I Corps was necessary if General Lee's grand vision for General Longstreet's battle-hardened corps was to be realized. After retracing their steps north to regain Herr Ridge once more and then going east before eventually again turning southward, Longstreet's Confederates finally resumed pushing south along a narrow country lane which ran down the low-lying valley of the swift-flowing Willoughby Run. This narrow valley would provide concealment for thousands of Rebels eager to strike General Meade's left flank. Now out of sight of Little Round Top thanks to the shelter of tangles of trees and dense underbrush bordering the creek and the tall timber covering Seminary Ridge to the east, the Confederates of the I Corps marched steadily southward undetected by the Yankees. Then General Longstreet's eight brigades finally gained the Wheatfield Road, and swung eastward in the final phase of the march toward the western slope of Seminary Ridge.

However, the price for ensuring the concealment of General Longstreet's flank march was not without cost. Patches of woods, jumbles of underbrush, deep ditches, rough terrain, and stone and rail fences broke up the marching column, slowing the trek southward. These delays resulted in an even longer and more time-consuming march. Additionally, the lack of a guide, a good map, or a thorough reconnaissance of the terrain by reliable Southern cavalrymen also delayed Longstreet's march southward.

But finally General Longstreet's troops gained Seminary Ridge. Then, the veteran brigades of the I Corps pushed southward and down the length of the ridge named after the Lutheran Seminary. At long last, General Longstreet deployed his commands on General Lee's far right. The altered plan of approach, the tardy, halting, and slow march of eight miles over rough ground combined with General Longstreet's passive reluctance to launch an assault had cost General Lee at least three precious hours. The loss of so much time bode ill for Southern fortunes on a day in which time would play a key role in determining winner from loser. Ironically, the lengthy countermarch by Longstreet's corps might have been unnecessary as the Yankees atop Little Round Top probably would have been unable to ascertain Longstreet's movements southward had he continued his flank march as originally intended. Longstreet's countermarch might have been one of the great Confederate mistakes at Gettysburg.[11]

A veteran commander who instinctively felt uneasy about any time-consuming delays or countermarching on the battlefield, Colonel Oates described how, "there was a good deal of delay on the march, which was quite circuitous; I suppose, for the purpose of covering the movement from the enemy." Alabama Brigade commander General Law also lamented the flank march south-

ward for "we moved very slowly, with frequent halts and deflec-
tions from the direct course—the latter being necessary to conceal
our movements from the Federal signal station on Little Round
Top."

All the while, the opportunistic General Meade was taking full
advantage of the Confederates's lack of activity. Granted a
reprieve, he continued to rapidly extend his left down Cemetery
Ridge, throwing more seasoned troops and batteries into line to
strengthen his already strong defensive positions along the high
ground. In addition, General Meade also hurried additional units,
like his V Corps, forward from the east to reinforce his left below
Gettysburg. Consequently, General Lee's original estimation of the
location of the Union army's left was becoming more obsolete with
each passing hour. No longer at the same location as when Lee had
formulated his battle plan, General Meade's left as originally
ascertained was in fact now at a point increasingly farther south
(or left) of the newly forming southern end of the Army of the
Potomac, as the tactical situation rapidly changed.[12]

Finally, in the sweltering heat and humidity of south-central
Pennsylvania around 3:30 P.M. and hours late in extending Lee's
line to the south, General Longstreet's two divisions belatedly
deployed along the Emmitsburg Road which ran along the ridge-
top. Atop the high ground of Warfield Ridge, the southeasterly
extension of Seminary Ridge, General Law hurriedly aligned
about fifteen hundred soldiers of his five Alabama regiments in a
lengthy battleline. This line was "formed at an acute angle with the
road, the right being in advance of it, between the road and the
mountain, and the left extending across and in rear of the road."

As the Alabama soldiers began to form in line behind the crest
of Warfield Ridge just east of the Emmitsburg Road, Longstreet's
veteran corps rapidly deployed in preparation for striking the
Yankees's left flank; Colonel Oates later described how "finally,
Hood marched across the rear of McLaws and would line on the
crest of a little ridge [Warfield Ridge], with [General Henry Lewis]
Bennings brigade [of Georgians] in the rear of his centre, consti-
tuting a second line—his battalion of artillery, sixteen pieces, in

position on the left. General McLaws then formed his division of four brigades in two lines of battle on Hood[']s left, and with sixteen pieces, in position on McLaw's left. This line was in the general direction of the Emmittsburg [sic] road and nearly parallel with it—the extreme right of Hood's line being directly opposite to the centre of the Round Top Mountain."

After emerging from the shadows of the humid woodlands of oak, cedar, and hickory along Warfield Ridge just west of the Emmitsburg Road and onto the open ground of the sun-baked fields atop the eastern side of the ridge, the 15th Alabama soldiers crossed the dirt road and took position on the high ground. There Colonel Oates formed his troops in the center of the Alabama Brigade's battleline. Spirits were high with Colonel Oates's men eager for the opportunity to turn Meade's left to exploit General Lee's July 1 success. To the Alabamians's left, or northeast, and within sight on the eastern slope of the valley of Plum Run stood the Michael Bushman stone house.

By the afternoon of July 2, the defensive-minded General Meade had his available units aligned in good defensive positions along Cemetery Ridge, as if inviting the Confederates to attack. Determined to exploit his success of the day before, the ever-aggressive General Lee continued to believe that he was presented with an opportunity to win decisive victory.

Aligned along commanding ground to solidly anchor the left end of the III Corps's line on the southern flank of Meade's line, the 10-pounder Parrotts of the 4th New York Battery, under Captain James E. Smith, were unlimbered along Houck's Ridge, or Rocky Ridge, which stood before or west of Cemetery Ridge. There, immediately northwest of the jumble of giant boulders called the Devil's Den, these roaring New York guns steadily hammered the long lines of Longstreet's Confederates, who remained motionless atop Seminary and Warfield Ridges under the relentless pounding. Colonel Oates recalled the opening fire on General Lee's far right when "both battalions of artillery opened fire [and] the Federals replied" with both enthusiasm and accuracy.

The New York cannoneers maintained a hot fire, hurling shells that screamed through the treetops above the heads of Oates's men who now lay prone to escape the storm. Shells smashing into the heavy timber made considerable noise, dropping limbs, bark, and leaves down in clusters upon the Alabama boys, and the iron shell fragments felled a handful of Alabama soldiers.

Held securely by the Army of the Potomac, Cemetery Ridge ran a length of around two miles southward below Gettysburg. The wooded ridge ended at two rocky hills called Little and Big Round Top, from north to south. About halfway between Seminary Ridge and its southern extension, Warfield Ridge, to the west and Cemetery Ridge to the east lay the shallow valley of Plum Run. Through this narrow valley ran not only the creek but also the Emmitsburg Road which angled northeastward toward the southern outskirts of Gettysburg. On July 2, Cemetery Ridge and the high ground around it had to be captured if Gettysburg was to become a decisive Confederate victory.

To his surprise, however, General Longstreet now learned that the high ground some six hundred yards to the northeast at the Peach Orchard was now held by large numbers of Federal troops and batteries of artillery. Indeed, the entire III Corps had advanced west before General Meade's main Cemetery Ridge line to deploy on better defensive and higher ground. Consequently, this advanced position on elevated terrain resembled anything but the weak and exposed left flank of the Army of the Potomac, as Generals Lee and Longstreet had earlier envisioned.

Countered by the Union III Corps's unexpected advance before Cemetery Ridge, the I Corps's flank march was now thwarted in achieving its initial objective of gaining the element of surprise and the tactical advantage by arriving adjacent to the Union army's left flank. By this time General Meade had steadily extended his line southward to Houck's Ridge around the Devil's Den and almost to the base of Little Round Top to cover more ground and protect his left flank along Cemetery Ridge to the east. Now the powerful III Corps occupied the commanding ground along the Emmitsburg Road at the Peach Orchard, effectively blocking

General Lee's designated avenue of attack up the Emmitsburg Road.[13]

Despite the changed tactical situation, General Longstreet prepared to strike up the Emmitsburg Road as ordered by General Lee. One of Hood's Texas soldiers to Colonel Oates's left before the Bushman farm later wrote how by this time "staff officers were riding in hot haste to the commanders of divisions and brigades, bearing the compliments of the General and with courteous salute delivering orders to attack the enemy at the signal." But a full eleven hours had passed since sunrise and what had been the Army of the Potomac's left was now its center.[14]

To additionally hinder General Longstreet's offensive effort this afternoon, the hard-fighting General Hood—Longstreet's most aggressive division commander—would shortly be eliminated from playing an offensive role on General Lee's right, when and where he would be needed the most. General Hood would fall early during the upcoming assault, when a shell from Captain Smith's New York battery on Houck's Ridge exploded above him. The fiery explosion would dehorse Hood in an orchard of the Bushman farm just west of the farmer's house.

Consequently, young General Law, only twenty-six but the senior brigadier general in Hood's Division, would shortly take over divisional command in place of the fallen General Hood. This sudden and unexpected leadership change amid the heat of battle would leave Colonel Oates and his 15th Alabama more or less on their own. In General Law's words, "As senior brigadier, I succeeded to the command of Hood's division, and directed its movements during the engagements of the 2d and 3d of July." As fate would have it, the Alabama soldiers who had recently brought up the Army of Northern Virginia's rear would shortly be thrust into playing the leading role during the "High Water Mark of the Confederacy" at the extreme right or southern end of Lee's line.[15]

While the angry New York cannons roared on the rocky elevated terrain of Houck's Ridge above the big rocks of the Devil's Den, Colonel Oates and his trusty "right-arm," Lieutenant Colonel Isaac Ball Feagin, made final preparations to lead their soldiers forward from their position on the high ground of Warfield Ridge just east of the Emmitsburg Road.

A promising officer in whom Colonel Oates had placed much faith and confidence, Lieutenant Colonel Feagin had originally served as the captain of Company B. At the regiment's organization, Feagin's skills were so well recognized that he was given command of one of the two 15th Alabama companies that were armed with Mississippi rifles instead of smoothbores. Alternating with Oates as regimental commander at various periods, Lieutenant Colonel Feagin had led the 15th Alabama during one major battle, Antietam, the one regimental commander in the brigade not killed or wounded. However, when the pursuing cavalry clashed with Lee's army while recrossing the Potomac during the withdrawal from Maryland on September 19, 1862, Feagin was hit in the skirmish at Boteler's Mill. Then Oates took command of the regiment while the handsome young lieutenant colonel recuperated. Along with General Hood's fall before the assault on Little Round Top began, as fate would have it Colonel Oates would also be handicapped with the early loss of Lieutenant Colonel Feagin, who would soon lose a leg and nearly his life.

With thousands of General Longstreet's Rebels deployed in lengthy battle lines, the Alabama Brigade's left now rested on the Emmitsburg Road, while occupying the high ground of Warfield Ridge. Meanwhile, the accurate artillery fire from the Parrott rifles manned by the hardworking New York artillerymen on Houck's Ridge intensified. The bellowing of these field pieces roared over the narrow valley of Plum Run like a summer storm raging across the muddy Chattahoochee. Private Jordan wrote how " . . . we were under heavy shelling [and consequently] the first order [had been] to lie down, as we were in full view of the enemy's artillery, and they were shelling us very closely . . ."[16]

There, amid the belt of oaks, hickories, and scattered cedars atop the eastern slope of Warfield Ridge, the veteran Alabama soldiers continued to endure the fierce cannonade. Many of these devout soldiers in gray now prayed to escape the leaden storm raining down upon them without mercy. Just east of the

Emmitsburg Road before the Alabamians lay open fields and meadows which plunged sharply down into the narrow valley of Plum Run. As if to assist Colonel Oates's upcoming advance down into the depths of the wooded valley, the local farmers had long ago cleared these fertile fields along the sloping terrain, removing rocks for cultivation. A sight rare in southeast Alabama's coastal plain, the Alabamians could see the neat stone fences which ran east down the slope and toward Plum Run. These rock fences divided portions of the tillable acreage for the cultivation of various crops.

In part because of the lengthy delays in getting into position, Colonel Oates's veterans instinctively did not like the looks of this fight. As demonstrated so often in the past, the men understood the bloody implications of yet another frontal assault in the Napoleonic tradition against the high ground on the other, or east, side of Plum Run. Consequently, Private Joseph Roberson was determined to get out of this fight at the first opportunity. Having seen one slaughter too many, he refused to risk his life in another offensive strike against a strong defensive position because Confederate leaders had too often thrown away the lives of Southern boys for no gain. Without a wound or even a scratch, therefore, Roberson went to his company commander and stated that he was wounded by a shell fragment. As hoped, Roberson was excused from duty with no officer bothering to check his "wounds" amid the fierce cannonade.

To save lives, Colonel Oates continued to keep his boys prone to escape the whizzing fragments from the bursting shells. This common sense logic came from an experienced officer who instinctively understood the importance of keeping casualty lists down before an assault in which every soldier would be needed.[17]

As Private Lary, now fatalistic after surviving some of the war's bloodiest engagements, described in a letter the inevitable cost for success that the 15th Alabama soldiers would have to pay on July 2, 1863: "There is now no retreat, 'forward march' is the command of fate . . . we will have to pay dear for the great boon of independence—it will cost us all our gems and gold—it will cost us the blood of our bravest men, poured out like water on the insa-

tiate earth . . . it is no time to count the cost [for] we must succeed
[and] persist though it [might cost] nine hundred and ninety-nine
[who] must perish and only one of a thousand survive, and retain
his liberty! One such freeman must possess more virtue than a
thousand slaves."[18]

From the wooded ridge-line of Warfield Ridge, the Alabama
soldiers could look eastward and plainly see the two elevations
before them called Big Round Top and Little Round Top. These
rocky hilltops stood like natural bastions on the opposite side of
Plum Run which flowed southward in the narrow valley below.
Directly in front of the prone Alabamians rose the heavily timbered southernmost end of Big Round Top, which stood directly
south of Little Round Top. To the view of the Alabama soldiers, Big
Round Top appeared about twice as high as Little Round Top.
From the commanding ground of Warfield Ridge, it was evident to
the woodsmen, farmers, and hunters from the Chattahoochee
River Valley that the jagged crest of Big Round Top was less heavily forested and bushy than at its lower elevations, consisting of a
crown of almost solid rock.

Closer and looming below them to the right on the west side of
Plum Run and just to the southeast was a flat knoll known locally
as the Bushman woods. To Colonel Oates and his men, this low hill
appeared only about one-third as high as Little Round Top.
Actually, the high ground of Bushman's woods was nothing more
than a flattened knoll. This timbered knoll was dominated by the
towering shadow of Big Round Top to the northeast on the other,
or east, side of Plum Run.

Meanwhile, the eight veteran brigades of the two divisions of
Longstreet's corps were aligned for hundreds of yards as far as the
eye could see along the north-south ridge which led northward to
the southern outskirts of Gettysburg. General Hood aligned his
crack division of eighteen infantry regiments into two battle lines.
In the front line on the division's right stood General Law's
Alabama Brigade, while the Texas Brigade was aligned in the front
rank on the division's left. In the second rank around two hundred
yards behind the Alabama Rebels were the Georgia brigades of

"Tige" Anderson and Henry Lewis "Old Rock" Benning. By any measure, the battle-hardened soldiers of Hood's Division were some of the finest combat troops in not only Longstreet's corps— which was "the cream of Lee's army"—but also in the Army of Northern Virginia. Hood's famous Texas Brigade, "Lee's Grenadier Guard," had earned reputations at an early date for combat prowess from Virginia to Maryland.

General Law described the dispositions of his five Alabama regiments: "the Confederate line of battle occupied a ridge, partly wooded, with a valley intervening between it and the heights held by the Federal troops in front." Before the formations of his 15th Alabama, Colonel Oates saw that General Law's Alabama Brigade now "constituted the right of Hood's line, and was formed in single line as follows: my regiment the 15th Alabama in the centre; the forty fourth and forty eighth Alabama regiments to my right and the forty seventh and fourth Alabama regiments to my left."[19]

Along the lengthy Alabama line, the sun flashed off the row of bayonets, and the red battle flags, torn by the bullets and shells from the savage fighting of Second Manassas and Antietam, stood limp in the suffocating heat and humidity of the sweltering July afternoon. It was becoming so hot that the Alabama soldiers must have sworn that the heat was as intense in south Pennsylvania as along the Alabama lowlands of the Gulf coastal plain.[20]

Confronting the twin hilltops on the opposite side of Plum Run, the Alabamians hoped that no sizeable numbers of Yankees stood on either of the two Round Tops which dominated the eastern horizon before them. Most of all, the Alabama men placed their faith in General Lee's flanking strategy to catch the Federals by surprise. Hopefully, they had marched far enough south down the ridge to now be in a position beyond the Union army's left flank. With its dominant position and size, Big Round Top stood before Colonel Oates's soldiers as the natural objective of the 15th Alabama rather than Little Round Top. Indeed, the larger of the Round Tops lay directly before Colonel Oates's regiment.

These savvy veterans from Alabama fully understood the frightful cost of attacking such high ground which rose before them like two ominous and imposing citadels. The worst scenario for the Alabama soldiers would be if rows of Union rifles and cannons were poised on either one of the two Round Tops. Big Round Top was not only the most elevated point on the battlefield but also the highest point in all of Adams County. General Law realized as much at first glance. He described how "the position occupied by the Federal left wing in front of us was now fully disclosed to view, and it was certainly one of the most formidable it had ever been the fortune of any troops to confront. Round Top rose like a huge sentinel guarding the Federal left flank . . . the thick woods which in great part covered the sides of Round Top and the adjacent hills concealed from view the rugged nature of the ground, which increased fourfold the difficulties of the attack."[21]

No 15th Alabama soldier could possibly have imagined or realized the importance of the upcoming clash on the smallest of these two elevations which stood before them. But, in fact, all of the past bloody battles across Virginia and Maryland had been fought in order to have these crack Alabamians placed in such a key situation as this. In many ways and as strange fate would have it, the unprecedented sacrifices and bloodletting of the past brutal campaigns of 1861–63 and the nightmarish fighting of Bull Run, the Seven Days, Cedar Mountain, Second Manassas, Antietam, Fredericksburg, and Chancellorsville by General Lee's veterans had set the stage for these Alabamians to have an opportunity to turn the Army of the Potomac's left during the most important battle of the war. Within the next few hours, more so than on any portion of the Gettysburg battlefield, it would be along the rocky and wooded slope of Little Round Top that much of the fate of this battle would be decided.

Ironically, with so much now at stake, the struggle for the possession of Little Round Top was about to be determined by a mere handful of soldiers—a dramatic showdown primarily between two regiments, the 20th Maine and the 15th Alabama. Never before or after in the Civil War would so few men on either side have such an opportunity to play a more dominant role to determine the outcome of a major battle.

This decisive confrontation about to erupt in unbridled fury across Little Round Top would be orchestrated by two young leaders: twenty-nine-year-old Colonel William Calvin Oates, a lawyer, teacher, and newspaperman who had opposed secession, and thirty-four-year-old Colonel Joshua Lawrence Chamberlain, a scholarly and introverted seminarian and college professor. Both of these young commanders now in their prime had made their livings with the written word and from the teaching of young minds. And now they would face each other at the southern end of their respective armies to decide which side would possess what was now the key to the battlefield, Little Round Top. Oates and Chamberlain represented two sections of the country which symbolically stretched to the far northern and southern borders of the American nation. And now symbolically these opposing commanders seemingly had been carried by fate to Gettysburg. During this forthcoming showdown between the 20th Maine and the 15th Alabama, it would be relatively minor and seemingly insignificant choices, tactical adjustments at the last minutes, and ever-changing circumstances on the battlefield beyond the control of the participants which would be magnified far out of proportion because of the tactical importance of Little Round Top. What would play a large part in determining victor from loser would be a host of intangibles. These intangibles could not have been calculated, measured, or fully understood at General Lee's headquarters at the Thompson House: the number of rounds in cartridge-boxes; the extent of fatigue among the men in the ranks; the amount of water in canteens; the character and quality of the combatants on both sides; the level of combat experience of the fighting men in the ranks; the level of leadership rising to the fore; the ability of noncommissioned officers to take the place of fallen lieutenants, captains, and colonels; the tenacity of the common soldiers in both blue and gray to do or die; and, perhaps most of all, fate, destiny, and simple luck.

As an experienced combat officer, Colonel Oates no doubt realized as much. Only twenty-nine and the youngest and most junior regimental commander in General Law's Alabama Brigade, Oates would very soon and quite suddenly and unexpectedly become the man of the hour for the Army of Northern Virginia. The frustrations of a troubled youth, an impoverished past, and the haunting memories of years of self-doubt and humiliation could be wiped away as if by magic if Colonel Oates was successful this day. What would soon be presented to Oates would be one of the golden opportunities of the war. Oates was about to lead his friends, neighbors, and relatives from the Chattahoochee Valley straight into the vortex of Gettysburg's most severe storm.

Along Warfield Ridge near the Emmitsburg Road where it angled northward to enter the valley between the two parallel ridges, Seminary and Cemetery, Colonel Oates stood before his Alabama soldiers. Sweating under the scorching July 2 sun, Oates's men anxiously awaited the word to move forward. These savvy veterans continued to dislike the look of the open ground before them—a natural killing field—and the imposing height of Big Round Top. After the exhausting morning march and the lengthy flank march to the south, Colonel Oates's Alabamians were in poor condition to mount the offensive on that targeted formidable high ground. A large number of soldiers, including Colonel Oates's younger brother, were sick and ailing. However, no one now wanted to remain behind with the surgeons, and some of the weakened and sickened Alabama Rebels stood with the regiment. Their tattered uniforms of wool were stained from the long months of hard campaigning across the South. Their throats were parched and dry, while lips were cracked and chapped from the lack of water and the intense heat of the July afternoon. Nevertheless, these Alabama soldiers remained in high spirits.

Company A stood on the 15th Alabama's left flank next to the 47th Alabama, which consisted of soldiers from such companies as the "Tallapoosa Tigers," "Jeff Holly Guards," and the "Goldwaithe Guards." To the right, Colonel Oates's other ten companies extended southward with Company K anchoring the right flank of the 15th Alabama. Below, or south, of Colonel Oates's right flank stood the 44th Alabama. Before Colonel Oates's ranks, meanwhile, three skirmish companies of the 47th Alabama hustled forward fading from sight to prepare the way for the advance into the valley of Plum Run.[22]

With each passing minute on Warfield Ridge under the shell-fire of the New York cannons, Colonel Oates realized that his boys could not take those imposing hills before him without a resupply of what his weary infantrymen needed most of all during a lengthy fight on such a hot and humid day—water. As a veteran commander, he understood that "water was as essential as cartridges." Most of the soldiers of Law's other regiments, such as the 4th Alabama, had already found water to refill canteens.

Consequently, Colonel Oates now gambled that a detail of soldiers—two men from each of his eleven 15th Alabama companies—dispatched on the double would be able to secure water at a well on the cedar-covered slope just south of the Andrew Currens house near the Emmitsburg Road. This sturdy two-story house of stone stood atop the ridge about one hundred yards to the southwest, or rear, of the 15th Alabama. The Currens house was not only beyond the Alabama Brigade's right but also beyond, or southwest of, the 48th Alabama's right, which anchored the right flank of Law's brigade.

Immediately on the west side of the Emmitsburg Road and bordering the dirt road which led northward to Gettysburg, the well water could provide the thirsty Alabama soldiers with a day-long supply. Colonel Oates was betting that these twenty-two soldiers would be able to complete their mission in only about fifteen minutes. This amount of time surely would give the detail sufficient time to return to the 15th Alabama's line before General Law gave the order to advance into the valley of Plum Run. Under the circumstances, the young colonel from Abbeville had no choice in making this decision. The Alabamians had already suffered severely from the lack of water during the march to Gettysburg on one of the hottest days of the year. And now the need for water was severe. No creek flowed from the top of their ridge so that they could refill canteens. Clearly, to dispatch the twenty-two-man detail to the front line to obtain water from Plum Run was out of the question. Rebel soldiers moving across the open fields leading to the small creek before Law's assault formations might draw fire—from Union artillery and infantry—or even cause a Yankee skirmish line to advance to contest the movement, while drawing attention to the direction of the upcoming assault. So Colonel Oates's water detail of almost company strength worked their way southwestward down through the sweltering woodlands of Warfield Ridge on the double with instructions to complete their mission as rapidly as possible.[23]

Before General Law's brigade advanced eastward into the narrow valley of Plum Run, some superstitious 15th Alabama Rebels tossed away their playing cards. Sin among the common soldiers suddenly became unfashionable with a big battle brewing, as thoughts turned toward God and salvation. No one wanted to meet their Maker with playing cards in their haversacks or pockets. Also in preparation for the attack, the veterans of the 15th Alabama took off blanket rolls and haversacks and piled their meager belongings in neat piles beside the line. A good many Alabama Rebels would never return to pick up this personal gear.

While lying prone on the crest of Warfield Ridge amid the nerve-racking rain of shells, other Alabamians placed the small soldiers' bibles from regimental chaplains in breast pockets for spiritual protection. These last-minute precautions now gave many religious-minded soldiers a measure of psychological and spiritual protection as they again readied themselves to meet the boys in blue.

In Company G's ranks, Corporal McClendon placed his faith in "the little Bible [that] I carried in my pocket through several warm engagements [but] it became so soiled from the effects of perspiration that I was afraid it would come to pieces [and] its teachings kept me from committing many sins." And Private Mitchell B. Houghton, an enterprising journalist with the Glennville Guards of Russell County, whose sergeant-brother would fight in the 2nd Georgia Infantry, Benning's brigade, during its savage assault on Devil's Den, was equally devout. The young, handsome soldier from the Chattahoochee River Valley had "a red Morocco bound little New Testament which I carried in my side pocket" throughout the tempest of Gettysburg. Facing the grim prospect of yet another frontal attack against formidable high ground, some Alabama soldiers felt apprehensive about the outcome of the upcoming attack—and they had good reason. In obeying General Lee's orders and implementing his aggressive tactics, more than 50 percent of the 15th Alabama would be killed, wounded, or captured within the next few hours. Now atop the commanding high ground of Warfield Ridge and lying prone with Company G under the intense bombardment, Private A. B. Bryant Skipper reflected, as he would later write, "I wonder[ed] if we po soldirs are remembered in the prairs at home."[24]

While Private Bryant Skipper was one of the youngest members of the 15th Alabama this day, Private Jack McDonald was the oldest Alabama soldier in Colonel Oates's regiment at Gettysburg at age forty-six. Within the next few hours, McDonald would fall wounded in the fight over possession of the little rocky hill. But many of Colonel Oates's soldiers were young, looking almost more like children than reliable fighting men who were veterans of some of the most severe campaigns across the South. These hardy boy-soldiers included noncommissioned officers with authority and respect like Sergeant William H. Hurt. Only sixteen, Hurt served as an inspirational leader of Company C. He was noted for leading his unit into the hottest fires with carefree abandon, and Gettysburg would be no exception. Known affectionately as "Sergeant Billie Hurt," the young man from Macon County was "one of the best young soldiers and non-commissioned officers" of the 15th Alabama, according to Colonel Oates. In the Alabamians's desperate effort to capture Little Round Top, Sergeant Hurt would be captured. Like so many other 15th Alabama boys destined to be taken prisoner this afternoon, he would survive the hell of a Northern prison to eventually return to his home and family in southeast Alabama.[25]

Finally, word from Generals Hood and Law passed down the line, informing Colonel Oates that now was the time to attack. With the orders to move out, Colonel Oates suddenly realized that he had lost his gamble in awaiting the return of his water detail—

he had not been granted the fifteen minutes needed for them to rejoin the regiment. Colonel Oates later lamented how "before this detail could fill the canteens the advance was ordered. It would have been infinitely better to have waited five minutes for those twenty-two men and the canteens of water, but generals never ask a colonel if his regiment is ready to move [and] the order was given and away we went."[26]

With the beating of drums and the blaring of bugles which echoed across the narrow valley of Plum Run like thunder on a rainy summer morning in the Wiregrass country so far away, the five regiments of Law's Alabama Brigade finally pushed off the high ground of Warfield Ridge with gear rattling in the hot stillness. After unleashing a cheer, the Confederates of the 15th's center surged forward in the center of Law's battle line around 4:30 P.M. with red battle flags waving in the bright sunshine. On the far right of the I Corps's line, the Alabama Brigade initiated Longstreet's attack in echelon, which would roll-up the corps's line from south to north. Each of Longstreet's eight brigades were scheduled to surge forward only after the unit on its right advanced first. Therefore, after being launched from right to left, or from the south to the north, General Longstreet's assault would be staggered and disjointed minimizing its strength. As General Law described the long-delayed advance, " . . . the movement [began] on the right, my brigade on that flank leading, the other commands taking it up successively toward the left."

In near perfect step and at a time when morale was "never better," wrote Colonel Oates, the Alabama Rebels swarmed off the ridge-top and across the open ground into the valley of Plum Run as gear clattered noisily. Colonel Oates's soldiers swung down the eastern slope of Warfield Ridge in a neat formation, flowing forward with the smooth ease of veterans. The long rows of thirsty Alabamians advanced toward the Run, while pushing through the hot cornfields and wheatfields along the west side of the valley of Plum Run. At least for the moment, the launching of the assault made the Alabama Rebels forget about their fatigue and thirst. With pride, Colonel Oates never forgot how "our whole line advanced in quick time, under the fire of our guns . . .," without knowledge or information of Union positions or intelligence about the terrain ahead from either Rebel cavalry or scouts. The tangles of trees and underbrush, lowness of Plum Run's valley, and the valley's depths hid Plum Run from the Alabamians's view both when atop Warfield Ridge and during the advance down the open eastern slope of the ridge.[27]

Maintaining their tight attack alignment, the Alabama soldiers surged down a fairly steep slope, descending eastward and ever closer toward Plum Run. The eastern slope of Warfield Ridge was so steep that only halfway down if any of Colonel Oates's men looked back, they would have been unable to see the crest of Warfield Ridge behind them. Additionally, they also would not have been able to see the full height of Big Round Top directly before them on the other side of Plum Run. All the while, artillery shells from the New York cannons around the Devil's Den area, a quarter of a mile northward and farther up the meandering course of the small stream, exploded above the surging ranks. These bursting shells showered the onrushing Alabama ranks with a deadly rain of shrapnel, occasionally dropping an attacker.

One 15th Alabama Rebel to fall in the artillery fire was Corporal George E. Spencer, age twenty-three. He went down with a severe wound when shell fragments ripped through flesh and muscle. Understanding how the eerie geography of the boulder-covered land of Adams County now worked to the advantage of Federal artillery, General Law lamented how, "the spurs and ridges trending off to the north of [Big Round Top] afforded unrivaled positions for the use of artillery." The bursting shells only served as a warning that much hard work yet lay ahead for the Alabama soldiers.

The whitish-colored swirls of smoke from exploding shells stood motionless above the advancing waves of Alabama Rebels amid the hot sky and the thick layers of humidity blanketing the valley of Plum Run. Not unnoticed by the Alabama soldiers was a sense of eerie foreboding, but all the while the Alabamians continued to push relentlessly across the sun-drenched land as the exploding shells brought down more soldiers.[28]

After crossing the steep eastern slope of Warfield Ridge at the southern edge of the Bushman farm, the Alabama assault formations continued onward. Snarled clumps of oaks, cedars, pines, and hickories were cluttered along the edges of the creek as it ran south below the Slyder house and along the pasture on the creek's west side. But immediately before the advancing Alabama ranks, the valley of Plum Run was mostly open. Marshy and lined with green, moss-covered rocks, the swift-flowing little stream was clear and cold. Originating from springs, this creek flowed in a meandering north-south course through the narrow valley which lay between Seminary Ridge and the Round Tops. Farther south, Plum Run entered the expanse of dense forest at the northern edge of Bushman's woods, running between Big Round Top and the flattened knoll of Bushman's woods.

For many of General Hood's attackers north of the Alabamians, this lengthy valley between the two parallel ridges— Seminary and Cemetery—would soon become "the valley of death." In some places, the ground was so rocky that trees could not grow. Private Jordan described the open avenue on the east side of Plum Run just above the Slyder house as the valley broadened north toward the Devil's Den: "This valley had no undergrowth, had a few trees dotted about, no rocks for protection in the valley but the mountains and ridges had great precipitous rocks." Despite the unknown ground and unknown enemy positions which lay before General Law's brigade, one Alabama soldier later described how the soldiers continued forward with confidence in jaunty fashion, almost "as if at a game of ball."

Colonel Oates described how his Alabama Rebels poured "through the valley which lay spread out before us at the foot of the range of mountains or hills, with a small muddy, meandering stream running through it—near midway." Indicative of the diminutive number of attackers on the far right of General Lee's over-extended battle line, the 15th Alabama soldiers, and the remainder of General Law's Alabama Brigade, now advanced in a single assault line instead of the usual double attack waves. Because of the marshy and wet ground around Plum Run and the fact that the creek deeply cut several feet into the ground, General Law called a halt before reaching the watercourse.

In addition, the rough terrain and stone fences slowed and broke-up alignment. Consequently, General Law also decided to halt to rearrange his assault formations before crossing the rougher ground at the creek. With General Hood now down, General Law wisely took precautions, especially in attacking formidable high ground and having no idea "how far up the slope of Round Top the Federal left extended . . . as the woods effectively concealed from view everything in that quarter."

After surging through some light timber at the lower western slope of the valley, the single assault line of 15th Alabama Rebels halted before the creek as directed. There, on the open ground of the Slyder pasture and just southwest of the Slyder house, Colonel Oates began to rearrange his regiment's ranks before continuing onward. Officers in gray hurriedly went along the line, adjusting and tightening alignment before meeting the Yankees.

During this abrupt halt to rearrange ranks fate seemingly intervened to place the 15th Alabama in *the* key position in the assault line on Lee's far right. Hence Colonel Oates's regiment would soon be in the most advantageous position to strike the Army of the Potomac's left flank. This sudden and unexpected tactical development resulted when the 44th Alabama and the 48th Alabama, to Colonel Oates's right, were ordered to shift to the left of Law's brigade to fill a gap in the advancing line of Hood's Division. These two fine Alabama regiments were now ordered northward and up to the mouth of the valley of Plum Run and toward the Devil's Den, slightly northwest of the Round Tops.

This ad hoc redeployment was made not only to meet ever-changing tactical developments on the battlefield and to fill the gap in the division's line but also to adjust to the rough terrain. But most important in tactical terms, the maneuver was to plug the increasingly widening gap between the Alabama Brigade and the

Texas and Arkansas Brigade to Colonel Oates's left, after the terrain fragmented the advancing lines.

Under the command of a former superintendent of the East Alabama Female Institute at Tuskegee, which was probably a source of envy among his men, Colonel William Flake Perry, the 44th Alabama was a reliable regiment, despite coming into existence at Selma, Alabama, relatively late in May 1862. Defending General Lee's hardpressed center, the 44th's casualties at Antietam had been nearly a staggering 50 percent.

On the double, Colonel Perry's soldiers now hustled north to take position in line on the extreme left of General Law's Alabama Brigade. Tough and reliable, these veteran Alabama soldiers hailed from Bibb, Calhoun, Shelby, Wilcox, Chambers, and Dallas Counties. Colonel Perry also took command of Law's entire Alabama Brigade, after General Law took charge of General Hood's Division.

While the 44th Alabama hurried northward to join General Benning's attack on the Devil's Den on the north end of Law's line, the 48th Alabama briefly served as the reserve, or second line, of Law's brigade beyond the 15th Alabama's left flank. But the 48th Alabama, known as one of the "twin regiments" because it had been organized at Auburn, Alabama, on the same day, May 22, 1862, as the 47th Alabama and both units fought together throughout the war, would maintain its role in support of Colonel Oates for only a short time. This was an unfortunate development for the outcome of Colonel Oates's attempt to capture Little Round Top. The 48th Alabama was a good regiment, that had served under Stonewall Jackson and fought at Cedar Mountain, Groveton, and defended the bloody railroad cut at Second Manassas. The 48th Alabama consisted of such companies as the "Cherokee Grays," the "Mills Valley Guards," the "Jeff Davis Boys," the "Mountain Rangers," and the politically named "Jacksonians" of Company E.

Leaving Colonel Oates and the 15th Alabama behind, the soldiers of the 48th Alabama would soon double-quick northward. Instead of linking with the right of the advancing Texas and

Arkansas Brigade to plug the gap between the two right-most brigades of Hood's Division, however, these two Alabama regiments advanced too far north. Then after mingling with General Jerome Bonaparte Robertson's Texas and Arkansas troops, they also joined in the bloody assault through the maze of giant boulders known appropriately as the Devil's Den.

These last minute tactical readjustments before Plum Run brought additional delay to the Alabama Brigade's advance, when invaluable time was running out on Confederate fortunes on July 2. Indeed, this additional delay caused an increasingly uneasy Colonel Oates to long regret how, "the advance was not skillfully made in all respects." Ironically, long after Gettysburg, Oates would leave his beloved 15th Alabama to command the 48th Alabama, which consisted primarily of northeast Alabama soldiers. But now this unexpected redeployment would leave the 15th Alabama on the extreme far right of the Army of Northern Virginia.

Meanwhile, the 47th Alabama remained to the 15th Alabama's left. Bonded together by close ties of blood and sacrifice, Colonel Oates's 15th Alabama soldiers could count a good many friends and relatives in the 47th Alabama. But at this time the 47th Alabama was twice as small as Colonel Oates's own diminutive regiment. And thus would provide relatively limited support to the 15th Alabama during the struggle for possession of Little Round Top.

In addition, the 47th Alabama was now without three of its most reliable companies. Almost as if playing a part in setting up the clash between the 15th Alabama and the 20th Maine, three companies of the 47th Alabama had continued to advance as skirmishers on the right of Law's Alabama Brigade to drive away some of Colonel Hiram Berdan's sharpshooters. These pesky Yankee marksmen were taking pot shots with impunity at the graycoat gunners of the six-gun 1st North Carolina Battery, the Rowan Artillery, under Irishman Captain James Reilly. While the Tar Heel artillerymen worked their guns on Warfield Ridge just east of the Emmitsburg Road and provided fire support, the Alabamians had seen some of these North Carolina gunners hit by the marksmens' fire. When the Alabama Brigade had belatedly aligned on Warfield Ridge to the left of the battery which had been firing on its own without support for some time and suffering in consequence, these North Carolina artillerymen had sarcastically cheered the late-arriving Alabamians. But now the Rowan Artillerymen hoped that the Alabama Rebels would wipe out the hated sharpshooters.

The absence of the three skirmish companies of the 47th Alabama left only seven diminutive companies advancing on the 15th Alabama's left. These seven companies were also under Colonel Oates's command, but all remained well below average strength. Major John M. Campbell, for instance, explained how these seven 47th Alabama companies to the 15th Alabama's left consisted of only around 150 men. For the formidable task of rolling-up General Meade's left flank and capturing Little Round Top, consequently, Colonel Oates could only count on this small group of soldiers to act in conjunction with his 15th Alabama. Additionally, the command structure of the 47th Alabama was in shambles at this time. As Major Campbell explained, "there was some confusion in these companies, owing to the fact that in the charge the lieutenant-colonel expected the colonel to give all necessary commands, and the colonel remained so far behind that his presence on the field was but a trammel on the lieutenant-colonel [South Carolina-born Bulger, a gray-haired, fifty-seven-year-old Creek War veteran, planter, and politician from Dadeville, Alabama,] because the colonel [Georgia-born physican James Washington Jackson who had a Georgia military school education and would resign on July 16, 1863] having been left behind . . ." Such leadership "confusion" among the remaining seven 47th Alabama companies would work to Colonel Oates's disadvantage for the remainder of the day.

Before the sun of July 2 dropped over the horizon, consequently, Oates would hold a golden opportunity in his hands because of the 15th Alabama's placement at the southern end of Lee's battle line despite a host of disadvantages. But even now, Colonel Oates was beginning to regret the wasting of so much precious time and the lengthy delays, which were combining to help sabotage his bid to turn the left flank of the Army of the Potomac.

On a frothing horse, General Law, the handsome young officer from Tuskegee, galloped over to Colonel Oates at the head of the 15th Alabama in the valley of Plum Run. Yet scarred by the fury of First Bull Run from two Julys before and having somehow survived leading his troops into the holocaust at Gaines's Mill and Miller's Cornfield at Antietam, General Law pulled up amid a swirl of dust. Some Company C soldiers of the "Macon County Commissioners" knew the dashing General Law, who was raised on a South Carolina plantation, as a friend and neighbor because he also called Macon County, Alabama, home. As indicated in a letter of Lieutenant Barnett Hardeman Cody, General Law fully recognized the elite quality of the 15th Alabama at an early date, declaring that William C. Oates's old Company G " . . . was the finest in the [Alabama] brigade."

Like Colonel Oates, the youthful Darlington, South Carolina-born Law was an aggressive commander, yet in his twenties, and a first son of a Deep South family. Most of all, Law was a fighter who engaged in almost as many clashes with Confederate officers over matters of honor and rank as with the Yankees. General Law's antebellum experience had been gained as a student at the Charleston Military Academy and then as a Professor of Belles Letters at the King's Mountain Military Institute at Yorkville, South Carolina. By the time of Gettysburg, General Law was a young officer of promise and high expectations, having earned his general's rank in the fall of 1862. One of his staff officers described how General Law's " . . . skill and daring had added luster to Longstreet's name on every field from Cold Harbor to Gettysburg."

Now commanding Hood's battle-hardened division after the general's fall, Law faced a serious dilemma. Without cavalry or time to reconnoiter, the young Alabamian still did not know "how far up the slope of [Big] Round Top the Federal left extended . . . " Like Colonel Oates, General Law was now forced to make the best of a confusing battlefield situation, relying upon a strong blend of natural and tactical instincts.[29]

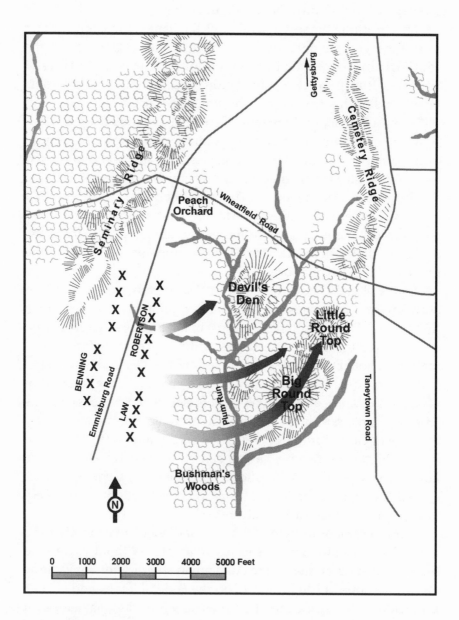

CHAPTER VI

Defiance of Orders

"This part of the line [which] was held by Hood's division . . . was really the key to the whole position of Gettysburg."

—General Evander Law

*U*nder General Law's orders, Colonel Oates and the Alabama Brigade had launched their assault straight eastward toward the looming Round Tops. This contradicted the assault orders of General Lee who had directed the advance northeastward parallel to the Emmitsburg Road. Despite the added responsibility of now commanding a division in a key battlefield situation, only a self-confident officer of sound judgment and considerable tactical and battlefield experience like General Law would have openly defied General Lee's orders. Relying on natural instincts and the tactical lessons of the past, General Law had sought to gain a tactical advantage on his own initiative by ordering his Alabamian regiments to advance straight eastward and not parallel to the northeast-running Emmitsburg Road in an oblique assault as General Lee had directed.

General Law had instinctively realized that the high ground of the Round Tops had to be in Confederate hands on July 2 if Gettysburg was to become a decisive Southern victory. If the

Federals gained the Rounds Tops, then nothing could push them off these formidable heights. Consequently, he took what actions were necessary for the best chance to lay claim to the two highest elevations on the battlefield. But before the assault began, General Law had attempted to do what he felt was tactically correct under the circumstances.

Sensing the possibility to exploit the opportunity on General Meade's left flank, the young Alabama general had earlier hand-picked and dispatched half a dozen of his best scouts to gather intelligence about the mysterious high ground before him on the other side of Plum Run. Many years later, General Hood confused the leader of these Alabama scouts with intelligence-seeking scouts from the 4th Texas of the Texas Brigade, who were dispatched earlier by General Hood on the identical mission to ascertain the exact location of the Union army's left in the Round Top area. In fact, it was General Law and not General Hood who chose a 4th Alabama noncommissioned officer, Sergeant Phinias K. McMiller, a scout par excellence and a "gallant and meritorious" soldier, as the leader of the Alabama scouts, not the Texas scouts. Lieutenant John McPherson Pinckney and five other 4th Texas soldiers scouted the Round Top area before the Alabama scouts. However, both scouting parties were equally effective on their respective missions.

Without knowledge of the terrain, General Law was "blind." He, therefore, relied upon the reports of the six Alabama scouts to develop a winning tactical plan amid a fluid battlefield situation. Making a smart move, General Law " . . . further instructed the scouts when they reached the summit [of Big Round Top] to observe carefully the state of affairs on the other side [east], and to send a 'runner' back to me with such intelligence as they might be able to gain [and] they moved off at a trot."

As directed by General Law, the mission of these trusty scouts was "to gain information upon this important point [by moving] as rapidly as possible to the summit of [Big] Round Top, making a detour to their right, and 'feeling' down from that point, to locate the left of the Federal line [because] the entire absence of Federal cavalry on our right, as well as other indications leading to the same conclusion, convinced me that the Federals, relying upon the protection of the mountain, considered their flank secure; that it was therefore their most vulnerable point."

General Law, a sage prophet whose battlefield instincts would rise to the fore on this afternoon of decision in south-central Pennsylvania, would soon be proven correct in his keen assessment of the tactical situation at that time. Indeed, the twin Round Tops before the Alabamians were at that point in time unoccupied by the Yankees. If the twin Round Tops were gained by General Law's Deep South soldiers, then the Alabamians would be securely in a commanding situation and in an advantageous position to strike the vulnerable left flank of the Army of the Potomac. Before any other Confederate officer on the far right of Hood's Division, it was General Law who had first sensed that this golden opportunity now lay before his advancing soldiers.[1]

Additionally enlightening General Law and confirming his beliefs, the advantageous tactical situation before the Alabama Rebels was confirmed even before the return of his half dozen Alabama scouts. "A few moments [after the scouts] had started, I saw in the valley [of Plum Run], some distance to our right, several dark figures moving across the fields from the rear of Round Top in the direction of the Emmitsburg Road," penned Law of the potential source of information. Immediately, General Law saw his opportunity to gather additional intelligence and hurriedly dispatched a party of Rebels to capture the two Yankees.

Heading toward what they thought was the army's rear with surgeon's disability certificates when captured, these two hapless Union prisoners informed General Law that on the east side of the Round Tops "the medical and ordnance trains [of the Army of the Potomac] 'around the mountain' were insecurely guarded, no attack being expected at that point," wrote Law. In addition, the prisoners also indicated that "the other side of the mountain could be easily reached by a good farm road, along which they had just traveled, the distance being a little more than a mile." Confirming his astute estimations on the tactical situation, General Law then began to realize the extent of the vulnerability of the unprotected left flank and rear of the Army of the Potomac. He now became more convinced that the Round Tops had to be secured that afternoon and at any cost.

Because General Meade's defensive line was over-extended along the high ground and curved like a fish-hook for a considerable length southward below the town, General Meade was unaware that Longstreet's corps had marched southward to turn his left; and because General Daniel Sickles had shifted his III Corps forward beyond the main Cemetery Ridge line to occupy the high ground of the Peach Orchard along the Emmitsburg Road, the Round Tops did indeed stand unoccupied on the Army of the Potomac's left. Therefore, this vulnerable area behind the Round Tops had been seen as a safe haven for General Meade to place the army's trains in the army's rear south of Gettysburg, which had been the vortex of the storm throughout July 1. With the battle expected to once again rage around the town of Gettysburg on July 2 as the day before, neither Generals Lee nor Meade were overly concerned about the two obscure Round Tops, which were about two miles south of Gettysburg and seemingly far from the main action. To the top generals of both armies, ironically, these two twin hills below Gettysyburg seemed unlikely bones of contention that afternoon.[2]

With the intelligence gained from the two talkative Yankees, General Law had immediately mounted up, and ridden toward the Texas Brigade to meet with General Hood to convey the news of the golden opportunity. On the ride northward, General Law had suddenly spied a messenger—one of his handpicked scouts— who was returning from the soldiers under Sergeant McMiller, 4th Alabama, scouting the Round Top area, to report more mind-boggling news to General Law.

As ordered by General Law, these Rebel scouts had reached the summit of Big Round Top after a long climb up the steep and timbered slope. The messenger informed General Law of an ideal scenario for Confederate fortunes which verified General Law's early estimation of the tactical situation on Meade's left flank: "There was no Federal force on the summit" of Big Round Top, the highest ground in the area that completely dominated the Gettysburg battlefield. Law was now more convinced of the urgent necessity of taking possession of the Round Tops because, wrote the Alabama general, this information "confirmed in every particular the statements of the prisoners I had just captured . . ." With the Round Tops unoccupied by Federal troops, this was the golden opportunity that General Law had envisioned for decisive Confederate success at Gettysburg.

The scouts had also discovered that the large ammunition, medical, and supply train of the Army of the Potomac now stood far from Gettysburg and only a few hundred yards east of the hollow between the Round Tops. Additionally, these invaluable trains had few blueclad guardians in the entire area. And best of all, the scout also informed Law that a good farm road led directly to the trains, and, most important, the rear of General Meade's army. Just beyond the parked trains was the Taneytown Road, which ran north toward Gettysburg and behind Cemetery Ridge and the Union army's rear. Clearly, the last place that General Meade was expecting an attack was on his left and especially his rear.

Lusting at the opportunity and hoping to strike before it was too late, General Law now fully understood that "if there had previously been any question in regard to the policy of a front attack, there now remained not a shadow of doubt that our true point d'appui was [Big] Round Top, from which the Confederate right wing could be extended toward the [north-south running] Taneytown and Baltimore [just east of the northeastward-running Taneytown Road] roads, on the Federal left and rear." General Law remained determined to make the most of the golden opportunity which lay before Colonel Oates and his Alabamians—and this called for striking eastward and not parallel to the Emmitsburg Road as ordered by General Lee.[3]

General Law now realized that "this part of the line [which] was held by Hood's division . . . was really the key to the whole position of Gettysburg." Before launching his attack, however, General Law attempted to obtain official approval for his against-orders attack and a change of General Longstreet's plan of assault. He had galloped over to General Hood, who as usual was near his Texas Brigade, to plead his case in person, begging for a modification of the plan of attack. General Law attempted to convince General Hood, who needed no convincing. Indeed, Hood did not like the looks of this fight and in fact had already twice appealed to General Longstreet in vain for a change of Lee's plan of attack. Both generals fully understood the wisdom of not launching an attack northeast, parallel to the Emmitsburg Road as ordered by General Lee but instead striking eastward and farther south to capture the Round Tops.

Before he fell wounded near the Bushman house from a bursting shell, the hard-fighting division commander fully agreed with General Law's tactical reasoning which was dominated by common sense, logic, and tactical insight. Indeed, after deeming the Union high ground positions as "impregnable," General Hood certainly realized the folly for his attackers if they followed General Lee's assault orders to the letter. Hood knew that by advancing northeastward up the Emmitsburg Road, the attacking formations of his division would be enfiladed from the high ground to the east and hard-hit from a murderous flank fire for little, if any, gain. In opposing General Lee's plan of attack because of the changed tactical situation on the battlefield, General Law boldly filed an official protest against obeying General Lee's orders.

General Law explained the changed tactical situation to General Hood with clarity, and:

> "pointed out the ease with which a movement by the right flank might be made [but Hood stated] that his orders were positive to attack in front . . . I therefore entered a formal protest against a direct attack [northeastward up the Emmitsburg Road as ordered by General Lee], on the grounds: 1. That the great natural strength of the enemy's position in our front rendered the result of a direct assault extremely uncertain. 2. That, even if successful, the victory would be purchased at too great a sacrifice of life, and our

troops would be in no condition to improve it. 3. That a
front attack was unnecessary—the occupation of [Big]
Round Top during the night by moving upon it from the
south, and the extension of our right wing from that point
across the enemy's left and rear, being not only practicable,
but easy. 4. That such a movement would compel a change
of front on the part of the enemy, the abandonment of his
strong position on the heights, and force him to attack us in
position."[4]

Earlier, General Hood had met with Longstreet's chief of staff,
Moxley Sorrel, and asked him to attempt to convince "Old Pete" to
modify his tactics. But now thanks to General Law's words of wisdom, General Hood decided to make one final appeal—his third—
to General Longstreet. Hood then sent a young staff officer,
Captain James Hamilton, who first listened to Law's rationale, to
General Longstreet's headquarters with Law's written protest
along with Hood's own endorsement. General Hood included his
own endorsement of General Law's tactical views of the present
situation after signing the Alabama general's written protest.

Throughout the day, General Longstreet was also convinced
that a movement farther south to gain the Round Tops was necessary for victory at Gettysburg, realizing that "here was offered a
chance to slip around the Union flank and get in the rear." In fact,
General Longstreet advocated a tactical plan to march the entire
army farther south and far beyond General Meade's left flank to
establish the Army of Northern Virginia in a good defensive position between the Army of the Potomac and Washington, D.C.
Then, General Longstreet hoped that General Meade's army
would destroy itself by launching frontal assaults against a strong
defensive position: ironically, the scenario General Lee would do
in reverse on July 2.

According to one account, General Hood had implored
General Lee in person that "my scouts report to me that there is a
wagon road around Round Top [leading up the east side to the
crest of the mountain and linked with the Taneytown Road east of

Big Round Top], at its foot, which has been used by farmers in getting out timber, over which I can move troops. I believe I can take one of my brigades, go around this mountain and simultaneously attack from the flank or rear, with the men in front, and capture Round Top." This incident was recorded by William Youngblood, a Pike County private in the "Quitman Guards" of Company I, 15th Alabama, before serving as one of General Longstreet's couriers, after boldly approaching "Old Pete" on June 23 and requesting the assignment on his own.

But Law's and Hood's rational alternative tactics to gain the Army of the Potomac's flank and rear were not sanctioned by General Lee. The final word on the matter finally came ten minutes later to Generals Hood and Law with Captain Hamilton's return from Longstreet's headquarters. With Captain Hamilton was General Longstreet's adjutant, Captain John Walter Fairfax, who emphasized that General Lee's assault orders must be obeyed.

While General Longstreet unofficially agreed with the wisdom of General Law's tactical revisions, he would not take responsibility in modifying Lee's orders. General Law was disappointed but undeterred upon hearing from Captain Fairfax that General Longstreet had reconfirmed General Lee's directive "to begin the attack at once" and as earlier specified in orders. Therefore, an equally frustrated General Hood barked out the words that the Alabama general from Tuskegee most of all had dreaded to hear, "You hear the order?" A frustrated General Law made no reply. Hoping to make the best of a bad situation, Law turned his horse and galloped off to rejoin his Alabama boys, who had a hard day's work ahead.

Because neither Generals Hood nor Longstreet would alter the orders from the army's commander, General Law now chose to hurl his troops eastward in defiance of General Lee's orders to strike up the Emmitsburg Road, hoping to exploit the tactical advantage and opportunity in a bid to secure the high ground on General Meade's left flank. Because the assault of General Longstreet's corps was in echelon and the Alabamians occupied the line's southern end and would serve as the brigade of direction for the division's advance along the line from south to north, General Law was the first officer to send his troops surging eastward.

Early military training at the Citadel in Charleston, South Carolina, where he graduated at age twenty with high expectations, had been put to good use. And now General Law envisioned taking possession of the Round Tops to gain the Union Army's flank and rear and capture those vulnerable ordnance and munition trains. After gobbling up these prizes, the left flank of the Army of the Potomac could be turned by his Alabamians, rolling-up Meade's line with a sweeping flank attack from the south. Despite being yet a month short of his twenty-seventh birthday, General Law would perform this day with more personal initiative, flexibility, and imagination than the majority of General Lee's most esteemed West Pointers. The hard-hitting team of General Law and Colonel Oates would prove a good combination throughout this afternoon in Adams County.[5]

By refusing to get his boys killed in a suicidal attack up the Emmitsburg Road and across open ground as ordered by Lee, General Law demonstrated the type of tactical insight which was in limited supply among the Confederate army's top commanders many years his senior. Relying on his own tactical sense and best battlefield instincts, young Evander McIver Law had early realized that sending his troops surging up the Emmitsburg Road was little more than a suicidal attack. Consequently, to General Law, the possibility of striking farther south than General Lee's orders dictated and beyond General Meade's left flank held the promise of decisive victory.

Ironically, Generals Longstreet, Hood, and McLaws all readily agreed with the wisdom of the revised tactical plan of General Law, dreading Lee's orders to launch a frontal attack. After General Hood appealed to "Old Pete" directly, General Longstreet had sought in vain to convince General Lee of the wisdom of swinging farther south to capture the Round Tops and turn Meade's left flank. But General Lee remained unconvinced of the plan's wisdom, refusing to alter his decision to attack up the Emmitsburg Road from the southwest.

According to his battle plan as earlier established, General Lee's oblique assault in echelon was designed to sweep northeastward up and parallel to the Emmitsburg Road to gain the lower, or southern end, of Cemetery Ridge, where the commanding general planned to smash into the left flank of the Army of the Potomac. General Lee's tactical plan called for General Longstreet's two divisions of the I Corps to surge forward—about halfway between Little Round Top and the Emmitsburg Road—in a bid to strike the Union army's left flank, after gaining the high ground between Seminary and Cemetery Ridge at the Peach Orchard to exploit the advantage of terrain. Meanwhile, General A. P. Hill's corps was to pressure the Union center to keep reinforcements from rushing to the assistance of General Meade's left. And General Ewell's corps on the north was to strike in conjunction with General Longstreet's corps on the south, helping to set the stage for success on Meade's left flank.

Confident from his past successes on battlefields across Virginia to Maryland, General Lee was most of all determined to exploit his July 1 success. By attacking up the Emmitsburg Road, he hoped to retain the initiative and the momentum by striking hard at the Army of the Potomoc. Lee was gambling that General Meade had significantly strengthened his right before General Ewell's corps at the expense of his left flank. Consequently, with pressure simultaneously exerted on Meade's right and center, General Lee's plan of attack centered on hitting General Meade's left above the Round Tops, with Longstreet's Corps rolling diagonally up the Emmitsburg Road from the southwest.

The ever-aggressive General Lee had based his battle plan on the belief that the Round Tops were devoid of Federals, believing the vulnerable open end of the Union battle line lay just north of the Round Tops. If Lee's tactical reasoning was correct, then General Meade's vulnerable left flank would be outflanked by Longstreet's two divisions steamrolling northeastward up the Emmitsburg Road. According to General Lee's plan, the battle of July 2 would be Chancellorsville all over again, with thousands of howling Rebels ripping into a weak flank of the Army of the Potomac and bringing decisive victory on Northern soil.

But in reality, this tactical formula for decisive Confederate success as earlier envisioned by the ever-optimistic Lee was no longer feasible. Since General Lee had first planned the attack, the tactical situation had changed with the extension of the Federal line southward. This extension pushed the Union left flank farther south to the Devil's Den, just northwest of the Round Tops, and well below the Peach Orchard sector. Without the assistance of Jeb Stuart's cavalry to ascertain the exact location of Meade's left flank, General Lee was blind and groping. However, such disadvantages failed to hamper General Lee's aggressive instincts. Lacking knowledge of the enemy's positions and dispositions, General Lee was hoping for the best without the advantage of intelligence, which was normally forthcoming from his army's trusty "eyes and ears," especially in launching the tactical offensive.

In truth, however, the Confederates had only ascertained the tactical situation on Little Round Top after the blueclad guardians of the previous night had departed and before the arrival of the V Corps replacements. Hence, Little Round Top would be devoid of Yankees only for a short time. But more important for the future outcome of General Lee's plan of attack, Meade's left was not northeastward up the Emmitsburg Road where he expected to find it but southward at the Devil's Den.[6]

Consequently, General Longstreet's top lieutenants, General McLaws and Hood, were initially astounded to discover that they were not beyond the expected location of Meade's left flank after deploying for the attack. It then became clear that the flank march had failed in its objective of gaining a position from which to roll-up the Union left. This sudden realization came to a shocked General McLaws with the startling sight of thousands of General Sickles's Yankees and lengthy rows of artillery of the III Corps, after advancing west from the Cemetery Ridge line, aligned on the dominating terrain before McLaw's brigades. General Lee and his battle plan had been checkmated almost before the first shot in this sector had been fired. As fate would have it, Longstreet's corps had completed a time-consuming and lengthy flank march in the belief that it would find "nothing in [their] front [for they would] be entirely on the flank of the enemy."

But the flank march which was to have won the element of surprise to rekindle the glories of Chancellorsville had been lost to Longstreet's "rock" corps, even before it took position on Lee's right. General McLaws now found that the Peach Orchard—Lee's primary high-ground objective in the first stage of the offensive to strike Meade's left on Cemetery Ridge—was held by a full Union corps. Because General Dan Sickles was as unorthodox and unconventional as General Law in terms of altering his commanders' battle plan to more effectively meet battlefield requirements, the III Corps now occupied the key high ground of the Peach Orchard.

A stunned General McLaws could only lament that there now existed "a state of affairs which was certainly not contemplated when the original plan or order of battle was given . . ." However, the inflexibility of Confederate leadership at the highest levels on July 2 meant that Southern leadership—with the exception of General Law—would not adapt to the altered tactical situation. Generals McLaw's and Hood's Divisions had failed to reach an advantageous position from which to strike the left flank of the Army of the Potomac as envisioned by General Lee. As fate would have it, it would now largely depend upon General Law and Colonel Oates to accomplish what had been assigned to Generals McLaw and Hood: rolling up the Union army's left flank.[7]

Because of the disadvantageous tactical situation and the failure of Confederate leadership to alter an obsolete tactical plan, General Law believed that "just here the battle of Gettysburg was lost to the Confederate arms." This was an undeniable realization to General Law because General Lee "made his attack [on July 2] precisely where his enemy wanted him to make it and was most fully prepared to receive it."

Indeed, even as Hood's and McLaws's Divisions aligned to attack northeastward as directed, the Federal line stretched so much farther southward that the Army of the Potomac's left already overlapped the right flank of some of Longstreet's attack columns advancing from the southwest up the Emmitsburg Road. Because of the changed tactical situtation, therefore, General Longstreet's assault formations would be hit on the right flank by enfilading fires from the high ground to the east. General Longstreet's soldiers, ironically, were about to do exactly what General Meade most desired Lee's over-confident army to do at Gettysburg: the ultimate folly of launching ill-advised and suicidal frontal assaults against high ground held by thousands of veterans and well-positioned batteries poised in all but impregnable defensive positions. As General Meade and his top lieutenants realized, this was the guaranteed recipe for Confederate defeat.

Making the best out of a bad situation, therefore, General Law had been forced to act on his own out of necessity, siezing the initiative. The young general had ordered his five Alabama regiments to advance straight eastward toward the Round Tops. Most of all by this time, General Law fully realized that the Confederate advance up and parallel to the Emmitsburg Road was a death-trap. Thus he risked his career by making his own decision in advancing eastward and striking farther south than ordered to gain the Round Tops and the enemy's flank and rear. Such bold personal initiative and tactical flexibility was what won battles, and Law possessed a natural instinct for securing victory on the battlefield with aggressive action, such as at Gaines's Mill. On July 2 in this crucial situation with so much at stake, Law's rational disobedience of General Lee's obsolete orders made good sense to this practical general from Macon County, Alabama.[8]

Because of the altered tactical situation on the Union army's left and due to the tactical flexibility of the free-thinking General Law, the young general's hard-hitting Alabama Brigade on the far right, ironically, would now have the best chance to fulfill General Lee's original tactical plan of striking and turning the Army of the Potomac's left flank. This fact, of course, was completely unknown to General Lee, as was the altered dispositions of the Union army, thanks in large part to the absence of General Stuart's cavalry.

To the Alabamians's left, meanwhile, General Robertson's four regiments of Hood's old Texas Brigade, including the 3rd Arkansas Infantry, soon followed the Alabamians's example by striking eastward instead of attacking northeastward and parallel to the Emmitsburg Road. Against orders and unlike McLaw's Division which now targeted the Peach Orchard beside the Emmitsburg Road for capture to fulfill Lee's orders, General Hood made preparations to hurl his troops north of General Law's Alabama Brigade, eastward and away from the Emmitsburg Road and toward the Devil's Den: a testimony to the wisdom of General Law's tactical innovations as developed on the battlefield.

Hence, General Robertson's Texas and Arkansas soldiers charged eastward, like Oates's Alabamians, and toward the Devil's Den and the western side of Little Round Top with the conviction "to do or die," wrote one Texan. Because Law's Alabamians began General Longstreet's echelon assault from right to left, these Trans-Mississippians launched their attack after the Alabamians surged forward with battle flags waving in the late afternoon sunlight. The troops of Hood's old Texas Brigade would attempt to maintain contact with Colonel Oates's Alabama attackers to their right. Appropriately, Colonel Oates's men had many friends, neighbors, and relatives in these hard-fighting Texas regiments, which were some of the best units of the Army of Northern Virginia. During the antebellum period, the native Alabamians of the Texas Brigade had migrated west across the Mississippi to make a new life amid the rich lands of frontier Texas, before enlisting in these Lone Star State regiments. In addition, many Georgians of "Old Rock" Benning's Brigade also hailed from the Chattahoochee Valley and the thriving Chattahoochee River port of Columbus.

General Law had placed his faith in an altered battle plan because a frontal assault in echelon "promised nothing but desperate fighting, heavy loss, and probable failure." This, ironically, was the eventual tragic fate of the assaults of Generals McLaw's and Hood's Divisions on bloody July 2. Indeed, staggered infantry attacks in echelon over a wide front promised to diminish both strike power and momentum, while ensuring little support to exploit any success won by the attackers advancing under a brutal enfilade fire.[9]

Like a good West Pointer, General Longstreet was considerably less flexible than the opportunistic General Law. Consequently and regardless of the battlefield situation, Longstreet was determined to carry out General Lee's offensive instructions precisely as ordered and without adapting to the changed battlefield situation. But after General Hood's wounding and assuming division command, General Law led the Texas, Arkansas, and Alabama regiments of Hood's Division forward into the raging storm of the jumbles of big granite rocks known as the Devil's Den, striking eastward like Colonel Oates's Alabamians farther south before the imposing hill called Big Round Top.[10]

Even after moving forward, General Hood had yet protested Lee's orders when General Longstreet rode up, while expressing "his regret that he could not turn the Federal left." By this time, neither General Law nor Colonel Oates harbored such regrets. And when the wounded General Hood was taken rearward, he "could but experience deep distress of mind and heart at the thought of the inevitable fate of my brave fellow-soldiers, who formed one of the grandest divisions of that world-renowned army; and I shall ever believe that had I been permitted to turn Round Top Mountain, we would not only have gained that position, but have been able finally to rout the enemy" at Gettysburg. It was now up to the Alabama Rebels to do on their own what General Hood had been denied.[11]

CHAPTER VII

Alabama's Rebels
Resume the Offensive

"What business had he, a corps commander, to advance with the line of battle on one part of the field? Instead of taking a position from which he could see the progress of the battle all along the line."

—Colonel Oates speaking of General Longstreet's
actions on July 2, 1863

Only with General Law's unexpected arrival before the 15th Alabama on the far right was Colonel Oates enlightened about recent tactical developments on the field and General Hood's fall. Colonel Oates learned from General Law of the importance of both his position on Generals Lee's and Longstreet's far right flank and the key role that the 15th Alabama was now destined to play in the most crucial battle of the war. Colonel Oates must have felt a heavy burden of responsibility upon learning from General Law that it was the all-important mission of the 15th Alabama, now the sole regiment occupying the right end of Lee's advancing battle line, to turn the left flank of the Army of the Potomac.

As ordained by fate, the changed battlefield situation, and circumstance, Colonel Oates and only a few hundred of his Alabama soldiers had suddenly been handed the opportunity to wreck the career of the Union army's new commander, George Meade, before it really began. General Meade expected Lee to attack on the north at Culp's Hill and not Little Round Top. Consequently, General Meade had reinforced Culp's Hill at the expense of the southern end of his line, especially Little Round Top. If the Alabamians took advantage of this opportunity to capture Little Round Top and roll-up the Union left flank, then General Meade would simply be another on a long list of defeated Army of the Potomac commanders over the last two years.

But General Meade, the hard-nosed West Pointer who was defending his home soil of Pennsylvania, would rise to the challenge of Gettysburg. Without much fanfare, the business-like Meade had recently replaced "Fighting Joe" Hooker, who had lost his nerve and reputation against General Lee and Stonewall Jackson at Chancellorsville. Now fighting a defensive battle on good terrain on Northern soil, the recently defeated "Mr. Lincoln's Army" was a much different force than in the dark Virginia forests of Chancellorsville in early May 1863.

And as fate would have it, Colonel Oates's soldiers were about to pay a high price for the breakdown of communication among the highest levels of the Confederate army's top leadership as the lack of understanding between the offensive-minded Lee and the defensive-minded Longstreet continued throughout July 2. And when and where he was needed the most—to direct the Alabamians's effort to turn the Union army's left on the far right— General Longstreet was nowhere to be found. General Lee's previously successful policy of relying on a delegation of authority to enhance the personal initiative of his corps commanders was to prove ineffective at Gettysburg.

General Longstreet's passive, if not sullen, non-compliance would help to ensure that Colonel Oates's Alabamians would not receive badly needed support on this July afternoon. In part, however, this situation was also due to the Alabama Brigade's position on the extreme flank during an attack in echelon. And with Colonel Oates commanding too few troops for the assigned offensive task at hand, support was essential if the tide was to be turned in the Confederacy's favor on General Lee's far right.

At this time, Longstreet was moving forward with the South Carolina and Georgia troops of McLaw's Division toward the III Corps's defensive positions in the Peach Orchard, about a mile northwest of Colonel Oates's Alabama Rebels. For the remainder of the afternoon, the fury of the Peach Orchard and the Wheat Field would consume General Longstreet's attention. Consequently, to accomplish their vital mission, Colonel Oates and his thirsty, barefoot, and hungry men were on their own on the right end of Lee's line. Likewise, General Lee would remain absent from the far right, providing neither leadership nor guidance.

An embittered Colonel Oates later hotly denounced the lack of leadership demonstrated by General Longstreet on July 2, dooming his 15th Alabama to an unsupported, isolated, and inadequate bid to capture the strategic Round Tops. Oates asked rhetorically in an angry denunciation "What business had he, a corps commander, to advance with the line of battle on one part of the field? Instead of taking a position from which he could see the progress of the battle all along the line, and with the practiced eye of a great captain, taking in at once the whole situation, eager to discover and quick to take advantage of any mistake of his adversary, or weak points in his line, he was playing the part simply of a gallant brigadier, and advancing with his line of battle at one end of it, leaving the other to take care of itself . . ."

By this time and despite being General Law's most junior regimental commander, Colonel Oates was eager for an opportunity to strike an exposed flank and perhaps gain the Union army's rear on his own if necessary. As now ordered by General Law, the mission of the 15th Alabama was seek out, hit, and then roll up the left flank of Meade's army. General Law later indicated that another one of Colonel Oates's objectives on the far end of the Army of Northern Virginia's line was to anchor that weak flank: "In order to secure my right flank, I [ordered that it be] extended well up on the side of Round Top . . ." However, Colonel Oates recounted a more comprehensive set of orders. He stated that he was directed by General

Law to move forward and then to the left and "hug the base of [Big] Round Top and go up the valley between the two mountains" to pinpoint and then strike Meade's left flank on Little Round Top.

Hence, after pivoting his troops northward to follow the base of Big Round Top by way of "a left half wheel" maneuver, Colonel Oates's fundamental mission was to hit Meade's left flank whenever and wherever he found it. And at this time, General Law believed that the Union army's left was located somewhere between the two Round Tops. Then, General Law hoped that the 15th Alabama and the seven small companies of the 47th Alabama to Colonel Oates's left would be in an advantageous position to turn the Union army's left flank.

Indicating the importance of the Alabamians's mission to smash into the vulnerable left flank of the Army of the Potomac, Law then gave Oates orders he never forgot. With a gleam in his eye which betrayed his hunger for the possibilities of a successful assault, General Law ordered Colonel Oates to "do all the damage" that he possibly could to the Union army's left flank and rear. In the no-nonsense words of an average enlisted man in the ranks, Corporal McClendon described how General Law's directive meant that "our job was to kill or wound some more Yankees or be killed or wounded by them . . ."

Colonel Oates and his soldiers now allowed the intoxicating thoughts of this opportunity to drift through their minds, fueling their determination to succeed at any cost. And the mass of Union munition, ordnance, and supply trains were unguarded and alone, waiting to be taken by those bold enough to take them. With the bullet-shredded battle flags waving in the summer heat, Colonel Oates ordered his soldiers onward toward Big Round Top, after realigning ranks just southwest of the Slyder house and before the open pasture bordering the west side of the creek. At a quick pace which indicated the urgency of their mission, the Alabama Confederates pushed on with precision as steel bayonets gleamed in the bright sunshine of July. Finally, Colonel Oates's soldiers began to cross the deeply cut Plum Run at the valley's lowest point on the double. Wasting no time, these veterans in gray and butternut splashed through the clear water from the springs of Adams County, while trying to avoid tripping over the rocks or slipping in the mud. The threadbare Alabama boys attempted to maintain as tight an alignment as possible as they pushed through the mud and water. Amid the grassy pasture on the creek's west side, the 15th Alabama's ranks surged through the lowness of the valley below the Slyder house, while the noise of clanging gear filled the hot and humid air that was choking the lowlands.

Without halting, the onrushing Alabamians continued passing across the creek despite stubbing toes on rocks, slipping on the moss-covered rocks, and scrambling first down and then up the muddy bank. Even though their mouths and lips were parched and cracked from lack of water, not a single Alabama boy broke ranks to fill his canteen in the cool, clear waters of the stream—a testament to Colonel Oates's discipline.

Under the searing sun and with spirits high, the Alabamians unleashed their distinctive war cry from the Wiregrass and Chattahoochee River country of southeast Alabama's coastal plain. As during the hardhitting attacks of the past two years, the 15th Alabama was again proving itself to be "a good yelling regiment."

With only seven companies of about 150 soldiers of the 47th Alabama on Colonel Oates's immediate left, the task of striking the Army of the Potomac's left flank was primarily the 15th Alabama's mission. The 15th Alabama was overall more experienced and dependable than Colonel Bulger's command. Consequently, the younger—by almost thirty years—but more experienced Colonel Oates would continue to retain overall command of his regiment and the seven 47th Alabama companies for the remainder of the day.

As an ill portent of things to come in the upcoming struggle for Little Round Top, five skirmish companies of Law's Brigade vanished from Colonel Oates's front: the three skirmish companies of the 47th Alabama on the left veered southward and away from Colonel Oates and his regiment; in addition, the two skirmish companies of the 48th Alabama on the right advanced even farther south, evaporating like ghosts into the greenness and humidity-hazed thickness of the Bushman Woods: all destined to be lost to Colonel Oates during the upcoming struggle for Little Round Top. These five Alabama skirmish companies represented a significant loss of manpower—a full one tenth of the total strength of General Law's brigade and one-half of an entire regiment—on a day when every Rebel would soon be needed at Little Round Top.

Thus neither group of advancing Alabama skirmishers would provide any assistance to the 15th Alabama on this day of destiny. Ironically, the farther east that Colonel Oates advanced that afternoon, the more men he was destined to lose before meeting the first Yankee. And now the majority of the more than seventeen hundred Texas and Arkansas soldiers of General Robertson's "Grenadier Guard" brigade to the left, who were to have also assisted in the turning of Meade's left, were moving farther northeastward toward the Devil's Den. Instead of assisting Colonel Oates, most of these veteran soldiers of Hood's old Texas Brigade would fight hundreds of yards to the north.

But thus far, the gradual descent down the eastern slope of Warfield Ridge, into and through the narrow valley of Plum Run had been deceptively easy for the 15th Alabama attackers. Without the benefit of a protective skirmish line in front to lead the way Colonel Oates must have felt fortunate to have not yet met the enemy. With pride, Colonel Oates later described the assault: "Our line advanced in quick time under the fire of our guns, through an open field about three or four hundred yards and then down a gentle slope for a quarter of a mile, through the open valley of Plum Run [where] a small, muddy, meandering stream running through it near the base of the mountains."

Despite having seen only the backs of a few Yankees retiring eastward before the advancing waves of the Alabamians, not a single musket from either a Federal skirmish line or a regular line of bluecoats had been fired at the Alabamians. To Colonel Oates this seemed to indicate that no Federals occupied the high ground in his front east of Plum Run at the western base of Big Round Top. Indeed, by this time, Colonel Oates's advance completely overlapped the southern end of General Meade's left flank, and the

Alabamians surged beyond it. Initially the artillery fire from Captain Smith's New York Battery had exploded among Colonel Oates's attackers, but even this cannonade had ceased by the time the Confederates entered the depths of the low ground around Plum Run.

In fact, both the bloodless advance and the advantageous tactical situation seemed much too easy for the Alabamians in relation to the opportunity that was presented to them. To Colonel Oates and his veterans, the job of turning the Union army's left and gaining its rear now appeared more like a case of marching and maneuvering than hard fighting. It seemed that all the Alabama troops on the far end of General Lee's army now had to do was simply keep moving forward to reach the Round Tops. Nevertheless, this illusion of an easy success without cost gave some veteran Alabama soldiers an uneasy and anxious feeling. Indeed, these battle-hardened Alabamians almost instinctively sensed that such a seemingly easy scenario for Confederate victory on July 2 was far too optimistic. Colonel Oates's advance had been so easy that it seemed too good to be true, and it was.

The first Yankees encountered by the Alabamians on the east side of Plum Run would be those of the 2nd United States Sharpshooters. Without cavalry, Union General Sickles had been forced to extend the left flank of his III Corps with sharpshooters instead of horsesoldiers. Thus watching the Alabamians's disciplined advance through the belt of woods and fields of the Slyder farm, an awed Sergeant Wyman S. White, 2nd United States Sharpshooters, could hardly believe his eyes. He later described how ". . . a solid mass of rebels spilled over a ridge in our front [and] they came yelling and firing and struggling over fences and through the timber . . . they were dressed in butternut clothes they had the appearance of a plowed field being closed in mass formation . . ." Sergeant White and an advanced band of skirmishers therefore fell back before Colonel Oates's ranks before they were overrun. On the double, these crack marksmen retired from the cover of the house, barn, and smokehouse of farmer John Slyder, and headed toward Big Round Top to rejoin their comrades at their main line on the east side of Plum Run. Taking defensive position on a ledge of high ground which overlooked the creek bottoms and low ground to the west, they found excellent cover behind a stone wall with their companies. In preparation for meeting Colonel Oates's advance, the Federal marksmen leaned their rifles atop the stone wall, steadying their aim.

Thus Colonel Oates and his Alabamians were destined to run straight into what was little more than an ambush. There along the high ground overlooking the stream, this formidable stone wall position on the east side of Plum Run was manned by 150 crack sharpshooters. With the savvy of hardened veterans, these Yankee marksmen wisely held their fire in order to hit the onrushing Rebels when they were most vulnerable amid the marshy, low ground at the creek bottoms.

A sheet of flame suddenly exploded, pouring off the high ground with a vengeance. The eruption of gunfire burst from the wall of rocks, rippling down the line of sharpshooters. Unleashing an uncanny accuracy, these Federal marksmen never seemed to miss a shot. The Yankees busily loaded and fired with an accuracy never before seen by Colonel Oates's veterans in either Virginia or Pennsylvania, and Alabama soldiers began to fall, dropping to the ground like brown fallen leaves on a windy autumn morning.

As Colonel Oates described the situation, "when crossing the little run we received the first fire from the Federal infantry, posted behind a stone fence near the foot of [Big] Round Top mountain. Our line did not halt." With another cheer, the Alabamians continued onward with precision, almost as if on a drill ground before the homefolk in Abbeville. With the absence of the five skirmish companies, no skirmishers now advanced before the 15th Alabama, leaving the regiment vulnerable with no knowledge of the terrain or the enemy's location. Indeed, no Rebel scouts had learned of this lengthy line of Yankee sharpshooters to warn Oates of the danger.

The stone wall lay on a small ridge that ran roughly north-south and parallel to Plum Run. There, the high ground provided a fine defensive position for the sharpshooters to effectively protect the Union army's left flank. Spanning eastward from the level ground of the creek bottoms and the Slyder house, the stone wall followed a narrow farm lane that ran roughly west-east on the east side of Plum Run. Then, turning southeastward, it followed the natural contours of the western base of Big Round Top. These natural contours of the elevated ground and the stone wall running along its length rose gradually upward toward the tallest elevation in Adams County, which was actually more of a mountain than a hill.

The dense woods and underbrush on Plum Run's east side and along the rising ground on the western slope of Big Round Top concealed both the strength and location of the sharpshooters' defensive position. Local farmers had not cleared either the timber or rocks from the east side of Plum Run and a natural obstacle of rocks, trees, and saplings stood before the stone wall, impeding the Alabamians's attack up the gradual slope that led toward the higher ground.[1]

Exploding unexpectedly at close range, this murderous frontal fire hit the Alabama attackers hard. But the worst fire came from a southerly direction to rake the right flank of the 15th Alabama, which was enfiladed from the high ground. While the 44th and 48th Alabama Regiments continued to push northward and across the 15th Alabama's rear to reach the left of Law's line, the 15th Alabama soldiers continued east, attacking the concealed positions of the 2nd United States Sharpshooters.

Colonel Oates described how the sharp-eyed marksmen were "posted behind a [stone] fence at or near the [western] foot of Great Round Top [after] they reached that position as we advanced through the old field [the pasture running south along the west bank of Plum Run]. No other [Union] troops were there nor on that mountain at that time." Without immediate support either in his front, rear, or on either flank, Colonel Oates was on his own during his first challenge at Gettysburg long before ever reaching a place called Little Round Top. For when Colonel Oates looked rearward for immediate support he was shocked to discover that he was now without a reserve. Worst of all, he also understood the added tactical disadvantages that his exhausted soldiers now faced in overpowering a stone wall on high ground manned by sharpshooters, decreasing greatly his chances for turning General Meade's left and gaining the army's rear, when time was of the essence.

Colonel Oates explained the disadvantage which would play a role in determining Confederate fortunes on the far right during the upcoming struggle for Little Round Top: "I did not halt at the first fire, but looked to the rear for the Forty-eighth Alabama, and saw it going, under General Law's order, across the rear of our line to the left [which] left no one in my rear or on my right to meet the foe." Colonel Oates was now doubly vulnerable without support on either flank and rear. This tactical disadvantage also resulted because the Alabamians were forced to manuever in "a left half wheel" in order to confront the stone wall defenders.

Clearly, by this time, Colonel Oates needed the assistance of the 44th and 48th Regiments to have a chance of capturing the high ground, especially if large numbers of Yankees gained Little Round Top before him. However, the 44th and 48th Alabama continued northward on the double to plug the gap in General Hood's advancing line when the 4th and 5th Texas remained connected to the left of Law's Alabamians in the advance eastward and the 1st Texas and 3rd Arkansas attempted to follow the Emmitsburg Road in a northeastward direction. Meanwhile, the left of General Robertson's Texas and Arkansas brigade pushed northeastward to strike the Devil's Den, while the Texas Brigade's right continued advancing eastward toward the western slope of Little Round Top.

What most of all now pulled the more than seven hundred soldiers of the 44th and the 48th Alabama northward and away from Colonel Oates's sector were the urgent calls of the hard-pressed General Robertson. The Texas Brigade's commander repeatedly requested General Law to send assistance to help him capture the Devil's Den and especially the lethal New York cannon aligned on the crest of Houck's Ridge, which proved to be a formidable obstacle. Consequently, these sudden developments and realignments meant that the 15th Alabama alone would have to drive the best sharpshooters of the Army of the Potomac from behind the stone wall on dominant terrain.[2]

With his men dropping from bullets whistling through their advancing ranks and enfilading the regiment's right flank and rear, Colonel Oates now "knew it would not do to go on and leave that force [of Union sharpshooters], I knew not how strong, in our rear with no troops of ours to take care of them; so I gave the command to change direction to the right." With his assault formations advancing roughly northeastward, Colonel Oates quickly shifted his men to the right or southeastward to try to eliminate the brutal flank and rear fire from the eagle-eyed marksmen of Company B, 2nd United States Sharpshooters. The rapidly firing Yankees of Company B held the far left flank, or the southernmost position, of the 2nd United States Sharpshooters line, and they poured an enfilade fire from the stone wall southeast of the Slyder house. This brutal fire streaming from the hardy backwoodsmen, loggers, and frontiersmen from Michigan was so severe that their musketry exploding from the stone wall became known as the "Hornet's Nest" at Gettysburg.

However, this new threat from the southeast or rear meant that Colonel Oates would have to ignore General Law's orders to turn to the left, or north, in order to ease through the hollow between the Round Tops to seek out General Meade's elusive left flank. Never before had Colonel Oates either questioned or disobeyed an order given on the battlefield. But he did so now. Clearly, the young colonel was maturing into an independent-minded, flexible, and free-thinking commander amid the crisis of battle and once again demonstrated the tactical flexibility needed to meet an ever-changing situation on the battlefield.

But the last-minute realignments during the 15th Alabama's advance combined with the thick timber and brush on the creek's west side and the scorching fire raining down on them now caused some confusion among Colonel Oates's troops. And when the 15th Alabama moved to the right, Colonel Bulger shifted his seven 47th Alabama companies and double-quicked them toward Colonel Oates's left in an attempt to maintain alignment with the advancing 15th Alabama, causing more confusion in the ranks which were already fragmented in crossing fences. In addition, leadership was lacking with Colonel Bulger not realizing that the regimental commander, Colonel James W. Jackson, had collapsed at the beginning of the advance. Also, Colonel Bulger incorrectly believed that his primary objective was to silence Captain Smith's New York guns on Houck's Ridge, and that he was not under Colonel Oates's orders as General Law had directed.

Angered by the mix-up on the battlefield, Colonel Oates later described how the 47th Alabama soldiers "got telescoped into our left and the men were mixed several lines deep." The confusion in the ranks of the 47th Alabama resulted in confusion in the 15th Alabama, impeding forward momentum and costing more precious time. Forty-two-year-old Sergeant William R. Holley, a tough noncommissioned officer and leader of the "Henry Pioneers," who no one wanted to cross unless they wanted trouble, was enraged by the confusion among his once neatly aligned ranks. Colonel Oates described this hard-fighting sergeant as "a brave soldier, but a very cautious, watchful, prudent, and sensible man." During the mix-up with the shifting ranks of the 47th Alabama, Sergeant Holley attempted to not only keep his men in line but also to straighten out the mess and confusion among Colonel Bulger's soldiers, even while under a hot fire. Meeting with little success, the frustrated Company G sergeant screamed in frustration to his commander who must have agreed with the sentiment, "Colonel Oates, make Colonel Bulger take his damned concern out of our regiment!"

Clearly, Colonel Oates had made the correct tactical decision to act on his own. The danger that the 15th Alabama's right would be additionally exposed to a flank fire if he turned to the left as ordered by General Law and not wanting to leave an unknown number of Yankees in his rear if he swung northward caused Oates to decide to act on his own. Consequently, he now led his attackers southeastward to drive the sharpshooters away from the stone wall at the western base of Big Round Top.

By this time, one reality could no longer be denied by Colonel

Oates: Generals Lee, Longstreet, and Law had all but abandoned the 15th Alabama to its own devices to win or lose on the far right of the Army of Northern Virginia. Indeed, while the 15th Alabama and the seven 47th Alabama companies surged southeastward against the flaming stone wall, the remainder of General Law's brigade attacked more in a northerly direction: an ill-timed division of force which would remain permanent on July 2, much to Colonel Oates's disadvantage.

The defensive stand made by the elite sharpshooters of the Army of the Potomac now played an important—even if forgotten—role in the overall struggle for Little Round Top. The fight for the stone wall caused General Law's advancing units to fragment, sapping offensive strength and momentum, while additionally diminishing an already limited amount of manpower. Even worse, more precious time was consumed and wasted, delaying the Alabamians's all-important mission of turning Meade's left flank and taking the Round Tops before the arrival of Union reinforcements. Because of the clash with Berdan's Sharpshooters, Colonel Oates and his men would now possess even less chance of winning decisive success in the upcoming struggle for Little Round Top.

CHAPTER VIII

Bloody Fight for a Stone Wall

". . . we took the matter coolly [and] many a brave Southron threw up his arms and fell. But they came on, shouting and yelling their peculiar yell . . ."

—one of Berdan's Sharpshooters describing the attack of the 15th Alabama before Big Round Top

By any measure, the Alabama attackers faced no ordinary adversary in charging the stone wall. Well-concealed behind it and poised in excellent firing positions along the high ground at the western base of Big Round Top stood the best marksmen of the Army of the Potomac—Colonel Hiram Berdan's Sharpshooters.

This was an elite special forces command and President Lincoln's deadliest riflemen. They originally had been recruited from newspapers across the country requesting the best marksmen in the North. The eight 2nd United States Sharpshooter companies were deployed in a line that spanned around a half-mile. Four companies were deployed north of the Slyder home, while the other four sharpshooter companies were aligned south of the house. The North's best sharpshooters now effectively protected the army's left, or the left flank of General Sickles's III Corps, which was anchored on the Devil's Den. Sheltered and well-hidden, these highly disciplined men in green uniforms stood firm to unleash a devastating fire.

Without exaggeration, these elite sharpshooters "undoubtedly killed more men than any other regiment in the Army" during the four years of war. One shocked Confederate soldier long remembered the horror which could be inflicted by the rapid fire of these crack marksmen: "Those Yankee Sharpshooters were marvelous [and] they rarely missed a man at a mile . . ." These deadly men now fought tenaciously under the inspired leadership of regimental commander Major Homer S. Stoughton. In buying precious time and delaying the Alabamians's advance toward the vulnerable left flank of the Army of the Potomac, the capable major led the 2nd United States Sharpshooters with distinction that July day, rising to the challenge of confronting Colonel Oates.

No sharpshooters on July 2 would play a more important role at Gettysburg than these marksmen who were now standing firm before the 15th Alabama. This invaluable purchase of precious time and the depletion of Oates's already limited manpower would play a key role in determining the outcome of the upcoming struggle for Little Round Top. The other regiment of Berdan's Sharpshooters—the 1st United States Sharpshooters—fought to the north at Pitzer's Run on July 2, and ironically received widespread recognition for their role there. These sharpshooters conducted a much better publicized delaying action—ironically against other Alabama soldiers—in which they would claim to have sabotaged Rebel success at Gettysburg by delaying General Longstreet's advance before the Peach Orchard salient. However, the little-known role of the 2nd United States Sharpshooters in delaying Colonel Oates's advance on the far right of General Lee's line was more important. Clearly, Major Stoughton's marksmen deserve more recognition for helping to save the day at Gettysburg on the Confederate right flank rather than what the other sharpshooters accomplished to the north.[1]

Many good Alabama soldiers went down to the blazing rifles

of these snipers. Among those 15th Alabama boys falling to the sharpshooters' fire were Privates A. Kennedy of Company B, and William Trimner, a Company G teenager who had recently recovered from a serious Fredericksburg wound. Both enlisted men were killed in the torrent of bullets. Other graycoats, including Company D's George E. Spencer, dropped seriously wounded. The blistering fire punished additional Alabamians, who were boxed-in along the deeply cut creek, which ran southward at the lowest point of the valley.

Sergeant White, one of the sharpshooters in a green uniform that day, recorded the extent of the destruction delivered upon the onrushing Alabama soldiers. He never forgot how: ". . . we took the matter coolly [and] many a brave Southron threw up his arms and fell. But they came on, shouting and yelling their peculiar yell . . ."—that piercing yip-yip of the Rebel Yell mingled with the cries of pain from Alabamians who were cut down by the scorching fire pouring off the high ground.[2]

One of Oates's most trusted officers now rose to the fore in leading his men forward against the wall of fire—Lieutenant Colonel Isaac Ball Feagin. With inspired leadership demonstrated on battlefields across the South, the handsome young officer had won his rank on May 1, 1863, serving as Oates's top lieutenant by the time of Gettysburg. A thrifty merchant from Midway, Alabama, Feagin was a dependable officer, barely two weeks away from his thirtieth birthday, and recently recovered from his Maryland campaign wound. Colonel Oates described Lieutenant Colonel Feagin, a young man with a fine physique who wore a fashionable goatee, as "courageous and faithful, and commanded his company in every engagement of the regiment, up to a short time preceding the second battle of Manassas, when, being senior captain present, he commanded the regiment through the fighting at Manassas Junction, on the Plains, at Chantilly Farm, at Sharpsburg, and at Shepherdstown."[3]

General James A. Walker wrote in his Maryland campaign report how "Captain Feagin, commanding 15th Alabama Regiment, behaved with a gallantry consistent with his high reputation for courage and that of the regiment he commanded [, proving to be] a gallant officer" on the battlefield.[4]

Now Colonel Feagin led the howling soldiers onward into the vortex of the storm. The cheering Alabamians charged onward, firing and loading on the run. All the while, the marksmen of the 2nd United States Sharpshooters blasted away with their deadly .52-caliber Sharps rifles. The seven-shot, breechloading rifles with open sights were especially lethal in the hands of these veterans known far and wide for "good eye & nerve." Wearing new green uniforms which were issued in January and Prussian-style knapsacks of cowhide covered with horsehair, the sharpshooters looked neat compared to Colonel Oates's ragged soldiers. And the most prized possession of these marksmen were their refurbished lever-action Sharps rifles which had been issued in March 1863. In addition, Major Stoughton's sharpshooters possessed new bayonets for hand-to-hand combat.

Colonel Oates now realized that he had run into a buzz saw. This was a hornets' nest of stinging sharpshooters, who were angry and delivering a good deal of punishment on the onrushing Alabamians. Minute after minute, the disciplined sharpshooters continued to blast away at the long line of Alabama men with cool, business-like efficiency. In a relatively short time, the green-clad marksmen riddled the attack formation much like when they had cut down a good many young North Carolina soldiers and Alabamians in the nightmarish "Bloody Lane" of Antietam. And now less than ten months later, these same greenclad marksmen, who had cut down Alabama Rebels with a destructive flank fire on September 17, 1862, were taking a heavy toll on Oates's Alabamians in a bloody repeat performance.[5]

Even though armed with new Enfield rifles from blockade runners and from the capture of Harpers Ferry, the 15th Alabama soldiers could not match the sharpshooters' rapid rate and volume of fire—a deadly rate of about ten shots per minute. Unlike the Alabama men who carried the standard forty rounds, these Yankee sharpshooters could fire more rapidly and longer because they usually carried sixty rounds. And this day these elite soldiers possessed even more rounds, with some marksmen carrying as many as one hundred cartridges.

One Confederate later admitted without exaggeration that "the Sharpshooters were the worst men we have to contend with" at Gettysburg. By any measure, no Yankees during the brutal three days at Gettysburg dealt out more punishment in proportion to their numbers than the reliable 150 "Green Coats," deployed behind this stone wall. These elite soldiers now shot down Alabama Rebels as easily as hitting targets at a turkey shoot. Watching his expert marksmen perform effectively in protecting General Meade's left, Major Stoughton described how "the enemy then advanced a line of battle covering our entire front and flank. While they were advancing, the Second regiment did splendid execution, killing and wounding a great many."[6]

But ignoring the escalating casualties, the 15th Alabama soldiers continued onward amid this hail of lead. Twenty-one-year-old Color Sergeant James R. Edwards now encouraged the Alabamians forward with his inspiring presence before the onrushing line of his fellow Alabamians. Colonel Oates wrote how "there was no better soldier in the regiment than 'Jim' Edwards [who was] a hard fighter and always conspicuous in action [and] as brave a man as ever went upon a battlefield."[7]

But the high cost of tangling with the 2nd United States Sharpshooters was increasing not only because of their accurate fire at close range but also because the Alabamians made such good targets in crossing the mostly open ground around Plum Run: a natural killing field for these trained professionals. The sharpshooters' dark green uniforms blended in well with the natural foliage of summer, which covered the base of Big Round Top like an emerald shroud. And even the green moss-covered rocks of the stone wall helped to camouflage the defenders. Consequently, the Alabama attackers had difficulty catching sight of the marksmen, and these unseen Yankees shot down Alabamians with methodical efficiency in the lower end of the "Valley of Death."

Leading his cheering soldiers onward with a waving saber and encouraging words, Lieutenant Colonel Feagin was soon hit by this blistering fire of Berdan's sharpshooters. Marksmen who had already earned legendary reputations for shooting down Rebel colorbearers and officers, both on foot or horseback, continued to do the same this afternoon. With the struggle for possession of Little Round Top imminent, Lieutenant Colonel Feagin's fall was a severe blow to the entire regiment. Lamenting the tragic loss at a most inopportune time, Colonel Oates described the fall of his dependable "right arm" before the blazing stone wall. Oates penned how "soon after the advance began the gallant Lieut.-Col. Isaac B. Feagin was shot through the knee, which [later] necessitated amputation of the limb. . ." Feagin was down and in severe pain, but he was not out for the war's duration.

Lieutenant Colonel Feagin would have his right leg amputated at the thigh not once but twice, first at a Gettysburg field hospital and then later in a Northern prison. However, the tough young man from the small town of Midway would survive the nightmarish ordeal of dual amputations. Eager to rejoin the struggle, Colonel Feagin would be exchanged in early 1864. Despite the loss of his leg and fated to hobble on crutches for the rest of his life, he would join the Invalid Corps, after a disability discharge in December 1864.

In addition to the loss of Feagin, Colonel Oates was also handicapped because the third highest ranking officer of the 15th Alabama, who had considerable combat experience, was also unavailable to him this afternoon. Colonel Oates lamented how "the major was voluntarily with the wagon-train . . . consequently I had no field officer to assist men" for this stiffest challenge to date.

Colonel Berdan's marksmen put up a tough fight and a determined resistance at their stone wall. But the Alabama Rebels relentlessly surged up the gradual slope of the western base of Big Round Top. While loading and firing on the run and closing in upon the enemy, the Alabama soldiers were surprised by the sight of adversaries not in the customary Yankee blue but uniforms of green.[8]

The scorching fire of the Union sharpshooters especially

caused damage among the 15th Alabama partly because the three 47th Alabama skirmish companies continued "not [to be] in the battle of July 2," complained Colonel Oates of the critical absence of manpower. According to Colonel Oates, these three skirmish companies of the 47th Alabama continued to ease "to the right of the southern front of Great Round Top, and passed around it to the right on the eastern side."

Colonel Oates explained the tactical confusion of a badly coordinated offensive effort which would prove extremely costly to Southern fortunes that day: "The attack, instead of being straight forward, as the skirmishers doubtless believed it would be, was a left half wheel, but of which the skirmishers were not informed, so they went to the right and the line of battle to the left." Consequently, these three Alabama skirmisher companies continued to ease around the south end of Big Round Top and away from Colonel Oates, encountering no Yankee troops and providing no assistance to the 15th Alabama. As events would soon prove, the loss of such invaluable manpower would come back to haunt the Confederate effort to turn Meade's left flank.

Colonel Oates blamed the confusion among the Alabama skirmishers on a breakdown of communication, unspecific orders, and the lack of "a competent field officer [instead of only two captains who were in] command of the skirmish line of the brigade . . ." The other two skirmish companies from the 48th Alabama also continued to flounder in the Bushman Woods far from the battle raging for the stone wall.[9]

Thus as fate would have it, Colonel Oates continued to fight without either adequate support or assistance on the most important afternoon of the war: a disadvantageous situation which would continue the entire day for the hard-luck 15th Alabama. But the initiative, experience, and fighting prowess of the men in the ranks rose to the fore, especially after Lieutenant Colonel Feagin's fall. One attacker in gray described how "every fellow was his own general; private soldiers gave commands as loud as the officers with nobody paying any attention to either."[10]

But the howling Alabamians poured onward to finally overpower some of the toughest defenders that they had ever encountered. Private Jordan described the moment of triumph, with the 15th Alabama's first victory at Gettysburg—a forgotten but important clash on the afternoon of July 2. The hard-fighting enlisted man stated how "with a resolute determination we cleared everything before us, scaled a stone fence, and pursued the enemy across a narrow valley and drove them into the mountain . . . . I fired deliberately and stepped behind a small tree to reload my gun, their bullets were cutting close, expecting to be shot every second loading my gun . . ."[11]

Then surging forward in one final push to victory, the Alabama soldiers drove the last elite marksmen from the stone wall. Later, General Longstreet described without understatement how "the attack was made in splendid style . . . and the Federal line was broken by the first impact. They retired, many of them, in the direction of Round Top behind bowlders and fences, which gave them shelter . . . this was an unequal battle," won by Colonel Oates, however.

With the onrushing Alabama Rebels moving onward without wasting time to celebrate their success or rest, the Yankees fell back all along the line. Pushed aside by Colonel Oates's attack, the Union marksmen were forced to retire from the stone wall in two sections. Under heavy pressure, the left wing of four companies, A, E, F, and H, retreated eastward and up Big Round Top. Meanwhile, to the north, the right wing of four companies of the 2nd United States Sharpshooters retired northward beyond the right flank of the advancing seven companies of the 47th Alabama. These right wing marksmen eventually joined their comrades in the defense of the Devil's Den area. Other greencoat sharpshooters of the withdrawing right wing would retreat northeastward to ascend Little Round Top and play a role in its upcoming defense. These marksmen would help to slow the Alabamians's advance on Colonel Oates's left during the struggle for Little Round Top. The four companies of sharpshooters continued to fire while withdrawing up Big Round Top, raining down a hail of lead on Oates's victors.

Colonel Oates's men would continue to primarily clash with

these deadly marksmen under Major Stoughton. As in the defense of the stone wall, Major Stoughton remained with the four companies during the combination flight and fight up the steep slope of Big Round Top. Despite being chased from the stone wall, Major Stoughton provided invaluable leadership during this firing withdrawal resulting in additional Alabama casualties.

Savoring his hard-earned success, Colonel Oates described how "the sharp-shooters retreated up the south front of the mountain, pursued by my command." Maintaining the momentum by avoiding the temptation to halt, rest, or regroup his troops who felt the intoxication of success, Oates's aggressive nature kept his soldiers moving with the Yankees on the run. But the fighting on Big Round Top was far from over for the Alabamians. All the while, Major Stoughton and other greenclad officers instructed their withdrawing sharpshooters to keep "firing as they retired" up the largest mountain in all of Adams County.

The victory in overrunning the stonewall at the base of Big Round Top had been costly for the hard-fighting Alabamians. Private Jordan wrote, "in the charge a great many [of the 15th Alabama men] were killed and wounded, many did not get over the stone fence, or through the valley [of Plum Run] to the base of the next ridge." These were the forgotten casualties, the men who would not play a role at Little Round Top. The 15th Alabama's officers' corps had been shot-up by a tough adversary armed with the most murderous weaponry in the Union army. The high casualties among regimental leaders left Colonel Oates with even more command responsibility and less chance for success on July 2. Hereafter, Colonel Oates would be forced to continue to try to do his best without the benefit of his top two lieutenants, the second and third highest ranking officers of his regiment, while on his own without assistance or advice from his superiors or support troops.

But though the capture of the stone wall at the western base of Big Round Top was the forgotten first phase of the struggle for Little Round Top, as events would soon prove this hot fight played a key role in determining the winner on this day of destiny. The

fight for possession of Little Round Top cannot be fully understood or explained without first taking into account this forgotten
struggle for the stone wall. So deadly was the fire from Berdan's
crack sharpshooters that one of General Law's Alabama regiments,
the 4th Alabama to Colonel Oates's left, nearly broke under the
punishing fire. In contrast, the 15th Alabama never came close to
breaking under the storm of lead even though attacking a more
formidable defensive position than encountered by the 4th
Alabama.

As if an ominous sign of events to come atop Little Round Top,
one of these sharpshooter companies which had made such a stiff
fight was from Maine. The Alabamians had received their first
hard-earned and bloody lesson on the fighting caliber of Maine
soldiers. Throughout this afternoon, Colonel Oates's Rebels would
continue to learn that Maine Yankees were as tough as any of the
best soldiers in Longstreet's corps.

Now after a victory cheer that echoed over the two Round
Tops, the Alabama soldiers continued onward through the trees
and underbrush of the western and southwestern base of Big
Round Top. Breathless and sweaty the Alabama soldiers stopped
briefly, then some men rested their rifles on rocks and trees to
return fire. Exacting a measure of revenge, Colonel Oates's veterans now relished the opportunity to shoot those hated marksmen
who had cut down so many friends and relatives.

Union Sergeant White described the effectiveness of the
Alabamians's fire, which raked the retreating sharpshooters who
fell back across a rough terrain which was "mostly wooded and
large boulders and granite were thickly set in so they gave us a
splendid cover from which to oppose the enemy's advance. But
with all our advantage, our loss was considerable for the enemy
kept up a terrible fire and we fell back no faster than we were
obliged to, so when we skipped from one boulder to another the
rebels had very good opportunities to get in their murderous
work." By this time, the Alabama Rebels were highly proficient at
"their murderous work."[12]

CHAPTER IX

Conquering Big Round Top

*"[Big] Round Top is 116 feet higher than Little Round Top . . .
and only about 1,000 yards distant from the latter, which is almost in
a direct line from the summit of Round Top with Cemetery Ridge,
which was occupied by the Federal line of battle; so that it is manifest
that if General Longstreet had crowned Round Top with his artillery
any time that afternoon [then] he would have won the battle."*

—Colonel William C. Oates

The fast-moving 15th Alabama soldiers continued to surge up
the slope of Big Round Top. After the victory at the stone wall, the
onrushing Alabamians felt confident that the day could be won
with more hard fighting whenever and wherever they met additional Yankees, including Colonel Berdan's Sharpshooters. Then
the glorious name of Gettysburg would join the list of victories like
Second Bull Run and Chancellorsville, becoming yet another
sparkling success for General Lee and the hard-hitting Army of
Northern Virginia. By this time Colonel Oates's soldiers felt that
not only the army's combat capabilities but also the struggle's
righteousness ensured decisive victory at Gettysburg.[1]

But while swinging forward with flags snapping in the muggy, hot air of summer and ever-closer to the imposing heights, some Alabama boys felt an eerie sense of foreboding upon obtaining a close look at Big Round Top. Now swarming with Major Stoughton's retreating sharpshooters, this large and heavily forest-ed hill stood like a mountain before the onrushing Alabamians. Both of the Round Top elevations possessed a strange look to the average soldier from the Coastal Plain of southeast Alabama, rising above the gently rolling terrain around Gettysburg, commanding and dominating the entire area for miles around.

After the savage fighting of the first day when he lost the town, General Meade had aligned his corps in good defensive positions, mostly south and east of Gettysburg, along Cemetery Ridge. Cemetery Ridge gradually decreased in elevation as it ran south-ward until reaching the low point of snarled woodlands and marshy land before, or north of, the two Round Tops. Then these twin hills suddenly rose up just below the sprawling length of Cemetery Ridge.

Because of their height and the jumbles of large boulders and the green shroud of thick forest covering Big and Little Round Top, they seemed so unsuitable for either infantry or hauling up artillery that such a precaution had been largely overlooked by Union leadership. Indeed, General Meade and his top lieutenants did "not think that the occupancy or defense of Little Round Top was then thought of, for it appeared almost inaccessible."

Imposing Big Round Top, rising 350 feet from its base, was to the Alabama soldiers from the Chattahoochee Valley of southeast Alabama a most formidable mountain. And it looked even more ominous and commanding from the low valley of Plum Run, tow-ering up to dominate the eastern horizon like a forested citadel.

A conical hill and rocky spur of Big Round Top just to the northeast, Little Round Top rose about 170 feet from its base. It was distinguished by its bare western side, which was devoid of both timber and underbrush. In contrast, the southern and eastern sides of Little Round Top were heavily wooded and rocky. Little Round Top also had a rocky and timbered spur at its southern end, which would become known as Vincent's Spur. Both of these rocky hill-tops below Gettysburg were evidently the weathered remains of ancient volcanos. The gently weather-worn and rounded cones of the round tops betrayed this turbulent, fiery past millions of years before, which both armies seemingly were determined to resurrect this day.

With its barren and boulder-strewn crest, Little Round Top stood just slightly northeast of Big Round Top. The larger of the two mountains was known to the local German farmers as Sugar Loaf, Round Top Mountain, Wolf Hill, and Stony Point. Big Round Top was more densely timbered, rocky, and boulder-strewn than Little Round Top, providing a far greater obstacle to the advancing Alabama Rebels. In addition, Big Round Top was also steeper than the smaller elevation. In fact, Big Round Top was so steep as to even impede the passage of white-tailed deer from a direct ascent uphill at its steepest grade to the peaked crest of solid granite.

However, Little Round Top was the most unique elevation in terms of a more distinctive geography. Without exaggeration, one Federal described how "it is impossible to conceive a scene of greater wilderness and desolation than is presented by [Little Round Top's] bare and mottled figure, up-piled with granite ledges and masses of rock and strewn with mighty boulders . . ." The past fall, the hardworking Weikert brothers, who lived imme-diately east of the Round Tops, had cleared off Little Round Top's western face in the cool of autumn for winter firewood and to make a small profit from timber sales. They had hauled the tim-ber—oak and hickory—along a narrow dirt road which ran down the eastern face of the mountain.

However, neither Generals Lee nor Meade knew of the pres-ence of this narrow, dirt road which cut through the woods to reach the crest of Little Round Top. In Jeb Stuart's absence, General Lee continued to be hampered with the lack of intelligence-gather-ing cavalry on his right: a fact which would continue to work all day to Colonel Oates's disadvantage.

To the 15th Alabama's left, meanwhile, an amazed Colonel Perry, the 44th Alabama's commander who now led the Alabama

Brigade after General Law took divisional command with Hood's wounding, described the most eerie landscape that he had ever seen in his life: "Large rocks, from six to fifteen feet high, are thrown together in confusion over a considerable area, and yet so disposed as to leave everywhere among them winding passages carpeted with moss. Many of its recesses are never visited by the sunshine, and a cavernous coolness pervades the air within it. A short distance to the east the frowning bastions of Little Round Top rise two hundred feet above the level of the plain. An abrupt elevation, thirty or forty feet high, itself buttressed with rocks, constitutes the western boundary of this strange formation."

One 5th Texas soldier of General Robertson's brigade to Colonel Oates's left, wrote how along the western slopes of Little Round Top "the ground [was] covered with large boulders from the size of a wash pot to that of a wagon bed . . ." And another Texan described " . . . boulders from the size of a hogshead to the size of a small house" covered the slopes of Big and Little Round Top. Dotting the valley of Plum Run and the slopes of the Round Top, these thickly clustered clumps of granite rocks and boulders presented an ominous appearance to the attackers, promising to break-up advancing ranks.

The jumbled maze of large rocks and boulders rose eerily from the patches of grass amid the surreal landscape both on the eastern half of Plum Run's valley and across the slopes of Little Round Top, giving this area a mysterious and eerie appearance. But most forboding of all, the terrain leading up to Little Round Top had the ominous look of a cemetery, with the rocks and boulders resembling tombstones. Without exaggeration, one Yankee described in a letter how " . . . the field was covered with jagged rocks and huge broken stones of every conceivable shape,—the ugliest looking place for a battle, or anything else that one could easily select."

Another Texan of Hood's crack division, who was accustomed to the sight of the sprawling cotton plantations along the river bottoms of the Trans-Mississippi, described one boulder "as big as a 500-pound cotton bale." One Alabama Rebel, a veteran who did not like the looks of what he saw, understood after a close view at

Little Round Top how "a long line of large boulders cropping out of the mountainside [were in fact] forming a natural breastwork."[2]

Colonel Oates later described the importance of both the position and the situation in this sector on the far right of General Lee's surging battle line. He wrote how "[Big] Round Top is 116 feet higher than Little Round Top—the latter being 548 feet and the former 664 feet high—and only about 1,000 yards distant from the latter, which is almost in a direct line from the summit of Round Top with Cemetery Ridge, which was occupied by the Federal line of battle; so that it is manifest that if General Longstreet had crowned Round Top with his artillery any time that afternoon [then] he would have won the battle."

Confederate artillery emplaced on either Round Top could have enfiladed Meade's lines to the north, inflicting considerable damage from the commanding heights. Despite being much smaller than its forested twin to the south, Little Round Top commanded and overlooked a wide area, offering a breathtaking panoramic view of the sprawling countryside for many miles around and in every direction. The length of Seminary Ridge and the valley of Plum Run could be seen to the west, and the gold-hued Wheatfield to the northwest, and the quaint town of Gettysburg in the distance to the north. Even the distant clump of trees—the target of "Pickett's Charge" on the next day—could be seen from the commanding summits. But most important of all, the lengthy expanse of Cemetery Ridge upon which the Army of the Potomac was aligned was in clear view to the north from the crest of Little Round Top.[3]

Meanwhile, with the Union left flank vulnerable, Colonel Oates was eager to gain the advantage. The mere thought of such a golden opportunity was a dream-come-true to these hard-fighting Alabamians so far from home. Other than the retreating sharpshooters who steadily retired up Big Round Top, there were "no other troops [now] on that mountain at that time." With his fighting blood up and knowing the importance of his mission, Colonel Oates was determined to continue driving the Yankees. Like a good commander who understood the wisdom of exploiting the hard-won tactical advantage and not wasting time, he refused to call a halt for his men to rest despite their exhaustion.

But Colonel Oates continued to advance in a direction not specified by General Law's orders. Driving the Yankees up Big Round Top meant ignoring General Law's directive to hug the western base of Big Round Top, before easing into the low ground between the Round Tops to strike Little Round Top from the south. However, the rapidly changing battlefield situation made General Law's orders obsolete to Colonel Oates's way of thinking. Now leading an independent command far from headquarters or support, Colonel Oates made his tactical adjustments on his own out of necessity with no high ranking officers available to indicate otherwise.

As proven repeatedly in past combat situations, Colonel Oates was a gifted commander largely because he was not only aggressive and flexible but also ambitious. And now these were necessary characteristics for success on the right end of Lee's line. Colonel Oates, therefore, continued to lead his troops up the western and southwestern slope of Big Round Top to take advantage of the Union left's vulnerability. In less than an hour, the Alabamians's advance had already covered around seven hundred yards before reaching the base of Big Round Top. Colonel Oates knew that victory would now only come if he made the correct tactical decisions at this point in time. He also realized that success could only be won if his Alabamians maintained iron discipline, and fought harder than they had ever fought before. But most of all, he knew that everything now depended upon his taking possession of the two rocky hilltops in Adams County.

Ironically, Colonel Oates officially only retained a major's rank while undertaking what was now the most important assignment in the Army of Northern Virginia on July 2. But without the lieutenant colonel and major of the 15th Alabama by his side, Oates continued to be on his own while developing his tactics on the far right of Lee's battle line. Handicapped by the ever-changing battlefield situation, the breakdown of the effectiveness of Confederate leadership, and the poorly coordinated and ill-timed attacks

of Longstreet's corps, it was now the role of this young junior officer from Alabama to turn the left flank of the Army of the Potomac
largely on his own.

As never before, Colonel Oates understood that his hard-fighting 15th Alabama now possessed a chance to play a leading role in
determining the outcome of the most decisive battle to date. Ever
the optimist, Oates later explained his personal philosophy in
regard to the challenge at Gettyburg: "I am not a fatalist, nor a
believer in destiny, and hence cannot say of Gettysburg as Victor
Hugo did of Waterloo, 'that God passed over the battle field.' I
believe in responsibility for human conduct, and although the
Federals greatly outnumbered the Confederates, yet the disparity
was not so great as on many other fields where the latter had been
completely victorious. The army under Lee was never much
stronger numerically, nor its condition better than at Gettysburg.
The rank and file were never more confident of success."[4]

Bolstering his confidence for success, Colonel Oates described
how he "had the strongest and finest regiment in Hood's division." However, Colonel Oates could only now count around 450
men as a result of hard marching and summer campaigning, but
he yet felt confident that he could turn General Meade's left flank
with this cadre of hardened veterans.

But continuing the sabotage of the chances for Confederate
success at the south end of Lee's line, the Alabama regiments of
General Law's hard-hitting brigade remained divided and widely
separated. While the 15th Alabama and the 47th Alabama ascend-
ed Big Round Top in pursuit of Berdan's Sharpshooters, General
Law's three other Alabama regiments surged northeastward
toward the western and southwestern side of Little Round Top.
This crucial division of strength on Lee's far right flank sapped the
Alabamians's striking power.[5]

Facing his greatest challenge to date and having now been
thrust with more responsibility than ever before in his young life,
Colonel Oates continued to encourage his soldiers forward while
they surged up the western and southwestern slope of Big Round
Top. On the way up, the highest ground in Adams County became

gradually more steep and rocky. As the Alabama men moved upward while loading and firing at the retreating sharpshooters, the steep slope of the southwestern and western face of Big Round Top was covered with larger rocks and boulders. And gradually more extensive clusters of boulders were encountered by the Alabamians farther up the hillside. While toiling ever higher up the steep slope, Colonel Oates's soldiers breathed and sweated more heavily, gasping for air in the steaming heat of the early July afternoon.

All the while, the elite marksmen of Major Stoughton's left wing retreated up the western and southwestern base of Big Round Top while blasting away at their Alabama pursuers. At this time, Colonel Oates attempted to maintain alignment as best he could but the rough terrain made the task impossible. With the Alabamians encountering larger rocks, more clusters of fallen and heavy timber, and thick underbrush higher up the steep slope, the assault formation broke down. Separate groups of Alabama Rebels now struggled uphill as best they could.

Natural firing positions behind fallen timber and boulders offered ideal places from which the green-coated sharpshooters could shoot down on the advancing Alabamians. More so than Colonel Oates's men, these Yankee marksmen blended in perfectly with the forested surroundings, benefiting from the natural camouflage of the hillside during the close-range, uphill skirmish.

While catching their breath in the suffocating heat, Colonel Berdan's Sharpshooters laid their Sharps rifles on the moss-laced fallen logs and rocks to unleash shots which could not miss at such close range. The Alabamians learned the hard way that these "Green Coats" were expert marksmen who could fight and inflict punishment from a stationary position behind a stone wall or while on the move, as they shot rapidly with their breechloaders, firing from the hip or unleashing quick snap shots.

Battling these stubborn sharpshooters, who never seemed to miss a shot, while ascending the rough terrain of Big Round Top under a scorching fire was certainly "one of the most onerous labors of the war." And the Alabama soldiers were now also combating their own body-numbing fatigue and unquenchable thirst, as the scorching sun of the blistering day continued to shine brightly on Big Round Top.

After having remained behind the advancing ranks to blast away at the angry swarm of sharpshooters, Private Jordan described the fighting on the 15th Alabama's left: "As soon as I had loaded, [I] looked ahead of me to the front, across the valley, I saw that some of my company [B, 15th Alabama] had got across the valley to the base of the mountain or ridge, behind large rocks, I suppose it was about 150 or 200 yards across the valley, where a part of my company had advanced. I was in a very exposed position at that time, I did not hesitate, but was determined to go to them as speedily as possible, as I was determined to go as far as any of my command, if possible."[6]

All the while the piercing Rebel Yell continued to echo across the imposing mountain. The distinctive war-cry of the 15th Alabama "was always accepted as a signal of victory and tended to restore confidence." Amid the whizzing bullets of the blazing Sharps rifles as the green-uniformed sharpshooters hopped from rock to rock and tree to tree during their ascent up through the steamy woods, the 15th Alabama veterans continued their surge up the southwestern and western slope, returning fire when ascertaining a target amid the thick forest. Victory for Colonel Oates's soldiers on Lee's far right now depended upon advancing as rapidly as possible and wasting no more time. Indeed, too much precious time had already slipped away, steadily eroding Confederate chances for success at Gettysburg on July 2. Colonel Berdan's Sharpshooters continued to do their part in slowing the Alabamians's advance when time was of the essence. Sweat ran down the Alabamians's faces as they continued forward. But with each passing minute Colonel Oates's soldiers were increasingly separated and isolated from the bulk of General Hood's troops, including the remainder of General Law's Alabamians, who were either assaulting the Devil's Den or approaching the western edge of Little Round Top to the northwest.

Oates felt a measure of added reassurance though because of

the presence of his younger brother, Lieutenant John Alva Oates, who was now beside him. Despite his lingering sickness which had grown worse, Lieutenant Oates continued to lead the "Henry Pioneers" of Company G, the crack Henry County unit. Two years younger than his colonel-brother, Johnny Oates was the colonel's favorite sibling. They had grown up together, fought schoolyard bullies, allied against their disciplinarian father, and were insepa- rable for most of their lives. Johnny was William's "best friend, his closest confidant, and his ally in all of his adventures . . ." And for years they had fought together in some of the bloodiest battles of the war. William and John were much more than simply brothers linked by ties of blood. They were more like soul mates who need- ed each other whenever the going got especially tough. As Colonel Oates explained the close bond which could never be broken in life, "we were not only brothers, near the same age, but had been reared together, and no brothers loved each other better."[7]

This tie between the Oates brothers had been forged in both good and bad times. During Oates's free-spirited wanderings and wild adventures as a rambunctious youth, John had traveled from southeast Alabama to Texas in a long odds attempt to find his trou- blesome older brother. Dispatched by his loving mother, the younger Oates's mission had been to try to convince William to return to southeast Alabama. Just west of the Louisiana border, the two brothers had finally met by chance at Henderson, Texas, when ironically Oates was headed back east. There, they had had a joy- ous reunion and his brother then joined him on the road for awhile, encountering more adventures on the unruly Southwest frontier before returning to Alabama.

But as strange destiny would have it, the Oates brothers were now far from home in south-central Pennsylvania wearing the uni- forms of a new nation born in violent revolution. And the brothers' close bond would only be broken by a Yankee bullet. Lieutenant Oates, a young, handsome bachelor and successful Abbeville lawyer like his older brother, would not live to see his twenty- eighth birthday. Like so many 15th Alabama soldiers, "Johnny" Oates was destined to die during the raging storm of Gettysburg.[8]

In hurling the obstinate 2nd United States Sharpshooters from behind the stone wall and chasing the four companies up the heavily wooded slope of Big Round Top, many good Alabama soldiers in gray were cut down to rise no more. Cheering the boys of Company G onward, Lieutenant Oates now helped to fill in the gap for men dropped by the torrent of Sharps .52 caliber bullets. In bad shape and ill, John Oates had been one of the last regimental members to reach the field of Gettysburg. Ironically, Lieutenant Oates was now scaling Big Round Top on this sweltering afternoon primarily because of his brother's earlier assistance. Refusing to abandon John in enemy country, Colonel Oates had sent one of his horses back to retrieve his younger brother, who had fallen out of column and straggled far behind the fast-marching Alabama soldiers.[9]

The mere thought of dying in a Northern prison had been a strong motivation to keep Johnny Oates trying his best to reach his command at Gettysburg. But in fact, he had been so ill that he had to lay down behind the 15th Alabama ranks near the Emmitsburg Road before the attack. Colonel Oates never forgot how when he had first stepped behind the Alabamians's line and "found him lying on the ground in rear of his company, with a high fever. I told him that when the line moved forward he was not to go, but to remain where he was. He raised up, and his black eyes flashing fire he replied, 'No, brother, were I to do that it would be said that I avoided the battle and acted the coward. No, sir; I will go in with my company though I know it may cost me my life!' These were the last words ever passed between us."

As proven on the gory battlefields from Virginia to Maryland, Lieutenant Oates was a fine officer, who was "very bright and popular with all who knew him." But by the time of Gettysburg, Johnny Oates had been sick for some time. But Lieutenant Oates refused to request a medical discharge; despite the cost, he would not forsake his friends and neighbors in Company G, and, most of all, his older brother.

Thus on one of the hottest days of the year and after one of the longest marches in regimental history, Lieutenant Oates was eager to continue fighting beside his Company G boys despite his sickly condition and weakness. With Colonel Oates commanding the regiment during a major battle for the first time, John was determined to provide as much support as possible. Ironically, Colonel Oates's special relationship and close bond with his younger brother was much like that of Colonel Chamberlain for his younger brother, Lieutenant Thomas Davee Chamberlain. Like John and William Oates, Joshua and Tom Chamberlain would also stand beside each other at Little Round Top on this day of destiny. In an odd twist, both the younger Oates and the younger Chamberlain would lead their respective Company Gs in their older brothers' infantry regiments.[10]

As the losses among the officer corps reduced the combat capabilities of the 15th Alabama, a number of natural leaders in the enlisted ranks took their places, filling in during the crisis without being told or ordered. Colonel Oates's ceaseless efforts in the past to instill discipline within his command were now paying dividends.[11]

In continuing to lead his men up the wooded slopes of Big Round Top, Colonel Oates was again defying orders. He defended his decision as a response to the changed tactical situation in his August 8, 1863, battle report, stating that he had received orders from General Law that he could not obey:

> "[I received the] order from Brigadier-General Law to left-wheel [or pivot] my regiment and move in the direction of the heights [Little Round Top] upon my left, which order I failed to obey, for the reason that when I received it I was rapidly advancing up the mountain [Big Round Top], and in my front I discovered a large force of the enemy. Besides this, there was great difficulty in accomplishing the maneuver at that movement, as the regiment on my left (Forty-seventh Alabama) was crowding me on the left, and running into my regiment, which had already creating considerable confusion [and] in the event that I had obeyed the order, I should have come in contact with the regiment on

my left, and also have exposed my right flank to an enfilading fire from enemy. I therefore continued to press forward, [or eastward to scale Big Round Top.]"

Once again, Colonel William Calvin Oates had been his own
man. He continued to do his own thinking, while making the best
decisions according to his assessments of an ever-changing tactical
situation in his immediate front. After so much effort had been
expended by his exhausted men in getting uphill and after high
losses, Colonel Oates understood the improbability of moving his
troops back down the mountain and through the dense woods and
jumbles of boulders to obey General Law's orders to swing northward instead of eastward. To Colonel Oates by this time, the most
sensible way down the mountain would be to move north instead
of west, after gaining the summit of Big Round Top.

On this decisive second day of battle, while General Longstreet
defied General Lee and General Law defied General Longstreet, so
Colonel Oates defied General Law. Such a leadership breakdown
during offensive operations would have resulted in disaster in
most battles. But on July 2, ironically, the defiance of orders on
General Lee's right was now vital to Confederate success. Indeed,
such leadership initiative, unorthodox decision-making, and tactical flexibility among a single team of lower echelon commanders—Law and Oates—would almost be enough to turn the battle
in the Confederacy's favor. Colonel Oates now had within his
grasp what the most ambitious West Point-trained Confederate
leaders could only dream of achieving: a golden opportunity to
capture the unoccupied Round Tops, the key to the battlefield, and
turn the left flank of the Army of the Potomac.[12]

So the advance continued up the imposing heights of Big
Round Top, with Oates attempting to maintain alignment as best
he could. Hard-hit 15th Alabama companies like Company G continued to function well, serving as a solid anchor on the regiment's right-center. This Henry County company was perhaps the
best in the entire regiment, thanks to the Oates brothers. One
Company G Rebel of the "Henry Pioneers," for instance,

described in a letter how "we have the praise of the finest company in this Regiment."

The able common soldiers in the 15th Alabama's ranks continued to compensate for fallen officers, picking up the slack by assuming leadership roles. Among those dependable soldiers taking the place of dead and wounded officers like Lieutenant Colonel Feagin were the Kirkland boys of Dale County. The Kirkland clan of the hard-fighting "Henry Pioneers" had already lost Calvin J. Kirkland, a twenty-two-year-old violin player who had often raised spirits with his lively tunes. He had been hit by a fatal bullet at Second Manassas. When brothers Aaron S. Kirkland, age thirty-five, and Cicero Kirkland now fell wounded at Gettysburg, the other fighting Kirklands quickly filled the void. Cicero had won recognition for gallantry at Second Manassas, standing tall before the Federal onslaughts.

Now even drummer boy Allen A. Kirkland, a dry-humored, mischievous teenager and one of Colonel Oates's best-liked soldiers who loved to unmercifully tease his comrades, slung his drum over his shoulder during the hard climb up Big Round Top to pick up a musket to fight the pesky sharpshooters during the uphill struggle. Never known to lose his temper or good humor during the war, the young man nicknamed "Old Betsy" had only served as a drummer boy since June 1863. Meanwhile, in the advancing ranks of Company G, Rance Kirkland, diminutive Pulaski or "Pulasky" or "Pugh" Kirkland, age sixteen, and Allen Kirkland continued battling the Yankee sharpshooters, as if to avenge their fallen relatives.[13]

On the regiment's right, meanwhile, Colonel Oates was yet developing his offensive tactics on the move, while encouraging his men forward. Relentlessly and with solitary determination to gain the Union army's left flank, Colonel Oates led his soldiers onward up Big Round Top through the sickening heat. In front of his men as usual, Colonel Oates advanced up the high ground with only one objective in mind: to move forward "until I found the left of the Union line, to turn it and do all the damage I could . . ." But the torturous climb up the steep and rock-strewn slope of Big Round Top was increasingly difficult for the already worn soldiers. Indeed, Colonel Oates's veterans had already had an exhausting day before even starting the climb. They had marched and advanced more than twenty-five miles since the early morning hours; fought crack Yankee marksmen behind a stone wall; drove the best sharpshooters in the Union army from a strong defensive position on high ground; and now fought most of the way up the highest mountain that most of these southeast Alabama soldiers had ever seen, all on one of the hottest days of the year. By any measure, this was an impressive list of accomplishments long before the Alabamians ever came close to reaching Little Round Top.

But amid the suffocating heat and dense underbrush, the 15th Alabama men continued to clamor over the maze of rocks, boulders, and fallen timber as best they could, while scrambling up Big Round Top with the determination to gain the flank and rear of Meade's army before it was too late. Only discipline and high motivation kept these hardened veterans toiling up the mountain, while ignoring hunger, mind-numbing fatigue, and a thirst which choked parched throats like a dry stranglehold. For these 15th Alabama Rebels, this was a case of do or die. The hard-fighting teenager, Corporal McClendon stated that he and his 15th Alabama comrades were "full of malice and hatred for the 'Boys in Blue' [and were] anxious to kill him . . ." Motivated to redeem and justify the loss of so many relatives, friends, and neighbors on the battlefields and in the filthy hospitals across Virginia and Maryland, this all-consuming anger served as a great motivating factor for the Alabamians.[14]

Colonel Oates described the close-range fighting which raged across the steep and timbered slopes during the hot pursuit that was a running fight: "The places the men had to climb up, catching to the rocks and bushes and crawling over the boulders in the face of the fire of the enemy, who kept retreating, taking shelter and firing down on us from behind the rocks and crags which covered the side of the mountain thicker than grave-stones in a city cemetery . . . we could see our foe only as they dodged back from one boulder to another, hence our fire was scattering" but effective.

Along the steep western and southwestern slope of Big Round Top, the fighting swirled through the jumbles of rocks and trees. Now the Alabama boys proved their skill in fighting frontier-style amid the dense forests. The Alabamians fired from behind trees and boulders at the devilish "Green Coats," inflicting damage amid the hot woodlands. Blasting away and loading on the move, the 15th Alabama attackers continued to unleash their high-pitched war cries. However, these yells which had unnerved Yankees on other battlefields now only pinpointed the Alabamians as targets for the stealthy snipers of the 2nd United States Sharpshooters. With the Alabamians gaining ground about halfway up Big Round Top, Major Stoughton divided his command into two squads, with one squad retiring to the mountain's east side, while the other squad withdrew westward and around the left of the 47th Alabama.

One fine officer now rising to the fore like Lieutenant Oates to help compensate for Lieutenant Colonel Feagin's loss was nineteen-year-old Lieutenant Barnett Hardeman Cody of Abbeville. He was the son of Georgia-born Reverend Edmund Cody, a highly-respected Baptist preacher of Henry County. In the war's early days, this fiery man of God had almost gone to the front with his boys to fight the Yankees. Lieutenant Cody had enlisted in Captain Oates's "Henry Pioneers" of Company G at age sixteen, forsaking a quality education in a fine school at Cuthbert, Alabama. Even younger at fifteen, Barnett's brother, William Henderson Cody, also enlisted in Confederate service. He was fated to die at Cedar Creek, Virginia, in October 1864. The Cody boys hailed from a wealthy family and a large Henry County plantation of sixteen hundred acres with a good many slaves, halfway between Abbeville and the Chattahoochee River. Thriving from the cash crop of cotton, the Cody plantation was known far and wide as "Pleasant Ridge." On that fateful July 2, 1863, a first cousin of the Cody boys was leading the Sixth Alabama Infantry as a colonel in General Ewell's Second Corps.[15]

Serving with distinction in the ranks as a teenage private and then sergeant at a mere ninety-five pounds, Barnett Hardeman

Cody had been promoted to an officer's rank for gallantry at Antietam. Such actions ensured Cody's rise to the rank of junior second lieutenant. In fact, Lieutenant Cody would have been promoted earlier except for his young age. In the words of the pious Lieutenant Cody, "[Colonel Oates] told me that he was afraid to put me higher, for fear that my age could not keep me there." Most of all, Lieutenant Cody was a fighter, and that fact mattered most of all to Colonel Oates.

Despite suffering from illness and in need of hospitalization as recently ordered by the regimental surgeon who was ignored, the young Henry County officer had written in a letter "but I am determined to fight if we can get to face the foe." Dr. A. E. McGarity, Cody's brother-in-law, scribbled without exaggeration in a letter that "a nobler boy or one more universally admired [and] to know him was to love him." And in another letter, Surgeon McGarity described how Lieutenant Cody "was universally admired by all who knew him, both for his manly and noble bearing and his gallantry." Lieutenant Cody had written in an early letter to his father: " . . . we all moved off from 'Old Henry' perhaps many of us may never return again, but hope and trust that the 'God' whom I always trusted in will safely land us safe back home again"—a hope never to come true for Lieutenant Cody and many other 15th Alabama soldiers from the Wiregrass country.[16]

After Lieutenant Cody was fatally cut down at Gettysburg, Lieutenant Thomas M. Renfroe wrote a sad letter to the teenager's father to inform him that he was sending a "few things that belonged to your Son." This included "a fishing line with which I have tied up his bundle [as] it was the last sport he was engaged in before the fatal fight" at Gettysburg. But more than anything else, the pious Lieutenant Cody was close to his God. As he penned in one letter that he "will never throw away the Bible which our Dear Mother gave me [for] I shall keep that as long as I live, and when I die I want it Buried with me." As a cruel fate would have it, this was Lieutenant Cody's last wish before meeting his Maker at Gettysburg. But it is not known if this well-worn

Bible was buried with Lieutenant Cody in his shallow grave in Adams County, Pennsylvania.[17]

Meanwhile, the long climb for the 15th Alabama up Big Round Top was becoming even more difficult. In the sweltering heat of July 2, the weight of canteens, knapsacks, haversacks, and .577 Enfield rifles slung across the Alabamians's shoulders seemed to increase each minute these soldiers toiled uphill. These accoutrements helped to make the torturous climb up the steep slope of Big Round Top in the blazing heat the most arduous physical feat of their lives.

Entirely barefoot or wearing worn-out brogans of thin leather, Colonel Oates's men lost their footing many times during the steep ascent, slipping on the moss-covered rocks and tripping over fallen logs and limbs, while loading and firing on the move. Piles of small granite stones likewise gave way, causing soldiers to slip and lose their balance. All the while, the Alabamians kept their eyes open for hidden Federals in green uniforms, and blasted away at the retiring Yankees whenever the opportunity arose. The heat and thirst were unbearable, sapping the Alabamians's energy and strength. Colonel Oates lamented the many tactical disadvantages that he faced because "my men could not see their foe, and did not fire, except as one was seen here and there, running back from one boulder to another." And he described yet another dilemma that sabotaged future success as "my men fainted from heat, exhaustion, and thirst."

Slowly but surely throughout July 2, the fighting capabilities and already weakened strength of the 15th Alabama continued to be steadily drained and sapped long before reaching Little Round Top and meeting the 20th Maine. Colonel Oates described how "my men in the ranks, in the intense heat, suffered greatly for water. The loss of those twenty-two men and lack of water contributed largely to our failure to take Little Round Top a few minutes later." Lamenting this lost opportunity at Gettysburg long after the war, Oates would continue to curse this hot day in south-central Pennsylvania that he would never forget. Consequently, for many years after the war, he would sullenly call Big Round Top "that awful hill."[18]

Despite fighting under a host of disadvantages, the Alabamians pushed a concentrated group of Federals up Big Round Top to the right, across the southern slope. As the tough sharpshooters in green were hurled eastward, their hot fire continued to rake the 15th Alabama's right flank and cause damage. Faced with yet another crisis in a fast-paced battlefield situation, Colonel Oates immediately responded to the blistering enfilade fire. He quickly made effective tactical adjustments to meet the threat on his vulnerable right flank now hanging in midair. Again demonstrating tactical flexibility in a battlefield situation, Colonel Oates hastily "deployed Company A, and moved it by the left flank to protect my right . . ."

Dashing off through the dense woodlands and fading from sight into the depths of the thick forest covering Big Round Top like a green blanket, Company A's soldiers from Russell County under Captain Francis K. Shaaff hustled southeastward on the double. Captain Shaaff was a good officer, who was remembered for shooting a Union major off his horse during the attack on the railroad cut at Second Manassas.

These fast-moving Rebels of Company A surged through the steaming woodlands, charging up and across the southeastern face of Big Round Top. Loading and firing on the move, the Russell County soldiers clamored through the underbrush in a running fight that grew in intensity. In chasing these pesky sharpshooters beyond the regiment's front, the soldiers of the "Cantry Rifles," or Company A, provided timely protection and assistance to Oates's vulnerable right flank.[19]

Now with his right flank safe from the enfilade fire of the sharpshooters, Colonel Oates continued to lead his soldiers higher up the steep face of Big Round Top. The timbered and rocky western and southwestern slope seemed to stretch upward forever to the exhausted and water-starved Alabama soldiers. Sucking in hot air like bellows and breathless in the suffocating heat, the worn Rebels, drenched in sweat and dirt, clutched at the mossy rocks, tree limbs, and clumps of bushes to scale the formidable heights.

To the 15th Alabama's left and despite the difficulty in doing so, meanwhile, the seven 47th Alabama companies continued to maintain alignment both within the regiment and with Colonel Oates's left flank. Surging up the northwestern slope of Big Round Top, Colonel Bulger's Alabamians had the relative advantage of encountering less steep terrain in following the slope's more gradual contours in contrast to the 15th Alabama, which pushed straight up the steepest and most rocky slope of Big Round Top.

Before the Alabamians reached the final third of the hard climb to reach the mountaintop, the slope leveled off for a short distance along the western slope at the foot of the almost vertical rise of the rocky summit. Upon gaining this small perch of level ground, the exhausted Alabama boys found that this less steep ground allowed tired muscles a brief respite. But then began the roughest climb of the day for Colonel Oates's Rebels, as his men pulled themselves up the steepest slope they had ever encountered. But out-of-breath and panting in the steamy heat of summer, the 15th Alabama Rebels finally reached the top of the imposing summit of Big Round Top. Attempting to catch their breath for the first time since the advance's beginning, Colonel Oates at long last called a halt. Many Alabama Rebels, drenched in sweat and without water, were yet struggling up the mountainous slope while others were either panting heavily or passed out. It would take time for every man to reach the summit, and Colonel Oates knew that he had to wait for them.

The Alabamians had advanced, fought, and climbed, most of the time under fire. Consequently, there were now much fewer Alabama boys in the ranks, for many fell to the fire of Colonel Berdan's Sharpshooters and the artillery shelling and the combined affects of the intense heat, sore feet, and worn-out bodies. Even worse for the outcome of Colonel Oates's vital mission, around seventy-five 15th Alabama Rebels, who had been dispatched from the regiment on independent assignments, had yet to rejoin the command.

Colonel Oates described the gaining of the summit after they "pressed forward untill [sic] I reached the top and the highest point on top of Round Top. Just before reaching this point, the Federals in my front as suddenly disappeared from my sight as though commanded by a magician." Upon reaching the summit, Colonel Oates and his soldiers were relieved to find Big Round Top unoccupied. One reason why General Meade was not overly concerned with Little Round Top was that "it appeared almost inaccessible" to the Army of Northern Virginia and beyond its reach. Nevertheless, the 15th Alabama soldiers had somehow managed to get themselves up the largest mountain in the entire county, which dwarfed Little Round Top, without water in canteens and while fighting the Union's elite marksmen. Meanwhile, the 47th Alabama soldiers to Colonel Oates's left had likewise advanced with the 15th Alabama, surging up Big Round Top. By this time, Colonel Bulger's exhausted men were a short distance away below the 15th Alabama along the slope of Big Round Top to the northwest.

Colonel Oates described in his battle report the tactical advantage that he had gained at this time: " . . . my right [was now on] the top of the mountain, on the right of the line." And this was no ordinary mountain. Colonel Oates realized that Big Round Top "was higher than the other mountain [Little Round Top] and would command the entire field" of Gettyburg.

Colonel Oates was now the master of the most imposing summit at Gettysburg. From this most commanding height for scores of miles around and at last free of the forest canopy, he could now look west to judge the time of day by the sun's position above the western horizon. Heavy firing to the northwest around the Devil's Den and farther to its right indicated to Oates that the Federal left was yet before him, and that he had gained a position dominating the Union army's flank and rear.

As far as the Alabamians could see, the patches of woodlands and the sprawling fields of lush grain crops spread out before them below Big Round Top. These sun-drenched fields of July were hued in the bright colors of summer along those sections of Warfield and Seminary Ridges and Plum Run's valley not covered in woodlands. While the scattered patches of forest were dark green at alternating intervals, the expansive fields of the local Pennsylvania farmers were yellowish-tan with luxurious crops of oats and wheat, which mingled with the green fields of Indian corn in a colorful natural tapestry.

Meanwhile, on the horizon as far as the Alabamians could see loomed the distant blue-hazed ridge-line of South Mountain. This lengthy ridge-line dominating the far western horizon seemed to hang heavy in the heat, humidity, and mist-like haze of summer. To the east, the Alabama Rebels could see a broader expanse of fields and scattered patches of woodlands which stretched seemingly for endless miles toward the hazy depths of southern Pennsylvania.

And even more bluish-tinted mountains could be seen eastward in the far-away distance beyond the narrow ribbon of dirt that led from the eastern base of Big Round Top. Suddenly strategic, this was the Taneytown Road which led southward from Gettysburg. North up the Taneytown Road and about halfway to Gettysburg stood General Meade's headquarters behind Cemetery Ridge. "From the top of the mountain a Federal soldier could not be seen, except a few wounded and dead ones on the ground over which we had advanced," marveled Colonel Oates. Feeling triumphant while standing atop the imposing height of Big Round Top, Colonel Oates fully realized the tactical advantage that he had gained for the Confederacy.

Hardly believing his eyes at the extent of this tactical advantage gained by him on the Federal army's left flank, Colonel Oates had yet to discover the exact location of General Meade's left, however. Therefore, he walked over to the rocky northern edge of the summit to ascertain the situation in the direction of Little Round Top to the north. This northern edge of the Big Round Top's summit consisted of a number of huge parallel boulders, which rose straight up like a wall. There it almost seemed to the young Alabama colonel that he was now on top of not only Adams County but also the world. From this commanding height, the distant horizons spanned in every direction as far as the eye could see.

After gaining the northern edge of the rocky summit, Oates

eased out to stand on the protruding high ledge of solid rock. This vertical wall of stone consisted of a high cluster of huge boulders, which rose upward about fifty to sixty feet from the ground like giant tombstones piled up by the gods. This protruding group of giant parallel slabs of rock would later become known as "the Sphinx" because the shape of this cluster of huge boulders bore some resemblence to Egypt's Great Sphinx of the Nile. These parallel boulders rose up and were clumped together like the man-made monuments, appearing eerily mysterious to the soldiers from the coastal plain of southeast Alabama.

From the rocky outcroppings of "the Sphinx," Oates continued to look north through the thick foliage of the trees. While peering toward Little Round Top, he could hardly believe his eyes. Atop the commanding summit of Big Round Top and while the struggle for Devil's Den to the northwest raged fiercely and the thin layers of smoke rose higher, Oates never forgot that moment when he "let [his men] lie down and rest a few minutes [and now] I saw Gettysburg through the foliage of the trees [and] I saw from the highest point of rocks that we were then on the most commanding elevation in that neighborhood."

Worn and hungry, many of the Alabama Rebels, with tongues swollen and lips parched from the lack of water, fell to the ground in exhaustion as they reached the rocky summit. These young men coughed and gagged, while sucking hot air into heaving lungs and exhausted frames. Many felt half-sick, nauseated, and dizzy from sunstroke and heat exhaustion.

Colonel Oates, consequently, called a halt on the towering summit of Big Round Top to allow his soldiers a well-deserved rest. On this sweltering day at Gettysburg not even a faint breeze stirred the green leaves of the tree's heavy foliage which lay limp in the humidity, as the blazing sun beat down on Big Round Top's summit without mercy. Colonel Oates yet hoped that his missing twenty-two-man water detail would reach the regiment. With empty canteens, the 15th Alabama soldiers felt like selling their souls for a single mouthful of water from the Slyder well or from Plum Run.

But Colonel Oates was hoping against fate for the arrival of the missing canteen detail. Unfortunately for the 15th Alabama, the small detail was attempting in vain to link with the regiment, after following on the 15th Alabama's heels. However, the detail and their precious water resupply would be captured that afternoon by the adjutant of the 2nd United States Sharpshooters and a dozen green-coated sharpshooters on the south side of Big Round Top. Thus the parched 15th Alabama Rebels would continue to suffer in the sweltering heat of the sun-baked summit of Big Round Top, receiving no resupply of water. With Colonel Oates's soldiers hovering on the Union army's left flank, this development would play a part in determining the final outcome of the most decisive small unit action of the war.[20]

Without a map, guide, or a higher ranking officer present to issue specific orders and with his men broken down from exhaustion, Colonel Oates decided to continue to rest his men. The young colonel took this opportunity to get his own bearings on the tactical situation, while assessing the extent of the tactical opportunities from his elevated position on the north edge of the rocky summit. Finally free of the tangled woodlands below the summit and with Little Round Top looming before him, Colonel Oates now began to contemplate exactly what to do next and the best way to do it.

From the dominate perch high above the surrounding terrain, Oates could now sense the exciting possibilities that could be exploited after capturing the summit. One close look told this opportunistic young colonel that if Confederate guns could be brought up Big Round Top, then this highest point in Adams County would not only dominate General Meade's line to the north but also would serve as an impregnable Confederate bastion on the Army of the Potomac's left flank.

Perched atop the forested mountain which dominated the area for miles around, in Colonel Oates's words, there was "a precipice on the east and north, right at my feet; a very steep, stony, and wooded mountain-side on the west. The only approach to it by our enemy, a long wooded slope on the northwest . . . within half an hour I could convert it into a Gibraltar that I could hold against ten times the number of men that I had, hence in my judgment it should be held and occupied by artillery as soon as possible, as it was higher than the other mountain [Little Round Top] and would command the entire field." Oates realized that Confederate guns emplaced atop Big Round Top could completely command the lower terrain of Little Round Top to the north.[21]

Colonel Oates could see the fighting swirling around the big granite rocks of the Devil's Den. In the distance, his Rebels continued to hear the distant rattle of musketry from where the smoke of battle rolled up from the valley of Plum Run like the thick white haze from a thousand campfires. There, the yelling Texas, Georgia, and Alabama Rebels were battling like demons for possession of the Devil's Den, driving the Yankees from the valley and the jumble of big rocks now strewn with bodies. Earning a hard-won success, these tough fighters of Hood's Division continued to uphold their reputations for fierceness on the battlefield after planting battle flags atop the largest boulders of Devil's Den in triumph and unleashing victory cheers. Most important, however, the long-sought vulnerable flank and rear of the Army of the Potomac now seemed to lay before Colonel Oates just a short distance ahead, and Little Round Top stood within easy striking distance.

But seemingly at the last possible minute and with the Alabamians's victory finally in sight, fate was in the process of intervening to sabotage the chances of Colonel Oates's bid for victory. As the Alabamians rested atop Big Round Top, hundreds of lumberman, loggers, and woodsmen of the 20th Maine double-quicked toward Little Round Top along with three other veteran regiments of their fine brigade of battle-ready troops. With rifled muskets on shoulders, these Union troops swung toward Little Round Top to deny the Alabama soldiers their long-awaited chance to reach out and take hold of their elusive dream of victory on the left flank of the Army of the Potomac. These two opposing regiments of young men and boys—one from Maine and the other from Alabama—were about to meet in a deadly clash. As destiny would have it, the stage was being set for the dramatic showdown between the 15th Alabama and the 20th Maine.

Events had begun to turn away from the Alabamians's favor when, only a short time earlier, General Gouverneur Kemble Warren, the chief engineer of the Army of the Potomac, had been astounded to discover that Little Round Top was unoccupied as the fighting swirled around the Devil's Den. Because of the thickness of the woodlands draping Big Round Top in a green shroud, General Warren could not ascertain how far General Lee's battle lines extended south below the Devil's Den. For all he knew, half of the Army of the Northern Virginia might be advancing south of the Devil's Den, swarming toward the Round Tops to capture those key heights. And then flashes of sunlight flickering off hundreds of Rebel bayonets confirmed General Warren's worst fears.

The vulnerability of an unoccupied Little Round Top had resulted from a series of key Union mistakes. On the afternoon of July 1, General Winfield Scott Hancock, Second Corps commander, had directed General John W. Geary's division to extend the army's left southward down Cemetery Ridge to occupy Little Round Top, anchoring the left flank on the high ground. This wise extension of the Army of the Potomac's line had been accomplished by the night of July 1. On the morning of July 2, however, Geary's division had been redeployed northward to Culp's Hill on the far right to face General Lee's expected attack, while General Sickles's III Corps was ordered to replace Geary on Little Round Top. However, the independent-minded General Sickles had moved his forces as he wanted and not as ordered on July 2.

Consequently, General Sickles's corps had advanced from the Cemetery Ridge line to form the exposed salient of high ground at the Peach Orchard. This caused the III Corps's line to extend southward from the Peach Orchard on the Emmitsburg Road to the Devil's Den, which now anchored the Union army's left flank. The III Corps's extension before, or west, of the army's main line of Cemetery Ridge ensured a shortening of General Sickles's line. Therefore, General Sickles's unauthorized readjustments of the III Corps's lines before the main army guaranteed an exposed left flank to the south. Hence, not enough III Corps troops were available to extend the line farther south to occupy Little Round Top.

And both Big and Little Round Top were left unoccupied by the time Colonel Oates and his Alabamians marched forth to exploit the tactical advantage.

General Sickles's bold decision to act on his own to advance his line westward to the high ground of the Peach Orchard along the Emmitsburg Road left the Army of the Potomac's left flank most vulnerable. Now the key to the battlefield, Little Round Top just southeast of the Peach Orchard, was about to become the primary bone of contention with much at stake.

Fortunately for General Meade, the 12,000-man V Corps lay in reserve around the Taneytown Road and near the army's left when needed the most on July 2. In position to meet the Alabamians's threat on General Meade's left flank was General James Barnes's 1st Division, V Corps, which had moved north along the eastern base of Little Round Top and now approached the Wheatfield to reinforce General Sickles at the Peach Orchard to the northwest.

Nevertheless, the crisis now brewing on General Meade's left flank was most serious for the Army of the Potomac. With Devil's Den, the Union army's left, now captured by General Benning's Georgians and Law's Alabamians, Little Round Top was there for the taking. Ironically, throughout the morning and early afternoon, neither Generals Lee nor Meade were overly concerned about the tactical importance of Little Round Top. Nor could either commander fully realize the all-important role that this small rocky hill would play in determining the battle's outcome during the next few hours of this afternoon in hell. Quite suddenly and unexpectedly and unrealized at the headquarters of either army, Little Round Top had suddenly become the key to the battle.

Unfortunately for Confederate fortunes at the southern end of Lee's battle line, however, General Longstreet had concentrated two-thirds of his veteran corps to overrun the Peach Orchard salient and Sickles's III Corps. This heavy concentration of Southern manpower northwest of the Round Tops came at a high price, explaining in part Longstreet's failure to provide the necessary support for Colonel Oates's effort to turn the Union army's left flank. For the entire day, General Longstreet would dispatch neither reinforcements nor artillery to the assistance of those relatively few Alabamians now assigned the most crucial task in Lee's army.

Hour after hour, the fierce struggle at the bloody Peach Orchard, and beyond toward Cemetery Ridge after the capture of the Peach Orchard, would continue to draw most of the attention and strength of Longstreet's corps away. And early success in capturing the Peach Orchard drew Longstreet's corps deeper into the storm to exploit a success that could not be fully exploited. In addition, General Lee's tactical plan focused too much effort on encircling the wrong Union flank, General Meade's right. To the north the Army of the Potomac's right at Culp's Hill, just southeast of Gettysburg, offered much less promise for a successful Confederate flanking movement than to the south at Little Round Top.

While the Army of the Potomac and its leaders were rising to the challenge as never before on the battlefield which negated even the collapse of the III Corps and the loss of the Peach Orchard salient, the leadership of the Army of Northern Virginia—unlike its fighting men in the ranks—was experiencing its worst day. There, on the battle's second day, General Lee's leadership corps was performing badly out-of-tune and far below expected levels when it mattered the most. In contrast, the Army of the Potomac and its conservative, solid commander, General Meade, was performing at their best in the decisive battle swirling around the little town of Gettysburg. In the words of one historian, "in retrospect Lee [and his top lieutenants] might just as well have been playing pinochle at Cashtown so far as any direct action on their part to influence the battle of the late afternoon was concerned."

Because General Longstreet had not forwarded Generals Hood's and Law's protests on to General Lee's headquarters at the Thompson House on the Chambersburg Pike on the northwest outskirts of Gettysburg, the commanding general was "left in ignorance of the true position of the enemy's [left] flank." Meanwhile, the storm that had consumed the Peach Orchard and the resulting breakthrough continued to draw the primary focus of

Longstreet's offensive effort, eliminating any assistance to the 15th Alabama.

In addition, the savage fighting which roared over the Devil's Den also drew the focus of General Law and the remainder of his Alabama Brigade. Ensuring the lack of brigade support for Oates, this struggle northwest of Little Round Top continued to hamper Colonel Oates's isolated effort to turn General Meade's left flank. And the poorly coordinated offensive tactics on both brigade and division levels additionally ensured that the upcoming task of rolling up the Federal army's left flank fell primarily upon the shoulders of Colonel Oates.[22]

Seemingly an unkind fate continued to orchestrate tactical developments this afternoon to Colonel Oates's and the Alabamians's disadvantage. No matter how hard the Alabama Confederates fought this day, Colonel Oates's soldiers would be at the disadvantage in attempting to turn Meade's left flank without assistance. The rapid course of events and tactical developments elsewhere on the field were beginning to make the vital mission of the 15th Alabama seemingly impossible by this time. But Colonel Oates had no way of knowing what was happening elsewhere to turn his advantages into disadvantages. Only later would he learn of the rapid course of events and tactical developments which sabotaged his chances for success. After initially discovering that Little Round was unoccupied except for a handful of signal corpsmen, General Warren, the army's chief engineer, had hurriedly sent word of Little Round Top's vulnerability to General Meade. Then the commanding general passed news of the danger down to General George Sykes, the new V Corps commander, who was pushing his units forward to support General Sickles's III Corps around mid-afternoon of July 2.

Unlike General Lee's sprawling exterior lines of nearly four miles in length, the advantage of Meade's interior lines combined with superior numbers would assist in the reinforcing of the vulnerable Union left flank at the last minute. This tactical advantage ensured a rapid shifting of Federal troops to threatened sectors with an ease only wished for that afternoon by General Lee. Acting quickly on his own to obey General Sykes's intercepted orders to General Barnes to send a brigade to occupy Little Round Top, Colonel Vincent rose to the challenge, taking immediate action. When needed the most on the Union side, Vincent had the initiative to move forward to occupy the hill himself, after departing the Cemetery Ridge sector north of Little Round Top. Only recently arrived at the east of Cemetery Ridge, the four regiments of Colonel Strong Vincent's brigade pushed toward Little Round Top on the double. Major Ellis Spear, who was now the second in command of the 20th Maine after the regiment's major became sick during the march through Maryland, described the regiment's maneuvers, ". . . with Little Round Top just to our left, we were near entering the wheatfield, when the head of our brigade was turned to the left, and we moved back & around, in rear of Little Round Top."

Colonel Vincent's brigade had been at the right place at the right time for Union fortunes that day. Consequently, Vincent's Maine, New York, Michigan, and Pennsylvania regiments were close enough to Little Round Top to quickly reach the elevation. Much like the aggressive General Law, Colonel Vincent, who was the same age as his Alabama counterpart at age twenty-six, possessed a clear understanding of the strategic importance of Little Round Top on this day of destiny.

On Big Round Top's commanding summit, meanwhile, Colonel Oates continued to survey the promised land below him to the northeast—Little Round Top, this obscure hill covered with rock, underbrush, and timber and, best of all, only a few Yankee signalmen. Without exaggeration, General Meade later stated how ". . . Little Round Top was the key point of my whole position and if they had succeeded in occupying that, it would have prevented me from holding any of the ground I subsequently held to the last." Farther north Colonel Oates also saw through the trees of Big Round Top beyond the summit of Little Round Top, the lengthy battle line of Sickles's III Corps to the northwest. The III Corps's line ran like a thin blue ribbon northwestward from the Devil's Den to the Peach Orchard, then turned northeastward to follow the Emmitsburg Road. Beyond the III Corps, General Meade's blue lines flowed northward along Cemetery Ridge which led southward from the outskirts of Gettysburg. From the commanding summit of Big Round Top on this cloudless day and despite the hot summer haze, Colonel Oates saw Gettysburg and Culp's Hill farther to the north.

Rolling-up General Meade's left flank now meant much more than simply once again thrashing the Army of the Potomac as at Second Manassas, Fredericksburg, or Chancellorsville. Colonel Oates and his Alabama Rebels were now determined to grasp the unprecedented opportunity that lay before them. Quite unexpectedly and in an odd twist of fate, the long-sought cherished dreams of the Southern people and nation were now within the sight and grasp of Colonel Oates and his 15th Alabama. And seemingly all that the Alabama soldiers now had to do was to reach out and embrace the great destiny of the Southern nation by also capturing Little Round Top and presenting General Lee and the Army of Northern Virginia with an opportunity to win decisive victory at Gettysburg.

As Colonel Oates envisioned the optimistic scenario leading to decisive success, Confederate artillery could be hauled up either or both of the Round Tops to sweep and enfilade the Union lines. This cannonade in conjunction with a flank attack would then roll up the left end of General Meade's line like an old carpet. After having already gone much too far and lost too much during this war, the Alabamians were not about to miss this golden opportunity.

As one V Corps soldier explained, the capture of Little Round Top by Colonel Oates's Alabamians "would have forced Meade to abandon his strong position in disorderly retreat." As in the primeval world of nature based upon the endless evolutionary struggle of survival of the fittest, the ever-optimistic Colonel Oates could now almost sense the death of one nation and the corresponding birth of another with the capture of the twin Round Tops.

Colonel Oates, tall, dignified, and handsome, was now the right man in the right place for the Confederacy. With both Big and

Little Round Top dominating the nearby Taneytown Road amid the level fields to the east, Colonel Joshua Chamberlain of the 20th Maine realized how "the Taneytown Road [was] perfectly commanded by the Little Round Top [and was the] road [which] opened the direct way to Washington" and perhaps the war's end. Indeed, if the Confederates cut the Taneytown Road, then accomplished the same feat in regard to the Baltimore Pike farther to the east, then the Alabamians would be between the Army of the Potomac and Washington, D.C.

About five minutes had passed on the barren summit of Big Round Top and the weary Alabama soldiers had barely had time to catch their breath when Captain Leigh Richmond Terrill, the assistant adjutant general on General Law's staff, reached the summit to everyone's surprise. At this time, General Law was leading his troops into the fiery storm of the Devil's Den, but had the presence of mind to dispatch Captain Terrill on his mission to reach Colonel Oates. By the time of Gettysburg, everyone knew better than to cross Captain Terrill if they could help it as he was hot-tempered and had strong influence with General Law and brigade headquarters. After apparently having been informed by the Texas scouts of the easiest way up the largest mountain in Adams County, Captain Terrill had found the narrow logging road leading up the east side of Big Round Top. Slipping through the wandering bands of Yankee sharpshooters, the young captain had galloped up the heavily wooded slope to find Colonel Oates and his boys on the summit.

Throughout the afternoon on General Lee's right, Captain Terrill had performed admirably. He had ridden to the front of the Alabama Brigade to launch its attack, and personally led the 4th Alabama forward during much of its advance. Now having somehow avoided running into the greenclad sharpshooters who were lurking in the woods on each side of Big Round Top, the captain informed Colonel Oates that General Law would continue to command the division, after General Hood had been cut down by the fire from Union batteries at the assault's beginning. Colonel Oates now learned partly why he had been on his own since the advance's beginning: General Law was busy leading his hard-fighting Alabama regiments against the Devil's Den northwest of Little Round Top.

Without protocol, an impatient Captain Terrill now bluntly inquired why the exhausted Alabama men were not immediately continuing the advance off Big Round Top. The captain was surprised to receive a curt reply from Colonel Oates in the form of a protest. Colonel Oates believed that a secure grip on Big Round Top would make Little Round Top untenable even if Union troops took possession of the hill. To Oates's way-of-thinking, another offensive effort to capture a position without knowledge of the terrain and without a thorough reconnaissance was a risky undertaking. Indeed, Colonel Oates had already been surprised both by the Yankees's presence and tenacity at the stone wall and in simultaneously advancing and fighting up the great height of Big Round Top.

In response to Oates's protest, Captain Terrill emphasized the urgency of moving northward to capture Little Round Top, stating that "General Law's order was for [Oates] and Colonel Bulger to lose no time, but to press forward and drive the enemy before us as far as possible." To bolster his case for remaining in a defensive position on Big Round Top, Oates emphasized the difficulty in continuing the advance and capturing Little Round Top, after so much marching and fighting by his exhausted and undermanned regiment now low on ammunition.

Without courtesy or diplomacy, Colonel Oates explained how wisdom and common sense now called for his Alabamians to remain securely in place to retain possession of Big Round Top on the Union army's left flank. Colonel Oates realized the necessity of not forfeiting the many hard-won gains of the day, especially with his command in poor shape by this time. Most of all, he understood the need to hold Big Round Top because it so completely dominated Little Round Top and the Union lines to the north. Both Oates and Joshua Lawrence Chamberlain were convinced that Big Round Top was far more important than Little Round Top and the key to the battlefield.

In addition, the huge rocky outcroppings on the northern edge of Big Round Top's summit—the "Sphinx"—prevented the Alabamians's direct advance northward down the timbered northern slope of Big Round Top. Even more, to the colonel's way-of-thinking, moving his soldiers off the commanding summit and down into the low ground of the saddle between the two Round Tops would put his Alabamians in a most vulnerable position. Clearly, his almost broken-down Alabama boys were in no shape to continue offensive operations. Besides less than full strength, the 15th Alabama atop Big Round Top carried empty canteens, and no water was to be found on either Round Top, even if the Rebels captured the adjacent hill. Worst of all, Oates's regiment was without either the water detail or the missing skirmishers of Company A. Therefore, Oates hotly argued his case to Captain Terrill, who grew more irritated by the minute with this free-thinking junior officer.

Colonel Oates hoped that the water detail might yet link with the regiment atop the mountain. But at this time, these twenty-two soldiers had seemingly disappeared from the face of the earth. The water shortage was a severe problem, and by this time, the Alabamians's thirst was unquenchable, with the combination of nervous tension, blackpowder from biting paper cartridges, and the acid smoke of battle combining to parch mouths and throats. But worst of all, there would be neither a resupply of manpower or ammunition forthcoming for the isolated 15th Alabama. Colonel Oates's Alabamians continued to be out-of-sight and out on a limb at the southern end of General Lee's line.

Oates was convinced that Big Round Top had to be held at all costs. He realized that he now had possession of an impregnable perch which dominated the field, especially Little Round Top. Since Big Round Top so completely overlooked Little Round Top to command the surrounding area, Colonel Oates remained most reluctant to abandon his hard-won, high-ground prize.

Colonel Oates's pragmatic tactical assessment of the situation made sense to him. With the instincts of a good artillery captain, he understood how Little Round Top could not be controlled by the Yankees even if they gained possession, if Confederate artillery was up on Big Round Top by way of the logging road. Consequently, the Henry County colonel continued to spiritedly argue his point to Captain Terrill. Oates again questioned the wisdom of General Law's orders to keep moving forward because they had been issued before the capture of Big Round Top and without that consideration in mind. Oates believed that Big Round Top's capture had best fulfilled General Law's directive to gain the enemy's left flank because he now possessed the highest ground on the battlefield.

Colonel Oates's argument made such good sense that even Captain Terrill agreed with him. Captain Terrill saw the wisdom of the colonel's tactical assessment and the urgent need to hold Big Round Top and not take the risk of losing it by resuming the offensive without water or sufficient manpower. But Terrill also realized that he must follow orders from headquarters. He therefore abruptly concluded the increasingly heated exchange with Colonel Oates by emphasizing in firm tones that orders were orders. A frustrated Terrill was in a bad mood with General Hood's attack unraveling early on, and after helping to lead the 4th Alabama into action that afternoon. In a heated response, Captain Terrill finally shouted, "Lose no time, but press forward and drive the enemy as far as possible."

Consequently, Colonel Oates now began to realize that he would have to make the best of the situation by once again resuming the offensive. With General Law now on the left leading his soldiers who had their hands full at the Devil's Den, Colonel Oates would continue to be largely on his own to succeed or fail. Unfortunately for Oates, the struggle for the Devil's Den, just northwest of Little Round Top and at the southern end of the parallel ridge, continued to focus the attention of Confederate leaders away from the Round Tops for the remainder of July 2. As events on Little Round Top would soon prove, this was a most costly diversion.

Indeed, at this critical moment, neither Generals Lee nor Longstreet or now even Law, could be found on the far right to direct affairs or give up-to-date instructions either in person or by a competent staff system. For decisive success on the southernmost flank of General Lee's army, real-time directives of high-ranking officers were needed on the far right to coordinate offensive operations among the fragmented units of Hood's Division. Later lamenting the breakdown of the effectiveness of the army's leadership and the lack of communication on July 2, a frustrated, if not angry, Colonel Oates could only write with regret how Big Round Top was "the key-point of [the Army of the Potomac's] position [and] I felt confident that Law did not know my position, or he would not order me from it. I had not seen him or any other officer after I received Stoughton's fire, and did not see any general or staff officer, other than Terrill" on that fateful July 2.

Another Confederate likewise complained of the uncoordinated and unsupported effort to capture Little Round Top during one of the great lost opportunities of the war: "'O for one hour of Stonewall Jackson!' [for] if Jackson had been at his old place watching the firing line, Little Round Top would not have so easily escaped our capture." Perhaps even a few minutes of direct assistance or word from either Generals Lee, Longstreet, or Law to hold Big Round Top on the far right might have been sufficient to ensure a decisive victory for the South.

On the far right flank of Lee's Army, however, the twenty-seven-year-old Oates would be on his own this day, and he would have to make the best of it. He would be left by himself to wrestle with the monumental challenge of attempting to do the right thing and at the right time. And worst of all, if he now lead his troops down Big Round Top in an attempt to capture Little Round Top, Colonel Oates would unknowingly come face-to-face with the hundreds of blueclad troops of Colonel Vincent's brigade.

As Colonel Oates explained the confusing tactical situation at this time when so much hung in the balance:

"Notwithstanding my conviction of the importance of holding and occupying Big Round Top with artillery, which I endeavored to communicate to Law through Terrill (he never reached General Law until near the close of the battle), I considered it my duty to obey the order communicated to me by Terrill . . . but it was against my judgment to leave that strong position. It looked to me to be the key-point of the field, as artillery on it would have commanded the [Little] Round Top and the Federal line toward Gettysburg as far as it extended along Cemetery Ridge; but the order was to find and turn the left of the Union line, and that was on Little Round Top . . ."

Ironically, in the beginning, General Lee's primary objective at Gettysburg had been to place artillery on commanding high ground to dominate the battlefield. General Lee himself described his main objective on July 2 as "to gain a position from which it was thought that our artillery could be brought to bear with effect." General Lee believed that he had won the high ground position that he needed for decisive victory with the capture of the elevated terrain of the Peach Orchard by General William Barksdale's Mississippi Brigade, but that would not be the case. In reality, the high ground that General Lee needed to ensure decisive victory was southeast of the Peach Orchard at the Round Tops, and especially Big Round Top.

But General Lee and his top lieutenants were now unaware of the developments at both Big and Little Round Top on this most decisive day of the war. Consequently, Colonel Oates's Alabamians would continue to receive neither support, guidance, or assistance. There would be no high-ranking Confederate leaders on the far right to assess the advantages of retaining possession of Big Round Top, adjust to the ever-changing tactical situation, or explore the tactical options in Colonel Oates's Round Top sector. Hence, Oates would only be able to react to the rapidly changing tactical developments on his own as best he could under the difficult and disadvantageous circumstances.

But contrary to Colonel Oates's opinion, the barren openness of Little Round Top now might have made it more strategic and tactically important than Big Round Top, despite the latter's superior height. According to the generally accepted view, the steepness of the upper third of Big Round Top, the rocky summit, and the heavily wooded slopes would have made it all but impossible for Rebel artillery to reach the crest. And according to this interpretation, such a feat could have only been accomplished if the cannon were hauled up the steep mountain by hand, after soldiers exerted much time and effort in cutting down virgin timber which towered upward like giants on every side of Big Round Top.

In addition, it has been estimated that the overall firing distance for Confederate artillery atop Big Round Top to have shelled the Union lines, with the exception of nearby Little Round Top and the southern end of Cemetery Ridge, might have been too great to have been effective in breaking up General Meade's lines to the north. For example, General Lee's artillery on Seminary Ridge would prove largely ineffective at Gettysburg, especially the great cannonade that was to have softened-up the defensive positions of Cemetery Ridge before "Pickett's Charge" on July 3.

However, what has been overlooked by historians was the fact that the logging road leading up the east side of Big Round Top made the movement of Rebel artillery up the mountain a distinct possibility. Then, Confederate guns manned by veterans atop Big Round Top could have been turned northward to hurl shells as far north as General Meade's center at Cemetery Hill, which stood along the Baltimore Pike that ran southeast from Gettysburg. Thus Colonel Oates might well have been correct in his tactical assessment that it was now only necessary to hold Big Round Top to ensure Confederate victory at Gettysburg if Confederate guns could be brought up the mountain, especially with a Union brigade destined to soon be firmly placed in strong defensive positions on Little Round Top.

But Colonel Oates now prepared to move forward to capture Little Round Top, which stood just to the northwest. And Little Round Top promised to serve as a launching pad from which Meade's flank could be rolled up by way of concentrated artillery fire or an infantry attack. Victorious Alabama Rebels atop Little Round Top would dominate the weakening and increasingly vulnerable left of Cemetery Ridge, the main battle line of the Army of the Potomac. If Little Round Top was captured, the Alabama

Confederates would then find themselves in the vulnerable rear of the Army of the Potomac. Once captured, Oates planned to turn Little Round Top into a "Gibralter" like he had envisioned for Big Round Top.

After his sweat-drenched boys finally caught their breath in the sweltering heat, Colonel Oates launched the effort to capture Little Round Top. Ten precious minutes—five minutes of rest and then five minutes of attempting to convince Captain Terrill of the wisdom of retaining possession of Big Round Top—had passed with the worn Alabamians gaining some badly needed rest on the summit.

With his decision to abandon Big Round Top, Colonel Oates could not march his Alabamians straight northward down the mountain on the most direct course to reach Little Round Top because of the high outcropping of rock near the summit. He finally led his men in double ranks down the hill by the left flank. Out in front as usual, Colonel Oates led the way down the slope through the trees, heading for Little Round Top as ordered. No time could be wasted and therefore Oates moved his troops down the steep slope of Big Round Top without sending out a line of skirmishers to lead the way. The loss of the Alabama Brigade's skirmishers continued to haunt Colonel Oates. All in all, Oates made a good choice in pushing down the hill by this direction, because the wooded terrain along the northwestern slope of Big Round Top was less rocky, covered with fewer boulders, and less steep. The ground sloped more gradually than if Colonel Oates's soldiers had moved straight northward down the slope from the crest, where larger boulders and fallen trees lay to impede a rapid descent in formation.

Many of these large protruding rocks below the "Sphinx" on the northern slope were clumped haphazardly together. Because of Colonel Oates's tactical adjustments to cross more favorable terrain to save time, the Alabamians's descent down the northwestern slope of Big Round Top was a Sunday stroll compared to the laborious push up the western side. After bypassing the steepest terrain and largest boulders piled near the summit and littering the northern slope, Colonel Oates shifted his men to the right or eastward. With discipline and tight alignment, the Alabama Rebels marched toward the narrow saddle of level and wooded ground between the Round Tops at the southern base of Little Round Top.

To his dying day, the young colonel from Abbeville would never cease to regret abandoning his mountaintop perch at the summit of Big Round Top. Even while pushing toward Little Round Top, Oates continued to feel that he was perhaps making a mistake and that trouble lay ahead. He had been ordered to resume the offensive without sufficient support, advice, or those things that his band of exhausted soldiers on General Lee's far right needed most of all to ensure success on July 2—water in canteens, a resupply of ammunition, reinforcements, and rest.

Colonel Oates was nagged by the realization that if Captain Terrill had only given "his sanction I would have remained at that point [the summit of Big Round Top] until I could have heard from Law or some superior in rank inquired for Law." But that "sanction" had never come and now Oates was embarking on yet another demanding mission to take the second highest ground position around Gettysburg. Clearly, this task of turning Meade's left flank directly from the south should have been undertaken by a veteran combat brigade in good shape with adequate rest and manpower rather than an exhausted, depleted, and bloodied regiment. But worst of all for Southern fortunes, large numbers of Federal troops were also moving swiftly to take possession of Little Round Top. As fate would have it, the imminent arrival and alignment of hundreds of Union V Corps troops in excellent defensive positions on Little Round Top, in the words of Colonel Edward Porter Alexander, would "once in position, made it impregnable."

But Colonel Oates and his soldiers trudged northward with battle flags limp in the heat, pushing closer to the right of the advancing 47th and 4th Alabama, from right to left. These two regiments now surged toward the southwestern and western slope of Little Round Top, while the 15th Alabama pushed northward and down through the timbered slope of Big Round Top. And after fighting their way through the nightmarish piles of boulders that made one Texas soldier believe that "the Infernal regions was spending its fury in and around a spot so fitly named 'The Devil's Den,'" the embattled 4th and 5th Texas, from right to left, of Robertson's brigade also pushed mostly eastward toward the western side of Little Round Top to the Alabamians's left.

The 15th Alabama soldiers, meanwhile, continued to struggle down the rocky and timbered northern slope of Big Round Top, realizing that time was of the essence. All along the way, Colonel Oates's men crashed through the intertwined tangles of oak, dogwood, hickory, and redbud which were thickly scattered along the northern slope of the rounded mountain with Enfield rifles on shoulders, raising a faint cloud of dust along the steep slope under the canopy of virgin timber. As yet, not a single Yankee had been seen during the rapid descent, and the situation seemed eerily reminiscent of the scenario when the 15th Alabama was surprised by the sharpshooters at the stone wall. Growing more apprehensive as a result of not knowing the Federals's exact location or dispositions or anything about Little Round Top, Colonel Oates described how his men "passed to the left-oblique . . . down the northern side of the mountain without encountering any opposition whatever."

As they trudged down Big Round Top, before reaching the open woodlands of the level ground between the two summits, the Alabama Rebels finally spied the huge park of Union supply and ordnance trains about six hundred feet to the northeast. On the southeast side of Little Round Top, these long lines of parked and heavily laden wagons lay amid the broad grassy fields of the Jacob Weikert farm. Ironically, this wagon train had been placed in the rear at this point by a concerned General Meade for safekeeping. As General Meade explained in a 3 o'clock telegram to the worried officials in Washington, D.C., "expecting a battle, I ordered all my trains to the rear." On July 2, ironically, General Meade felt that the most secure location for his army's train was on the southeast side of Little Round Top now within Colonel Oates's sight and almost within reach.

A never-to-be forgotten spectacle, Colonel Oates described the unbelievable sight which was now presented to him at the south-eastern edge of Little Round Top and just off the Taneytown Road: "After I reached the level ground in rear of [the] Spur [the southern base of Little Round Top], in plain view of the Federal waggon [sic] trains, and within two hundred yards of an extensive park of Federal ordinance wagons, which satisfied me that I was then in the Federal rear, rapidly advancing, without any skirmishers in front." Awed by the sight and lusting at the golden opportunity, Private Houghton never forgot how "we were on a hill [and] within rifle range but between us [and Little Round Top] was a deep ravine. We could see they were in some confusion and their teams and army wagons ready for flight. The men in the ranks spoke of such a favorable opportunity to flank them on the left as that part seemed wholly unprotected."

In attempting to turn General Meade's left flank, Colonel Oates had suddenly gained an unexpected opportunity to achieve even more. Oates could hardly believe the breath-taking sight or the good fortune that had now seemingly been handed to the 15th Alabama. Clearly, at this time, they were practically in the rear of Army of the Potomac.

At long last, Colonel Oates had gained a supreme advantage and an ideal position from which he could "do all the damage I could" to the flank and rear of the Army of the Potomac, as ordered by General Law. Oates's ideal scenario for decisive victory was described by one Yankee who feared the worst: "In a word, Gettysburg might have been the greatest disaster of the war, and might have turned the scales in favor of the rebellion [if Little Round Top had been captured and] the principal ammunition train, which was parked about half a mile in the rear, would have been lost, the general line of battle would have been doubled up, and a disastrous defeat would have been almost inevitable."

Consequently, about one-third of the way down the northern slope of Big Round Top, Colonel Oates immediately handed Company A—nearly fifty Rebels of the regiment's crack skirmishers who had just finally rejoined the regiment near the summit of Big Round Top after chasing the sharpshooters around Big Round

Top—a special mission of much importance. Under the command of the reliable Captain Shaaff, the Russell County soldiers of the "Cantry Rifles" hustled eastward downhill on the double and through the dense woodlands on their mission to capture the mass concentration of army wagons in the Army of the Potomac's rear. Lusting to exploit this golden opportunity which had been suddenly presented to him, Captain Shaaff led his Company A Rebels forward to "surround and capture the ordnance wagons," which were concentrated and parked before them in numbers so large that they could not be counted.

However, in his eagerness to take full advantage of the opportunity, Colonel Oates had dispatched his top skirmish company on another independent mission taking away more good men from the 15th Alabama which was unknowingly about to strike Colonel Vincent's brigade. With General Law's and Captain Terrill's urgent orders in his mind not to delay or waste any additional time, Colonel Oates continued to lead his troops forward again without a company of skirmishers to screen the 15th Alabama's advance in the hope of securing Little Round Top before it was too late. But despite not having received specific orders from either Generals Longstreet, Hood, or Law to capture the ordnance train in the Army of the Potomac's rear, Colonel Oates simply could not resist this opportunity which would not come again for General Lee's troops for the remainder of the war. The breakdown in command structure and the disjointed Confederate attacks this afternoon continued to leave Colonel Oates with no choice but to make tactical decisions on his own. The ever-aggressive Oates, therefore, was once again relying on his own initiative, instincts, and tactical common sense. Most of all, he was obeying General Law's urgent directive to "do all the damage [he] could" on the left flank of the Army of the Potomac.

Colonel Oates's decision to attempt to capture the Union army's wagon train was a gamble worth taking with so much at stake. As demonstrated on previous battlefields, any hesitation or undue caution at this point might prove fatal to Confederate fortunes. Once again, therefore, Colonel Oates's well-honed instincts as a gambler on the southwest frontier rose to the fore on the Army of the Potomac's far left. Colonel Oates again was taking risks which promised more considerable gains, but only if the opportunity was exploited to the fullest. And now by advancing without skirmishers to cover his approach to Little Round Top, Colonel Oates apparently assumed that he would encounter no Yankees on Little Round Top.

Meticulous in obeying orders and demonstrating leadership ability throughout the past, the capable Captain Shaaff was a good officer for the assignment of capturing the Union army's wagon train. This Columbus, Georgia native was an experienced officer with years of service as a noncommissioned officer and regular in the United States Army. Only minutes before, Captain Shaaff and his Company A had rejoined Colonel Oates on the summit of Big Round Top after another job well done.

Indeed, these Russell County Rebels under Captain Shaaff's leadership had successfully driven Major Stoughton's sharp-shooters to the east side of Big Round Top to protect the right of the advancing 15th Alabama. Now excited about the possibilities contained in Colonel Oates's orders to capture the wagon train in General Meade's vulnerable rear, the double-quicking Russell County boys of the "Cantry Rifles" quickly faded away in the timber with gear clanging and echoing along the hillside while bayonets flashed from the slivers of sunlight cascading down through the trees covering the northern slope of Big Round Top. One of his most trusted subordinates after the fall of Lieutenant Colonel Feagin, Colonel Oates described Captain Shaaff as "a very remarkable man . . . slender, muscular, with a quick, nervous manner, and one of the best officers in the regiment [and] he would have made a splendid colonel." As cruel fate would have it, Captain Shaaff would die of thirst and exposure when once again fighting in Union blue against the Indians in the Far West long after the fury of Gettysburg became a memory. But now Captain Shaaff was determined "to deploy his company in open order to surround and capture the train of ordnance wagons," wrote Colonel Oates. However, Captain Shaaff's mission this afternoon was both ill-timed and ill-fated. The chances of Company A achieving its objective was largely negated even before Captain Shaaff's veterans dashed down the slope of Big Round Top, thanks to the advance of Colonel Vincent's troops on Little Round Top.

From his new high-ground perch on Little Round Top, Colonel Joshua Chamberlain would shortly dispatch his Company B downhill on the double and through the woods a short distance eastward from the southern base of Little Round Top to protect his left flank. These Maine soldiers from Piscataquis County would take a strong defensive position behind a stone wall amid the thickets that bordered a field that led eastward to the Taneytown Road. The soldiers of Company B, however, would compromise their primary role of guarding Colonel Chamberlain's left flank by taking cover at the stone wall which was just beyond effective supporting distance of the 20th Maine's left flank, which would be positioned on the high ground to the northwest. This detached company expected the Rebels to swing around Big Round Top and strike from the southeast instead of directly from the south. Major Spear, therefore, explained how Company B would be guilty of "advancing perhaps too far & too much to the left." Unfortunately for Colonel Oates this stone wall stood squarely between Captain Shaaff and the Union wagon train. Just southeast of the high ground defensive position soon to be occupied by the 20th Maine on the southern spur of Little Round Top, the stone wall would remain in Union hands throughout July 2.

Clearly, on a decisive day when he would rise to the challenge of facing Rebels on the Union army's flank, Colonel Chamberlain would make a wise decision in sending Company B eastward through the dense woodlands between the two Round Tops to guard the 20th Maine's left flank. Consequently, Captain Shaaff's Company A soon ran into a united front of concealed Yankees when they expected to find no opposition. Eventually the Federals at the stone wall would consist of Colonel Vincent's advanced skirmishers, Chamberlain's Company B, and Berdan's Sharpshooters. Clearly, stone walls and what lay behind them would play a large role in thwarting the efforts of Colonel Oates and his 15th Alabama this afternoon.

And consequently, the badly needed soldiers of Company A would not rejoin the 15th Alabama when it launched its attack on Little Round Top. In contrast to Colonel Chamberlain's decision to dispatch his Company B from the 20th Maine, Colonel Oates's sending of troops—not once but twice—from the 15th Alabama would pay no dividends on this day.

Despite advancing northward and toward the southern base of Little Round Top without his crack Company A skirmishers leading the way before the regiment as usual, Colonel Oates felt confident after spying the Union wagon train that he had gained the Army of the Potomac's flank and rear. Union General Abner Doubleday wrote of the worst possible scenario for Union fortunes if Colonel Oates and his Alabamians had secured possession of Little Round Top, emphasizing how "once [Little Round Top was] in their possession they would flank our whole line and post guns there to drive our troops from [Cemetery] ridge [therefore Little Round Top] was in reality the key to the battlefield . . ."

And a Confederate realized how Little Round Top "was the keypoint of that whole section of the battlefield [and] possession of this point would not only have placed Sickles' Corps in a highly perilous position, but have enabled [Hood's Rebels] to take the entire line in reverse." Despite being in poor condition to resume the offensive and undertake more arduous fighting, Colonel Oates's Alabamians continued to harbor high expectations for success upon once again meeting the Yankees. So far not a single Union soldier had yet been seen or heard amid the dense woodlands below Little Round Top, as hundreds of stealthy Alabamians eased down the northern slope of Big Round Top. But after his dependable skirmishers of Company A had been dispatched to capture the wagon train and because of the urgency of his mission, the young Alabama colonel simply did not have enough troops at hand to risk dispatching yet another company from the main body to lead the way as skirmishers.

After much effort, the Alabama soldiers, sweaty, dirty, and

tired, at last reached the narrow and densely wooded saddle between the Round Tops. There, the land was level, and less rocky and heavily wooded than the northern slope of Big Round Top. In addition, the trees were smaller amid the more brushy saddle and depths of this lower ground than along the higher northern slope of Big Round Top. Steamy and humid, the dense woodlands of the low-lying saddle between the Round Tops were quiet, as if no Yankees were within miles. But it was much too quiet.

No doubt some 15th Alabama veterans now sensed as much. The determined stand made by Colonel Berdan's tough sharp-shooters and the running—or more properly climbing—fight up through the forested, steep slope and boulders of Big Round Top had sufficiently delayed Colonel Oates's advance enough to ensure that the Alabama Rebels would reach Little Round too late on the afternoon of July 2.

Contrary to the view of some historians, it was not Colonel Oates's brief halt of his exhausted soldiers on the summit of Big Round Top which had most of all reduced chances for Confederate success at Little Round Top this afternoon. The real culprit was the many crucial hours wasted by General Longstreet's flank move-ment and countermarch which allowed plenty of time for the V Corps units to reach Little Round Top and only minutes before the Alabamians.

The elation felt by the confident Alabama soldiers in finally gaining the Union army's flank and rear and launching their attempt to capture the army's idle supply, ordnance, and munition trains, which now sat unprotected for the taking only a few hun-dred yards away, would soon diminish. Now moving along the low, wooded ground nestled between the two Round Tops, the weary Alabamians continued onward with visions of glory but they were about to be caught by surprise again. By this time, hun-dreds of well-trained and disciplined veterans from four of Colonel Vincent's regiments were poised in excellent defensive positions on the high ground of Little Round Top awaiting the arrival of the Alabamians who remained unaware of the Yankees's presence. Colonel Oates wrote of the shock in his early August

1863 battle report, "On reaching the foot of the mountain below, I found the enemy in heavy force, posted in rear of large rocks upon a slight elevation [the southern spur of Little Round Top] beyond a depression of some 300 yards in width between the base of the mountain and the open plain beyond."

Upon his first glimpse of the Maine soldiers, Colonel Oates no doubt believed that these previously unseen Yankees were members of Berdan's Sharpshooters who must have taken a second defensive position on the lower slope of Little Round Top. Clearly, the Alabama soldiers had no idea that they were coming face-to-face with hundreds of hardened soldiers of the veteran V Corps on Little Round Top, where only a few Union signalmen had been seen only minutes before.

Colonel Oates later described the shock for the 15th Alabama which set the stage for the struggle for Little Round Top. He wrote how, "advancing rapidly, without any skirmishers in front, the woods being open without undergrowth, I saw no enemy until within forty or fifty steps of an irregular ledge of rocks—a splendid line of natural breastworks running about parallel with the front of the Forty-seventh regiment and my four left companies, and then sloping back in front of my center and right at an angle of about thirty-five or forty degrees."

Worst of all for Confederate fortunes this afternoon, the southern slope, or spur, of Little Round Top was a natural and strong defensive position which was now most formidable. And thwarting Colonel Oates's lofty ambitions of easily occupying Little Round Top, the rocky spur now contained a good many determined young men and boys from Maine under the command of a scholarly but ambitious colonel named Joshua Lawrence Chamberlain.[23]

CHAPTER X

The Attempt To "Do All the Damage I Could"

"Never in the history of war was arrival more timely . . . a further delay of half an hour for any cause and [the Union V Corps's troops] would have found Little Round Top in Law's possession and Cemetery Ridge occupied by Longstreet and his Confederates. The Army of the Potomac would have been split into two fragments . . . and Lee master of the situation."

—Union soldier on the race for the
high ground, July 2, 1863

Clearly fate had not been kind to the fortunes of the 15th Alabama so far that day. By this time, the Confederate attack had broken down, with no high-ranking officer taking charge. General Law's brigade fought divided and widely seperated in five sections throughout the afternoon: the 44th and 48th Alabama fought at the Devil's Den; the 4th and 5th Texas approached the west and southwestern side of Little Round Top with the 4th Alabama to their right; five Alabama companies marched too far eastward and out of the battle; the seven companies of the 47th Alabama neared

Little Round Top slightly northwest of Colonel Oates and detached from the 15th Alabama's left; and the 15th Alabama continued to advance on its own.

In the words of one Texas Brigade soldier, "in making the long charge our brigade got 'jammed' [and] regiments overlapped each other and when we reached the woods and climbed the mountains as far as we could go, we were a badly mixed crowd [and] confusion reigned supreme everywhere [as] nearly all our field officers were gone [either killed or wounded and] by this time order and discipline were gone [as] every fellow was his own general."

But worst of all for the 15th Alabama, only a few minutes before the less than four hundred Alabama Rebels approached the rock-covered and wooded southern slope of Little Round Top, Colonel Vincent's four Union infantry regiments of the 3rd Brigade, 1st Division, V Corps—the 16th Michigan, 44th New York, 83rd Pennsylvania, and the 20th Maine, from right to left—took good defensive positions in a semicircular defensive line that followed the contours of the high ground, after double-quicking up Little Round Top around 4:30. Only a short time before, these bluecoats had been idle, standing in reserve behind the III Corps to the north, but Colonel Vincent's bold decision to occupy Little Round Top on his own changed all of that. General Warren had already ordered Colonel Vincent, in the words of one 16th Michigan soldier, " . . . to hold this point at all hazards, if he sacrificed every man of the Third Brigade." Thus Colonel Vincent's veteran Yankees were now ready and waiting along the southern and southwestern slopes of Little Round Top holding excellent firing positions behind the jumbles of rocks and trees. And Colonel Chamberlain's Maine Yankees held elevated terrain only a few yards below the commanding summit of Little Round Top, which was now the key to the battlefield.

After winning their race to gain Little Round Top before the 15th Alabama, these 20th Maine Yankees were confident of success. Colonel Chamberlain had placed his troops in fine defensive positions on high ground, demonstrating a good eye for good defensive terrain. Covered with trees, rocks, and brush, this rocky spur held by the 20th Maine now served as the solid anchor of the extreme left end of not only Colonel Vincent's brigade but, more important, the whole Army of the Potomac. And one of Colonel Chamberlain's best decisions was to send out dark-haired and long-jawed Captain Walter G. Morrell's Company B beyond the main line to guard the regiment's left flank. However, Company B took position too far to the east and beyond effective supporting distance of the 20th Maine's left.

Company H's Private Theodore Gerrish, a teenage farmer from Oakfield, Maine, recalled how "our men appeared to be as cool and deliberate in their movements as if they had been forming a line upon the parade ground in camp." This heavily wooded, rocky, and underbrush-covered spur rose only to a height of around fifty to sixty feet above the level ground of the low-lying saddle between the two Round Tops. But from the Alabamians's lower position amid the timber of the saddle, the elevated spur now crowned with Maine rifles suddenly rose like a wall of rock, stone, and timber.

Colonel Chamberlain was made somewhat uneasy by the appearance of the eerie-looking natural stage upon which the struggle for possession of Little Round Top was to be played out to the bitter end: "Earnestly we scanned that rugged peak [of Little Round Top] which was to be the touchstone of that day's battle. It bore a rough forbidding face, wrinkled with jagged edges, bearded with mighty boulders; even the smooth spots were strewn with fragments of rock like the playground or battle-ground of giants in the elemental storms of old. Straggling trees wrestled with the rocks for a foot-hold; some were in a rich vein of mould and shot up stark and grim. Altogether it was a strange and solemn place, looking forlorn and barren . . ." The simultaneous advance of the 15th Alabama and the 20th Maine to gain Little Round Top before the other was crucial, for "never perhaps was seen the winner of a race secure such a prize at so little cost." Unfortunately for Southern fortunes, the 15th Alabama lost that all-important race by less than ten minutes.

Consequently, the 1,350 blueclad winners of the race were now poised on the timbered and rocky spur of Little Round Top, calmly awaiting the arrival of the Alabamians. And unfortunately for the 15th Alabama this afternoon, the last regiment of Colonel Vincent's brigade which had raced up the hill had been the 20th Maine. Now these tough soldiers under Colonel Chamberlain had caught their breath, and made preparations for meeting the boys in gray. Most important, the Maine soldiers were in a better overall condition to face the Alabamians, who had already marched and battled for more than twelve hours that day.

Even worse for the Alabamians's fortunes, the earlier realignments of General Law's battle line in the valley of Plum Run had placed the 15th Alabama at more of a disadvantage in contrast to the 20th Maine, who could count on brigade support. These tactical readjustments had left Colonel Oates more unsupported and isolated than ever before, as did the collapse from heat exhaustion or sunstroke of two Alabama Brigade regimental commanders, Colonel Jackson of the 47th Alabama, and Colonel Lawrence Houston Scruggs of the 4th Alabama. Therefore, as he was about to strike Little Round Top from the south, Colonel Oates remained on his own and with only a relative handful of men to do a job that needed at least a full brigade. With all things considered, it would seem as if Colonel Oates's Alabamians would have little chance for success in the upcoming struggle for possession of Little Round Top.[1]

Oates's task was formidible. The Alabama Rebels were facing a very good regiment. Most 20th Maine soldiers had been issued Enfield rifles in the autumn of 1862 upon their arrival in Washington, D.C., before marching to the seat of war. And in a letter, a confident Colonel Chamberlain had described how "I believe that no other Regt. will *ever* have the discipline we have now." And in a November 1862 letter, Chamberlain explained to his wife: "We are all in fine condition for a fight. To be sure our Regt. is now reduced to about 550. But what there are left are of the right sort." Ironically, after learning of a Rebel withdrawal during this same period, the Maine colonel had lamented in another letter how,

". . . our opportunity of glory will have to be put off." But now positioned on their rocky spur of Little Round Top, a greater "opportunity of glory" had been presented to Colonel Chamberlain than he could have possibly imagined only an hour before for "to lose [Little] Round Top would be fatal," penned one 16th Michigan soldier.[2]

To the 20th Maine's right stood the reliable veterans of the 83rd Pennsylvania. This fine regiment was a more experienced, tougher, and, hence, more dependable fighting force than the 20th Maine by the time of Gettysburg. Indeed, no Union regiment lost as many killed and mortally wounded in the war than the 83rd Pennsylvania except one. Like Colonel Chamberlain's regiment, the veterans of Captain Orpheus S. Woodward's 83rd Pennsylvania now "posted behind rocks and stones hastily thrown up for defense" would rise to the challenge of Little Round Top. However, the 83rd Pennsylvania's key role in the defense of Little Round Top has been ignored and forgotten by historians, who have focused almost exclusively on Colonel Chamberlain and the 20th Maine.

The 83rd Pennsylvania, in which Vincent had served as a young major in the war's beginning, was the most reliable and battle-hardened unit on the left wing of Colonel Vincent's brigade. These disciplined and finely drilled soldiers from the Lake Erie country were tough and had forged an unbreakable bond with the 44th New York at an early date. Consequently, these two regiments had fought beside each other on all the bloody Virginia and Maryland battlefields leading up to Gettysburg and that would not change on this day. When the initial brigade deployment was to have placed the 44th New York on the line's far right and beyond alignment with the 83rd Pennsylvania's right, the New Yorker's Colonel James C. Rice pleaded with Colonel Vincent, "Colonel, the Eighty-Third and Forty-fourth have always fought side by side in every battle, and I wish that they may do the same today." Understanding the psychological and moral advantage gained from such a realignment, Colonel Vincent ordered the redeployment. The 83rd Pennsylvania and the 44th New York standing in line beside each other ensured an even more tenacious defense of Little Round Top.[3]

And the veterans of the 83rd Pennsylvania were highly motivated, if not inspired by fighting on home soil. By this time, these Pennsylvanians were especially eager for a fight, because their own Keystone State was swarming with Rebels "who had invaded and desecrated their soil," wrote Captain Amos M. Judson, who commanded Company E, 83rd Pennsylvania. Clearly, by the time of Gettysburg, the combat record of the 20th Maine, which had joined the brigade during the Antietam campaign less than a year before, could not compare to that of the more experienced 83rd Pennsylvania.[4]

The 83rd Pennsylvania soldiers liked what they saw at Little Round Top, a strong defensive position on high ground. Captain Judson described Little Round Top as "an irregular rocky rise of ground, sloping down on two sides, (the front and rear) to low marshy ground [and] it consisted of a huge, solid rock, covered over with a thousand other loose boulders of every size and shape, and was most admirably adapted for a defensive position."[5]

Meanwhile, determined to roll-up the Federal left flank, Colonel Oates relentlessly pushed his exhausted soldiers through the trees and underbrush of the level saddle between the two Round Tops. One 83rd Pennsylvania officer described the saddle "between the two hills [which] was a small vale (not a ravine as it is commonly called) about a hundred feet in width, and covered with trees, but rather open and underbrushed." Unfortunately, for the 15th Alabama, "this vale [would shortly deserve renown as] the Valley of the Shadow of Death." Instead of rolling-up General Meade's flank with relative ease as expected, Colonel Oates and his 15th Alabama were about to run into the left of Colonel Vincent's brigade. The Maine Yankees braced for the storm with orders on this decisive day "to hold that ground at all hazards." Ironically, General Law also implored his hard-fighting Alabama soldiers that day "to hold the place at all hazards."

The upcoming clash between the Maine and Alabama soldiers would be one of the most desperate small unit actions of the war.

After making his bold independent decision—much like the earlier solo tactical decisions of both General Law and Colonel Oates—
to ascend Little Round Top on his own, the Pennsylvania-born
Colonel Vincent had wisely resisted the temptation of establishing
his defensive line along the crest of Little Round Top. Hence, the
defenders would not be exposed against the skyline to the sharpshooting Alabamians. Such a tactical error by the Harvard-educat-
ed colonel would have jeopardized the overall strength of his
defensive position, while bestowing upon the Alabama Rebels a
better opportunity to flank Vincent's brigade. Fortunately for the
Union, Colonel Vincent had made well-conceived defensive disposition of his four regiments along the high ground. Following
the lower edges of first the southern and then western slopes of
Little Round Top in a curved line which angled up, or north,
toward Little Round Top's crest to the north and to the 20th
Maine's right stood the 83rd Pennsylvania and the 44th New York
on the northwestern edge of the spur. Meanwhile, farther north up
the slope, or to the right, was deployed the 16th Michigan, which
anchored the brigade's right flank. And the key to Colonel
Vincent's position and the entire defensive line on Little Round
Top was the 20th Maine, which held the line's left flank.

As one blueclad soldier analyzed, "never in the history of war
was arrival more timely. The advent of Blucher's army on the field
of Waterloo was not more opportune to the exhausted English . . .
a further delay of half an hour for any cause and [the Union V
Corps's troops] would have found Little Round Top in Law's possession and Cemetery Ridge occupied by Longstreet and his
Confederates. The Army of the Potomac would have been split
into two fragments . . . and Lee master of the situation."[6]

Amid the thick foliage and trees of the level saddle of ground
nestled between the twin Round Tops, Colonel Oates and his
Alabamians pushed onward and ever-closer to the concealed positions of the 20th Maine and Colonel Vincent's brigade. With
loaded Enfield rifles, the stealthy Rebels eased north and toward
the southern base when heavy firing suddenly erupted to Colonel
Oates's left, opening the struggle for Little Round Top.

After unleashing the "Rebel Yell," the 4th Alabama launched a futile attack against the left-center of Vincent's brigade, which occupied the western and southwestern slope of Little Round Top. One 83rd Pennsylvania defender recorded how "the enemy had had his eye upon this position, but he was too late [and] he was now determined to atone for the loss by driving us out of it . . . on came the enemy, running and yelling like fiends . . ." Formerly occupying the Alabama Brigade's far left before the 44th and 48th Alabama's redeployment and now on the left of the seven 47th Alabama companies to Colonel Oates's left, the 4th Alabama ran straight into a blazing hot fire primarily from the 83rd Pennsylvania.

Much of the front rank of the 4th fell like tenpins from the scorching fire of the veteran Pennsylvania boys. Among the defenders who severely punished the 4th Alabama boys were the men of the 20th Maine's right. Against the blazing high ground of Little Round Top, the 4th Alabama veterans achieved few initial gains. As described by Captain Judson, commanding Company D, 83rd Pennsylvania: " . . . a sheet of smoke and flame burst from our whole line, which made the enemy reel and stagger, and fall back in confusion."

Likewise, to the 4th Alabama's left, the 5th and 4th Texas also ran into trouble. These Texas soldiers recoiled from a murderous fire principally from the 44th New York. One 4th Texas soldier, John C. West, described how the futile assault was made "over rocks and boulders and timber [against an] enemy [who] were thick and well concealed [and therefore] it was more like Indian fighting than anything that I experienced during the war [and] they had sharpshooters in trees and on high places that made it exceedingly dangerous to appear in any open place." The hard-hit Texans would continue to attack the hill, but with the same bloody results and for no gain. In short order to the Texans's right, meanwhile one-fourth of the attacking 4th Alabama were cut down by the Pennsylvanians's musketry.

After reaching Virginia in May 1861, these 4th Alabama soldiers had first made a name for themselves at First Bull Run, where they repulsed several Union attacks and played a role in driving the

Federals from the field on another hot July day two years earlier. The 4th Alabama brought a proud legacy to Gettysburg, having been the first Alabama regiment to see action, and losing one-third of its strength at First Bull Run. But the 4th Alabama's distinguished past and fine reputation as one of the "best drilled regiment[s] in the army" was not at all now benefiting Colonel Oates's effort to capture Little Round Top. Despite the repeated efforts of the 4th to take the hill, each attempt was hurled back. Worst of all for the 15th Alabama, the heavy punishment delivered upon the 4th Alabama and the repeated repulses ensured that this hard-hit regiment would provide little support on the left for Colonel Oates's attack when such assistance would be needed the most. But it was more than the blistering volleys that was now thwarting these 4th Alabama attackers. Like the 15th Alabama, this regiment was in poor condition for offensive operations and had already suffered losses from the ranks before receiving the first fire from Colonel Vincent's defenders. One 4th Alabama soldier wrote how:

> "When we arrived there many of our poor fellows were fainting and falling [including the regimental commander who passed out], overcome with heat and weariness, and in spite of exhortations from their officers, the men in line felt that they must lie down and rest awhile before making that second climb and storming the enemy's position on the crest. Thus our line stopped its advance, lay down among the rocks and bowlders, and simply returned the fire of the enemy ... while the leaden hailstorm poured down upon us and filled my eyes with grit and gravel knocked off the big rocks about me ... fate was against us there."

After the repeated repulses of the 4th Alabama, which included such hard-fighting companies as the "Canebrake Rifles," the "Conecuh Guards," and "the Magnolia Cadets," it was now even more exclusively the responsibility of Colonel Oates to inflict the damage necessary on General Meade's left to secure victory at Little Round Top before it was too late.[7]

Advancing with resolve up the southwestern face of Little Round Top to the 4th Alabama's right and the 15th Alabama's left the less than 150 soldiers from the seven 47th Alabama companies, consisting mostly of men from east central and northeast Alabama, experienced a comparable bloody fate as the assault extended southward contrary to plan. Hit by the flaming sheets of lead pouring from the high ground of Little Round Top, these Alabamians took a severe beating in only a few minutes. Continuing a process begun earlier in the advance, the systemic fragmentation of assault formations also continued to contribute to Confederate failure in this sector. The bloody repulse of the 47th Alabama resulted partly because these seven companies were disconnected from the 4th Alabama's right, sapping the assault's momentum and strength. Hence, the 47th Alabama's left was riddled by the flank fire from the 44th New York and the right of the 83rd Pennsylvania, which poured off the higher ground to the north. Knowing that his 47th Alabama was in trouble because of the loss of contact with the 15th Alabama, Colonel Bulger was upset and for good reason. Therefore, when he received verbal orders from Thomas L. Christian of General Law's staff, to once again "charge that line," Colonel Bulger replied, "Tell General Law that I am charging to the best of my ability [and] for God's sake put in the Fifteenth upon my right and, my life for it, we'll drive them when we come to them!"

Then once again leading his 47th Alabama soldiers forward without the support of Colonel Oates's regiment on his right, the gray-haired Colonel Bulger was in the forefront of the attack. In his own words, when his Alabamians "emerged from the boulders that thickly dotted the declivity they engaged in a hand to hand conflict with the federals [and I] jumped upon a rock, waved [my] sword and cheered the boys on in the charge. While [my] sword was waving in [my] left hand [I] was struck by a ball which entered the left breast, passed directly through the lung and lodged under the muscle of the left shoulder [nevertheless I] steadied [myself] stepped back a few paces and eased . . . down by a tree that jutted out from the crevices of the rock." Colonel Bulger had suffered his third wound within the year.

Attacking uphill against the flaming slopes of Little Round Top, the 47th Alabama soldiers received a brutal enfilade fire, which would play a role in reducing Oates's chances for success. Soldiers of the 83rd Pennsylvania and the 20th Maine's right raked the exposed and vulnerable left of the 47th Alabama with a vicious fire. However, fighting spirit remained among the hard-hit 47th Alabama despite their second repulse. In the words of Captain Judson, 83rd Pennsylvania: "But soon rallying they advanced again to the assault [and] taking position behind the rocks, they poured in a deadly fire upon our troops [and] hundreds of them approached even within fifteen yards of our line, but they approached only to be shot down or hurled back covered with gaping wounds."

Assistance to the 15th Alabama from these 47th Alabama troops had been effectively minimized for the remainder of the day. Colonel Bulger's survivors took cover behind the rocks and boulders along the southwestern slope of Little Round Top, and continued to exchange fire with the Pennsylvania and Maine defenders. Now those 20th Maine soldiers on Colonel Chamberlain's right soon turned to shoot down Colonel Oates's men after repulsing the 47th Alabama.

Both the 47th Alabama's disconnect from Oates's left and the third repulse of the day were a serious setback on the 15th Alabama's left, ensuring that the Alabamians would be even more on their own. Despite a host of disadvantages and decreasing chances for victory, however, the possibility of achieving a decisive success yet existed if Colonel Oates could hurl Colonel Vincent's brigade off the high ground of Little Round Top by first unhinging the anchor of the brigade's line, the 20th Maine.

As ascertained by the increased and deafening volume of gunfire echoing across Little Round Top to the north, the 15th Alabama was about to be met by a barrage of fire from the Maine bluecoats. Colonel Oates lamented that the 20th Maine had "reached this position ten minutes before my arrival, and they piled a few rocks from boulder to boulder, making the zigzag line more complete, and were concealed behind it ready to receive us."

Hidden amid the thick underbrush and scrub oak along the rocky southern slope of the spur, these Maine soldiers were now well concealed in what were in fact entrenched positions on high ground. Major Spear described how the 20th Maine's "front was open and rocky and the west face [of Little Round Top was] like a broken down wall of boulders, large & small [while] the crest and the eastern slope were covered with open woods, and scattered over with boulders . . . from our position, the ground sloped to the south [and] our line thus formed on the higher part of the slope partly amongst boulders, and with boulders and trees on the sloping front . . ." Colonel Chamberlain's men took full advantage of the bountiful defensive assets of the rough terrain, making a strong natural position even more formidable.

Colonel Oates would have felt less confident had he known of the firm resolve of the Maine bluecoats that afternoon as the result of his counterpart's orders. Colonel Chamberlain implored his defenders along the high ground with a grim determination which indicated the serious work that lay ahead: "Boys hold this hill!" at all costs. Consequently, the Maine soldiers were determined to stand firm much like the Alabama soldiers they faced. Private Theodore Gerrish explained how "Little Round Top was [now the great] prize [and] every soldier seemed to understand the situation, and to be inspired by its danger."

Enhancing his defensive stance, Colonel Chamberlain wisely did not make the mistake of underestimating the fighting capabilities of the Rebels before him while overestimating his own soldiers' fighting prowess. In fact, he respected his enemy, writing in one letter how, "I expect[ed] a hard fight [as] they are admirably handled & fight with desperation."

But what Colonel Chamberlain was about to witness would far exceed anything that he had previously seen on any battlefield in terms of Confederate desperation to do or die. Major Spear, a schoolteacher from the community of Wiscasset, Maine, and another Bowdoin College alumni like his esteemed colonel, felt much like Chamberlain, believing that "the confederates were better commanded and better fitted for war [and] were on the whole of superior material for soldiers." Perhaps Private Gerrish best described the tactical situation at Little Round Top: "Imagine . . . three hundred men on the extreme flank of an army, there to hold the key of the entire position!"

The cultured, idealistic, and well-educated Colonel Chamberlain was about to meet his counterpart who was a very different type of man—more hot-tempered, pugnacious, and emotional than intellectual and scholarly. However, these two determined commanders from opposite ends of the republic possessed a number of common characteristics which would fuel the tenacity of the upcoming struggle for Little Round Top. Both leaders possessed a religious-like zeal which ensured a level of fanatical fighting, including hand-to-hand combat, which would be almost unmatched in this war. Both the Alabamians and Maine soldiers were determined to do or die today to fulfill their respective missions of capturing and holding the hill to the bitter end. It would be this moral and righteous intensity instilled by Oates and Chamberlain to their troops which would in part result in one of the most savage small-unit actions of the war. Clearly, both leaders were zealous crusaders for their respective causes. As the Alabamians believed they were defending the Deep South by pushing north of the Potomac, so the 20th Maine soldiers, wrote Major Spear, were inspired by defending Northern soil which "had [a] great affect in raising the spirits of the men [who were] now marching to battle in defence of our own."

Ironically, the final outcome of this greatest clash on the North American continent would perhaps be determined during this upcoming small-unit clash at the far end of both armies. And more than the famous generals now far away at their headquarters, the struggle for Little Round Top would be conducted and decided by civilian-soldiers and the common fighting men of the 20th Maine and the 15th Alabama. And the upcoming struggle for possession of Little Round Top would also primarily be a showdown between Colonels Oates and Chamberlain. In the next few hours, the final outcome of the battle of Gettysburg rested solely on the correctness, timeliness, and wisdom of the tactical decisions of these two young former teachers. And as in so many wars, a good many young men were about to die for possession of an obscure plot of ground which had relatively little meaning or significance only a few hours before. No one on either side yet knew the name of the eerie-looking hill of rock, underbrush, and timber, which no soldier in either blue or gray would ever forget after bloody July 2, 1863.[8]

One 83rd Pennsylvania officer wrote, "The enemy had everything to gain if they carried the position [and] everything to lose if they failed, and they fought most desperately and determinedly." These Alabama veterans had never yet tasted defeat, and were determined not to do so at Gettysburg.[9]

If the young ambitious attorney in gray who had so zealously upheld the law in Abbeville and firmly opposed secession in righteous indignation only a few years before could strike a blow to turn the Union army's left and if that success could be exploited by Lee's army, then the life of the new nation would be ensured. All that William C. Oates now had to do was to push the 20th Maine off this hill, capture the spur of Little Round Top, and turn the left flank of the Army of the Potomac to open the door to a decisive success.

Thus before his advancing soldiers as usual after he directed them to move by the right flank after reaching the foot of Big Round Top, Colonel Oates was now moving forward through the timber between the Round Tops perhaps with the unforgettable words of General Law's instructions yet ringing in his head to remind him of the importance of his responsibility and mission: " . . . to lose no time, but to press forward and drive everything before me as far as possible." All the while, the musketry to the northwest on the southwestern and western side of Little Round Top continued to roar. However, the southern end of Little Round Top remained bathed in quiet and few Yankees could be seen.

All illusions of easy victory for Colonel Oates, however, instantly vanished forever when the southern slope of Little Round Top suddenly exploded with fire and flame. A point-blank volley from the high ground was unleashed into the midst of the

15th Alabama soldiers, who were sandwiched and caught on the low ground of the saddle between the Round Tops.

Initiating this crucial small-unit action at the southern end of both armies, the Maine volley exploded from the jumble of rocks, trees, and thick green foliage along the southern edge of Little Round Top with a vengeance. In Company H's ranks, Private Gerrish described how with the blinding explosion of musketry, the flaming battle line of the 20th Maine "was mantled in fire and smoke." This unexpected fire could not have been more devastating to Colonel Oates's soldiers who were caught at a disadvantage on the low ground.

Colonel Oates never forgot the surreal horror of that first murderous volley from the hidden rows of Springfield and Enfield rifles of the 20th Maine and the left of the 83rd Pennsylvania, which punished the 15th Alabama as never before: ". . . they piled a few rocks [together to form a breastwork and consequently] were concealed behind it ready to receive us [and] from behind this [rocky] ledge, unexpectedly to us, because concealed, they poured into us the most destructive fire I ever saw."

However, this defensive strongpoint was not in reality a rocky ledge as described by the veterans on both sides after the war. Instead, it was the rocky southern edge of Little Round Top's slope immediately above its wooded base and above the level ground of the timbered saddle. Corporal Elisha Coan, of the 20th Maine's colorguard, described how hundreds of these Maine veterans were aligned before the "slight descent fringed by ledges of rock & our side of the hill was covered with boulders. Beyond this line of ledge and other rocks the eye could not penetrate on account of the dense foliage of bushes," which choked the level, wooded ground between the two Round Tops. Hard-hit at the southern base of Little Round Top, Colonel Oates's Alabamians were now paying a high price for General Longstreet's delays, the breakdown of the effectiveness of Southern leadership, and the disjointed offensive effort by both General Law's Alabama Brigade and Hood's Division, which allowed for the timely arrival of these V Corps units now holding strong defensive positions across Little Round Top.

Caught by surprise with the sudden explosion of fire, Colonel Oates was shocked by the terrible destructiveness of this initial volley. He had expected to encounter—at most—only a Union skirmish line. Such a skirmish line could have been quickly brushed aside by Colonel Oates's hardened veterans before they overran Little Round Top and plunged into General Meade's vulnerable flank and rear. Without the reliable graycoat skirmishers of Company A leading the way as usual, the 15th Alabama had once again walked into what in effect was an ambush. This scorching fire from the blazing Maine and Pennsylvania rifles was not only at close range but was also a plunging fire. Pouring downhill, this first great volley swept off the higher ground to rake the Alabama soldiers without mercy.

Colonel Oates later explained the superiority of the elevated position of the double ranks of Maine and Pennsylvania defenders, blasting away from behind good cover. These New England and Pennsylvania bluecoats were perched on "an irregular ledge of rocks—a splendid line of natural breastworks running about parallel with the front of the Forty-seventh [Alabama] regiment and my four left companies, and then sloping back in front of my center and right at an angle of about thirty-five or forty degrees." But Oates responded with alacrity. Awakened to reality, the confident Alabama soldiers had learned a hard lesson about not sending out skirmishers to lead the way. The unexpected and sudden fury from the point-blank volley exploding from the rocky, timbered spur was not enough to panic or repulse Colonel Oates's hard-hit soldiers, however. Such a surprise by a devastating volley at close range from large numbers of Federals well-concealed on commanding high ground would have been enough to wreck the cohesion of many other isolated regiments without support.[10]

But the disciplined Alabama soldiers held firm under the brutal punishment, even while the torrents of bullets pouring off the high ground was "so destructive that my line wavered like a man trying to walk against a strong wind," recalled Colonel Oates. These Alabama veterans, yet isolated and on their own, refused to break under the wrath of the leaden storm. Colonel

Oates was never more proud of his soldiers' discipline than now. He wrote with admiration how "our line halted, but did not break. As men fell their comrades closed the gap, returning the fire most spiritedly."

Colonel Oates now sorely missed the almost one-fifth of his regiment he no longer had. The earlier loss of the water detail of twenty-two men and the absence of Company A's detached skirmishers sapped the 15th Alabama's strength. Combined with the casualties lost from the contest with Colonel Berdan's Sharpshooters at the stone wall at the foot of Big Round Top, the 15th Alabama was seriously undermanned for the formidable task of hurling the 20th Maine off the high ground. An embittered Colonel Oates would lament that "when [Captain Shaaff] could not capture the Union ordnance train he should have speedily rejoined the regiment in its assault on Little Round Top [but] instead he remained with his company concealed in the woods but three hundred yards distant."

In addition, Colonel Oates lacked other key support when he needed it the most. The three skirmish companies of the 47th Alabama likewise were absent from the battle line, having moved farther away from Little Round Top. Consequently, Colonel Oates could now count on less than four hundred 15th Alabama soldiers to mount his supreme effort to capture Little Round Top and turn the left flank of the Army of the Potomac. And now many of these Alabamians were already down, either killed or wounded after the 20th Maine's first volley at close range.[11]

Withstanding the initial punishment delivered at point-blank range by Colonel Chamberlain's defenders, the 15th Alabama recoiled without giving ground. Colonel Oates was not surprised that his crack regiment did not falter because it had never done so before. An experienced commander made more effective by tactical flexibility, Colonel Oates now realized that he had encountered a sizable force of Yankees when he had thought that this hill was unoccupied. By demonstrating coolness and discipline amid the tempest, "as men fell their comrades closed the gap [in the hardhit lines], returning fire most spiritedly," the handsome, young

colonel in a gray, double-breasted uniform stood tall before his soldiers while under the shadow of the blazing muskets of the 20th
Maine. Ignoring the hail of lead, Colonel Oates inspired and
encouraged his boys with his exposed presence before the line,
shouting and waving his saber so that his soldiers would not falter.[12]

And once again, the hard-earned experience of the average
Alabama Rebel in the enlisted ranks rose to the fore with so many
good officers cut down. These veterans knew how to respond to an
emergency, and now they went to work in business-like fashion
without being told. The Alabamians's natural initiative and fighting instincts began to take over, allowing the Alabama Rebel to
quickly recover from the shock of the first volley and return fire
with spirit.

One such inspirational leader with considerable combat expe-
rience who took charge in this crisis was forty-six-year-old
Sergeant Josiah J. Wofford. He was a savvy veteran of the Mexican
War and one of the oldest and most experienced men in the 15th
Alabama. The inspirational example of natural leaders like
Sergeant Wofford helped to stabilize the regiment now caught in
its worst fix.[13]

Clearly, Colonel Oates did not like the looks of this fight, after
having been caught by surprise and with his men dropping
around him. The colonel's regiment was now caught on low
ground which made maneuvering with precision almost impossible, as well as escape from the scorching fire pouring off the high
ground. He realized that his regiment was now forced to fight
back under a host of disadvantages and handicaps in contrast to
the 20th Maine which enjoyed the advantage of the good defensive positions on high ground. Explaining how the murderous fire
from hundreds of Maine rifles continued to sweep downhill from
the maze of rocks and trees with a lethal effectiveness, Private
Jordan lamented the tactical disadvantage in simple common soldier terms: " . . . they could see every movement we made, they
would shoot down, we would have to elevate our guns . . . the
enemy had the drop on us . . ." All the while, the rapid "reports of

their rifles sounded like a canebrake on fire," described Private Jordan of the high volume of fire sweeping off Little Round Top.[14]

The roar of the Maine rifles echoed from men using two different types of rifled muskets which were effective killing machines. At this time, around one-third of the 20th Maine was armed with Springfield rifles and the remaining two-third with Enfields—the finely balanced and reliable weapons of choice. In the hands of veterans, these rifled muskets steadily unleashed a steady hail of lead, raking the Alabama soldiers who were trapped in the narrow saddle of level ground between the two Round Tops. An avalanche of bullets tore through saplings and underbrush to thud into the chests, shoulders, and thighs of Oates's men. The lead minie balls from the Maine rifles did extensive damage at such close range, ripping into flesh and smashing bone.

While the soldiers of the 15th Alabama's right directly below what became known as Vincent's Spur gamely held their ground and returned fire despite the heavy losses, Colonel Oates's left took a severe beating. On the more open ground strewn with boulders on the southwestern slope of the spur, the Alabamians suffered the same bloody fate as the repulsed 4th Alabama farther to the left. The survivors of Company B, 15th Alabama, on the left flank, finally took cover to escape the storm of lead. Then they fought back as best they could under difficult circumstances, loading and firing in return. But here the 15th Alabama's advance on the left was effectively blunted.

After already having passed safely through a hail of lead from the Sharps rifles of Berdan's Sharpshooters, Private Jordan described the grim situation in his hard-hit sector on the 15th Alabama's left: "I succeeded in getting to the base of [the] mountain untouched. Immediately Sandy McMillan, Ben Kendrick, and Sam Kendrick attempted to follow me. The first two soldiers . . . . fell killed about 30 feet in my rear, the latter at the same time was wounded in the foot, but succeeded in getting to me. There was eight of us that had succeeded in getting to a large rock at the base of the mountain [and] one of the eight had been wounded in the foot." On the 15th Alabama's embattled left, "we had a duel for about half an hour, the enemy being behind rocks on the side of the ridge [and] at the base."

Twenty-two-year-old A. P. or "Sandy" McMillan was often sick but he had recently recovered sufficiently to now charge up the hill to receive his death stroke. And the two Kendrick boys from Barbour County were also both cut down by the murderous fire, with only one destined to survive his wounds. However, the other surviving Kendrick boys in Company B's ranks—except Henry Jefferson Kendrick who had died the previous winter of disease— William B., twenty-one-year-old Private Daniel L., and Private Robert Samuel Kendrick, a teenager, continued to battle the Yankees from Maine. Soon hit by a rain of bullets, Sam went down with a broken leg, dropping among the big rocks covering the southwestern slope of the spur of Little Round Top.[15]

One teenage Maine soldier, Corporal Coan, described the superior defensive advantages of the Maine veterans on the high ground for "our side of the hill was covered with boulders. Beyond this line of ledge and other rocks . . . the eye could not penetrate on account of the dense foliage of bushes." From this natural breastwork, strengthened with piled-up rocks to form a defense line linking boulder to boulder among the twisted tangles of underbrush and trees, along the elevated southern edge of the wooded spur, the steadfast Maine veterans continued to pour forth a deadly sheet of flame. This plunging fire swept the level saddle with a deadly torrent of bullets, striking more Alabama Rebels.[16]

However, the scorching fire cutting the 15th Alabama to pieces only served as a catalyst for a greater effort by Colonel Oates to rise to the challenge. Instead of pulling back, the young colonel knew that he could not relinquish ground at the base of Little Round Top if the effort to yet somehow turn the left flank of the Union army was to succeed. Despite the punishment, Colonel Oates refused to retire as many other commanders in a comparable no-win situation would surely have done. Instead he continued to encourage his boys to stand firm and to keep up the fire as hot and as heavy as possible. Now increasing numbers of Maine soldiers began to be hit by .577 caliber balls from Enfield rifles and more bluecoats fell over the rocks and trees after tasting the Alabama lead which swept the spur.

Meanwhile, Colonel Oates surveyed the confused tactical situation as it slowly began to reveal itself through the layers of drifting smoke of battle and heavy foliage of summer. Soon he could see that the punishment delivered by his rapidly firing Alabamians at close range was beginning to unhinge a portion of the 20th Maine's line: "I could see through the smoke men of the 20th Maine in front of my right wing running from tree to tree back westward toward the main body . . . "

It was this sector which took the heaviest punishment from the blazing Enfield rifles of the Alabamians. Here, the Alabama Rebels prevailed in a deadly duel of attrition. In his battle report, Colonel Oates described the intoxicating moment of success amid the tangled, bloody, and smoke-drenched woodlands at the southern base of Little Round Top. "After firing two or three rounds, I discovered that the enemy were giving way in my front . . ." Despite the fact that the 47th Alabama's support on his left was defensive rather than offensive after its bloody repulse before the volleys sweeping off the southwestern side of Little Round Top, Colonel Oates was now determined to launch an aggressive effort to turn the Union army's left flank. Therefore, he now made adroit tactical adjustments to not only resume the offensive and regain the initiative but also to exploit his hard-won advantage. After formulating a bold plan, Colonel Oates led most of his Alabamians eastward on the double in a column of fours.[17]

With a haste born of desperation, Colonel Oates encouraged his troops to move swiftly by the right flank through the wooded and brushy hollow between the two Round Tops. While the sound of clanging gear of these graycoat flankers made a metallic clatter that could be heard despite the noise of roaring rifles, Colonel Oates wisely kept a front rank in position, loading and firing, to mask the flanking movement to the right. Penetrating deeper into the Union army's rear, Colonel Oates's bold gamble in maneuvering eastward through the length of the wooded saddle between the Round Tops held the promise of victory.

Later, one member of Colonel Vincent's brigade explained how this was no ordinary flanking movement. Indeed, most of all, "success there [was now] opened to [Colonel Oates]—vantage ground from which to operate on the flank and rear of our entire army." As the clanging of gear rattled over the southern base of Little Round Top, the Alabamians sprinted through the suffocating heat and woodlands choking the saddle. The sweating grayclads raced farther throught the thick green foliage of summer, surging eastward in their attempt to out-flank Colonel Chamberlain's stubborn regiment.

While pushing on the double to the right, Colonel Oates sensed the promise of a successful flanking maneuver as the level land to the east skirting the southern base, or spur, of Little Round Top gradually dipped eastward amid the thick woods between the Round Tops. This gradually sloping ground gave Colonel Oates a natural low-lying avenue by which his Alabamians could ease around the southern base of Little Round Top to get into a position to strike and turn the 20th Maine's left flank. More than anything else Oates was determined that "the name Gettysburg might only [be] known in history as that of the place where the Union cause made its grave."[18]

However, as fate would have it, Colonel Oates's rapid flanking movement eastward was not unobserved by the sharp-eyed lumbermen, loggers, woodsmen, and fisherman of the 20th Maine. These were men who knew how to hunt with skill in the hardwood forests of Maine and had considerable experience in spotting the slight flicking of a wary white-tailed buck's ear in the dense woods or a moose hidden in a thicket on a distant hillside. Consequently, they now spied flashes of rapid movement amid the jungled saddle below them.

In the ranks of Company H, Private Gerrish described the unnerving moment when, "'Look!' exclaimed half a hundred men in our regiment at the same moment; and no wonder, for right in our front, between us and our skirmishers [of Company B], whom they have probably captured, we see the lines of the enemy. They have paid no attention to the rest of the brigade stationed on our right, but they are rushing on, determined to turn and crush the left of our line."

In addition, at least one officer, Captain Orpheus S. Woodward standing on the high ground on the far left of the 83rd Pennsylvania, also spied Oates's not-so-stealthy movement through the low ground of the woodlands. He instantly realized that the target of the flankers was the 20th Maine's left flank, and dispatched a messenger to notify the Maine men in that sector of the danger. Captain Woodward knew that if Colonel Chamberlain's left flank was turned, then he would suddenly have a good many Johnny Rebs in the rear of his 83rd Pennsylvania. The Pennylvania courier returned to Captain Woodward with a request from Colonel Chamberlain for an 83rd Pennsylvania company to extend its line to bolster his left flank. With the 4th and 47th Alabama in his front, however, Captain Woodward declined to send any assistance to the 20th Maine. In regard to receiving reinforcements, both Colonels Chamberlain and Oates were now both on their own.

Commanding the five companies on the 20th Maine's left where "we were placed to guard against flank attack," Major Spear never forgot the moment when "the first indication of the presence of the enemy was the sudden appearance of their line of battle. Emerging from the woody side of Big Round Top, they burst through the bushes down the steep slope [and] I saw their legs first. They were so far to the left that they seemed about to overlap and flank us. They had not opened fire, and evidently had missed our skirmish line [Captain Morrell's Company B], which had gone too far to the left [to take position behind the stone wall]."

Colonel Chamberlain's soldiers now understood the full extent of the serious threat brewing in the smokey woodlands before them at the southern base of Little Round Top. With Alabama Rebels on the move, Private Gerrish wrote how Colonel Oates's flanking movement "was to turn and crush our left flank [as General Lee had] crushed our right at Chancellorsville." Leading the regiment for the first time in a major battle after becoming colonel in May 1863, Chamberlain might have had second thoughts about having written to his wife, Fanny, less than three months before how, "the most that troubles me now is that I may not be able to take part in the next fight."

Knowing that they were witnessing a flanking maneuver, the foremost Maine bluecoats continued to contemplate the implications of the rapid Rebel movements flickering between the trees, while watching the gray and butternut shapes darting eastward amid the dense green foliage of July. The blur of Confederate troop movements in the wooded valley between the two hills continued to be ascertained by these vigilant Maine soldiers, despite the front-rank Alabamians continuing to blast away to provide their masking fire. The startling news that a good many Alabama Rebels were now attempting to flank the Maine regiment's left was first relayed to Colonel Chamberlain by Lieutenant James Henry Nickols of Company K, which held the regiment's center.

Described by Colonel Chamberlain as "a brave & energetic officer," Lieutenant Nickols, who possessed a passion for liquor which had caused him to remain a lieutenant instead of a captain more than once, spied Rebel movement as easily as he could find a bottle of whiskey. Out-of-breath and excited, the lieutenant informed the Maine colonel that "something queer was going on in his front, behind those engaging us." Alarmed by the news and despite bullets whizzing by, Colonel Chamberlain immediately jumped atop a large rock to ascertain the truth of the alarming report of Alabama Rebels moving rapidly to flank the 20th Maine. There, in the midst of the firing line, he assessed the tactical situation before him as best he could from the embattled spur. Confirming his worst fears, the Maine colonel now saw what he dreaded most of all: a good many Alabama veterans moving on the double from his right to left in an attempt to turn his left flank.

About the same time, Major Spear from the regiment's left likewise informed Chamberlain that he saw Rebels on the move in his front. Major Spear not only explained the situation to his colonel but more important, he proposed a tactical solution to the 20th Maine's dilemma: " . . . I went quickly over to him and advised him of the situation, suggesting that it seemed best to bend back two companies to meet the threat upon that flank." At this moment of crisis for the 20th Maine at the far end of the Union line, Colonel Chamberlain never forgot how "thick groups in gray were pushing up along the smooth dale between the Round Tops in a direction to gain our left flank. There was no mistaking this. If they could hold our attention by a hot fight in front while they got in force on that flank, it would be bad for us and our whole defence."

Already Colonel Oates had accomplished more than simply swinging his men eastward on the double in a routine redeployment. Most important in tactical terms, he had turned and also advanced his 15th Alabama soldiers northward through the woods of relatively level ground to gain an advanced position on the eastern side of Little Round Top's southern spur, after pushing sufficiently far enough eastward through the saddle between the Round Tops. There, on the 15th Alabama's newly formed right, the Rebels had finally gained an advanced and more elevated position from which they could launch their attack. Despite adjusting to a host of disadvantages, Colonel Oates had finally gained the tactical advantage.[19]

CHAPTER XI

Turning the Left Flank

"I again ordered the advance, and knowing the officers and men of that gallant old regiment, I felt sure that they would follow their commander anywhere in the line of duty. I passed through the line waving my sword, shouting, 'Forward, men, to the ledge!' and was promptly followed by the command in splendid style."

—Colonel Oates describing the final Confederate
assault up Little Round Top

*A*fter swinging on the double eastward and then northward sufficiently to convince him that he had now gained an advantageous position beyond the left flank of the 20th Maine, Colonel Oates possessed his vantage point from which to strike his long-awaited blow. He now took immediate action to launch a strike to push the Maine Yankees off Little Round Top once and for all and prepared to strike westward to drive the Yankees from their strong defensive positions on the high ground.

Leaping atop a large rock to inspire his men, Colonel Oates hoped that his band of soldiers, despite exhaustion, lack of water, and low ammunition, could yet deliver the coup-de-grace into the left flank and rear of Colonel Chamberlain's regiment. Now only forty to fifty feet distance from the well-positioned Maine soldiers, the thin line of Alabama Rebels was now extended so far eastward as to completely lap around and cover the length of the southern base of Little Round Top, and then angled northward along the lower and gradually sloping terrain to face the southeastern base of Little Round Top.

As Colonel Oates explained the tactical situation at this time and the new set of orders given to his left flank: "Just as the [seven] Forty-seventh companies were being driven back, I ordered my regiment to change direction to the left [to face toward the west], swing around, and drive the Federals from the ledge of rocks, for the purpose of enfilading their line, relieving the Forty-seventh Alabama—gain the enemy's rear, and drive him from the hill. My men obeyed and advanced about half way to the enemy's position, but the fire was so destructive that my line wavered like a man try-ing to walk against a strong wind . . ." Once again, the scorching musketry of the Maine defenders was devastating, inflicting severe punishment on the Alabamians who continued to fight under less cover and at a greater disadvantage than their opponent.

Meanwhile, most of the 15th Alabama, the right and right-cen-ter, surged forward pushing up the wooded eastern slope of the spur. Besides the flanking movement, urgent tactical necessities elsewhere on the field now resulted in the over-extension of Colonel Oates's already thin line, including the faltering assaults of the seven 47th Alabama companies to Colonel Oates's left. Striking repeatedly, Colonel Bulger's attacking companies had angled off, shifting farther north and away from the 15th Alabama's left while assaulting the southwestern side of Little Round Top northwest of the 15th Alabama. Against each offensive effort, the 83rd Pennsyl-vania and 44th New York soldiers "stood as firm as the rocks by which they fought [and even] the drummers had thrown aside their drums, seized the musket, and taken their place in the ranks." This 47th Alabama repulse to his regiment's left additionally diminished Colonel Oates's overall strength, reducing his offensive capabilities. Hence, the already slim chances of turning Colonel Chamberlain's left were now even less likely with the over-extension of the 15th Alabama ranks at both ends of the line.[1]

Unfortunately for the 15th Alabama, the 20th Maine's vulnerability on its left as first ascertained by Colonel Oates now no longer existed. Played out on a much smaller scale on Little Round Top, this tactical scenario was in some ways not unlike the tactical situation—attempting to strike a flank that was no longer a flank—which had negated General Lee's original offensive plan of July 2.

Despite the rough terrain, the confusion, thick smoke of battle, and the Alabamians's hot fire, Colonel Chamberlain had already made adroit tactical adjustments. Acting on the sound tactical advice of Major Spear, Chamberlain changed fronts at the last moment to counter Colonel Oates's flanking movement. To checkmate Colonel Oates's latest maneuver to gain a permanent tactical advantage on the rocky hill, he ordered his left wing to the left-rear to redeploy on higher ground and behind the good cover of a rocky ledge to take advantage of the natural contour of the slope a short distance rearward, while extending the line by forming the troops in a single rank. With the Union regiments on his right engaged and under heavy pressure, he also extended his right wing to take position along the trees and rocks to cover a wider front.

To protect the left flank of not only the Maine regiment but also Colonel Vincent's entire hardpressed brigade, the Maine colonel successfully bent back the left wing of his line, under Major Spear, to form a right angle to meet Colonel Oates and his men. All of this was accomplished while the 20th Maine soldiers maintained a hot fire which continued to inflict damage among the attackers. Colonel Chamberlain's tactical manuever was disguised by the thick smoke and summer foliage, and the Alabamians knew nothing of the Maine line's realignment across the rocky spur.

As Colonel Chamberlain explained the tactical adjustment amid the heat of battle: "Keeping this movement of the enemy from the knowledge of my men, I immediately had my right wing take intervals by the left flank at 3 to 5 paces according to the shelter afforded by the rocks & trees, thus covering the whole front then engaged; & moved my left wing to the left & rear making nearly a right angle at the color guard company [F] this movement was so admirably executed by my men, that our fire was not materially slackened in front, while the left wing was taking its new position." Thanks to this successful last-minute tactical adjustment that extended his front to cover a wider area, Colonel Chamberlain was now able to protect his vulnerable left flank, which had been dangling in mid-air only minutes before.

Adroitly meeting Colonel Oates's tactical challenge, Colonel Chamberlain employed the refused Company F, the reliable color company, as the pivot at the southernmost point of the Maine line after the rapid extension and bending back of the left. Private Gerrish described how "Colonel Chamberlain with rare sagacity understood the [flank] movement they were making, and bent back the left flank of our regiment until the line formed almost a right angle with the colors at the [key] point . . ."

After successfully shifting the left half of his regiment to face east and closer to the regiment's right half to better defend not only the left flanks of both Vincent's brigade and the Army of the Potomac but also the rear of Colonel Vincent's defensive line, Colonel Chamberlain's regiment was now in a more advantageous position to receive Colonel Oates's next assault, checkmating his bid to out-flank the 20th Maine. Even more, the 47th Alabama's already disadvantageous situation on Colonel Oates's left was made even more precarious by Colonel Chamberlain's extension of his regiment's right wing in a more lengthy line to face west. In addition and in response to Colonel Chamberlain's timely realignment, the 83rd Pennsylvania also extended its line to the left "in cooperation with [the] leftward move of the 20th, permitting the Maine men to take a position that protected the left flank of the brigade and . . . the left of the whole Army of the Potomac."

Company F continued to pay a high price for playing the key role of anchoring the 20th Maine's defensive line, however, Company F would be decimated by the Alabamians's fire and repeated attacks up the hill. This advanced, or southernmost, position of the 20th Maine was transformed into an embattled salient.

Bolstered by the hardest fighting and most reliable veterans of Company F, this exposed salient pointed toward the southern base of Little Round Top. With Company F serving as the anchor, Colonel Chamberlain's rapid tactical adjustment to counter Colonel Oates's flanking movement to gain the 20th Maine's left flank resulted in a more compact defensive line. And this stronger and more compressed Union line was now solidly aligned along the high ground with Company F anchoring the entire defensive position, incorporating the best defensive positions among the maze of rocks, brush, and trees.

In tactical terms, Colonel Oates had been thwarted in only a matter of minutes. Corporal Coan described the swiftness of the manuever that consisted of "a left backward wheel of the left wing of the regt. with the colors for a pivot. This movement was quickly made. Then our left wing faced nearly at a right angle with the original line and with the right wing which retained its original position. This left the colors in the salient formed by these two facings." With the refused left wing of the 20th Maine now positioned almost at a right angle to the regiment's right wing, Colonel Chamberlain's new defensive line offered a more formidable challenge and obstacle for the fulfillment of Colonel Oates's tactical strategy.

Now the open end of the horseshoe-shaped Union line faced north, following the rocky and timbered contours of the spur at the southern slope of Little Round Top near its base. As the Alabamians approached, this recently refused left wing now stood firm facing east and parallel to the right wing's line, which now looked to the west. The 20th Maine's line was cut through the middle by the length of the north-south-running main ridge line of the spur with both sections firing in opposite directions and beyond the sight of the other.

Thanks to the refusing of the 20th Maine's defensive line, the 15th Alabama's already slim chances to turn the Union army's left flank became even more remote. From right to left and extending north beyond the color-guard soldiers of Company F, the refused Companies A, H, C, and G of Major Spear's left wing now held dominant firing positions on the high ground and behind another rocky ledge even farther and higher up the timbered and rocky slope. Company G anchored the extreme left of the 20th Maine's line. Thwarted by his tactically flexible counterpart and his quick maneuver of refusing the blue line, Colonel Oates seemingly would simply not have enough men to extend his own line sufficiently to turn the Maine regiment's left flank. Nevertheless, Colonel Oates and his depleted 15th Alabama were far from finished in their efforts to drive the Yankees off Little Round Top despite the tactical countermaneuvers and adjustments of the 20th Maine.[2]

Eager to strike a blow as quickly as possible from the east to exploit his flanking maneuver, Colonel Oates screamed "Charge!" He ordered his attackers forward after estimating that he had gained an advantageous position from which to smash into not only the 20th Maine's left flank but also Colonels Chamberlain's and Vincent's rear. With battle flags limp amid the July heat and humidity and suffocating smoke, the Alabamians on the center and right now surged toward Colonel Chamberlain's left wing. As Colonel Chamberlain described the situation, it was "not more than two minutes elapsed before the enemy came up in column of Regiments with an impetuosity . . . "

Besides having been checkmated by Colonel Chamberlain's refusing of his defensive line, probably now less than three hundred 15th Alabama men attacked the spur from both the east and south. With Colonel Oates encouraging his men forward waving a saber, the onrushing Alabama soldiers, "having speedily recovered [from the effect of the first fires] rush[ed] to the assault with the earnestness of men who have never encountered an obstacle without breaking it down." As if unleashed from a bent-up coil which had been tightly wound, the cheering Alabamians rolled uphill through the drifting smoke with bayonets flashing in the afternoon light.

Captain James M. Ellison, the twenty-four-year-old commander of the "Macon County Commissioners," who had earned his promotion to captain during the previous July, now led Company C forward through the bullets. Commanding Colonel Oates's third company from the left, Captain Ellison encouraged his Macon

County attackers into the face of the hottest fire streaming from the spur's southern end and toward Colonel Chamberlain's color company. By this time, the unceasing roar of battle had reached a volume "so great," wrote Colonel Oates, that Captain Ellison did "not understand me and put his hand to his ear and inquired. I repeated it." Then, Captain Ellison yelled to his east central Alabama soldiers, "Forward, my men, forward!" And the howling Macon County Rebels surged up the wooded slope in a desperate bid to hurl the Yankees off the high ground. Standing firm with the 20th Maine's colorguard, Corporal Coan long remembered that the ear-piercing "'rebel yell' once heard [was] never to be forgotten" by Colonel Chamberlain's defenders on this bloody day at Little Round Top.

But instead of charging straight into the exposed left flank of the 20th Maine and rolling up the battle line to smash into Colonel Vincent's rear as expected, the Alabamians attacking from the east once again ran straight into another murderous volley. This explosion of musketry poured from more than one hundred Maine veterans along the redeployed north-south line of the left wing.

This east-facing line of Major Spear's left wing now stood firm like a wall of fire before the onrushing Alabama Rebels. From behind rocks, trees, both fallen and standing, and boulders of this second defensive line looking down the spur's slope, the Maine bluecoats blasted away from another strong defensive position. Colonel Chamberlain described in his battle report how the Alabamians surged uphill with a confidence "which betrayed their anticipation of an easy triumph. Their astonishment was great as they emerged from their cover, & found instead of an unprotected rear, a *solid front*."

Seeking revenge for the December 1862 slaughter at Fredericksburg, these 20th Maine soldiers were determined to stand firm at any cost. The charging Alabama Rebels were once again hit hard by another close-range musketry which exploded in their faces. Nevertheless, ignoring their fallen comrades, the Alabamians kept moving forward amid the storm, charging up the slope. An amazed Colonel Chamberlain wrote how despite the severe punishment being inflicted by his men, Colonel Oates's Rebels "advanced however within *ten paces* of my line, making what they call a 'charge'—that is, advancing & firing rapidly."[3]

Firing his musket beside other color-guard members of the 20th's Company F, Sergeant William T. Livermore described in his diary the savage fighting which surged across the southern and eastern slope of Little Round Top's spur with renewed intensity: "They came to within four or five rods, covering themselves behind big rocks and trees, and kept up a murderous fire . . ." And Major Spear, commanding the regiment's left wing with distinction, recalled how the "enemy, or many of them, crept forward & took shelter behind boulders, and fired on us from some partial covering, but I think these fellows overshot us generally."

At the southernmost point of the Maine line, meanwhile, Colonel Chamberlain's color company was especially vulnerable along the embattled angle, standing firm at their exposed salient. These colorguard members inflicted as much damage as they received, which was considerable. Inspired by the example of their commander, Lieutenant Holman S. Melcher, the Company F defenders shot down Alabamians amid the thick brush and timber, as if shooting white-tailed deer in the forests around North Bay or Moosehead Lake.[4]

Amid the escalating carnage which was becoming more surreal with each passing minute, Colonel Oates continued leading his men forward with abandon. While before the surging ranks of Company C, Captain Ellison's yell of, "Forward, my men, forward!" were his last words. Wearing a new double-breasted coat of a Confederate captain which Colonel Oates had recently presented to him, young Ellison was hit and his resplendent uniform was splattered with blood, after minie balls ripped through him and knocked him to the ground.

Colonel Oates later recalled the death of one of the best officers of the 15th Alabama: "I was looking at him when a ball passed through his head, killing him instantly. He fell on his back, threw up his arms, clenched his hands, gave one quiver and was dead. I thought him one of the finest specimens of young manhood I ever beheld. His company [C] gathered around him, notwithstanding they were exposed to the most destructive fire at the time." Falling to rise no more on the body-littered slope of Little Round Top, Captain Ellison would never again see his Macon County homeland or his reverend father of the Wiregrass country so far away.[5]

After Captain Ellison's death, Colonel Oates quickly galvanized the Macon County soldiers of Company C amid the blistering fire. He immediately ordered twenty-three-year-old Lieutenant LeGrand L. Guerry, a pious leader of French heritage, to take command of the hard-hit company. Instantly, Company C's veterans rallied behind the young French lieutenant, who had an "exceedingly quiet and passive disposition" except during the heat of battle.

Lieutenant Guerry now led his screaming soldiers forward into the din, surging through the trees. Among these Company C Rebels charging up the timbered and brush-covered slope were the new company commander's brothers and relatives, John E. Guerry, Douglas D. Guerry, two teenagers, and Thomas J. Guerry. In addition, this band of "French" Rebels were related to an uncle who had first commanded the hard-fighting Macon County unit, Captain Peter V. Guerry, who had been killed at Gaines's Mill during the Peninsula campaign.[6]

Meanwhile, the contest continued to rage fiercely across the smoke-covered slopes. Private Gerrish described the savage struggle which swirled over the bloody spur of Little Round Top: "A terrible medley of cries, shouts, cheers, groans, prayers, curses, bursting shells, whizzing rifle bullets and clanging steel [while] the enemy was pouring a terrible fire upon us." For the most part, the 20th Maine was now fighting essentially two battles, with each wing of the regiment simultaneously engaged in its own deadly contest with the relentless Alabama attackers. While Colonel Chamberlain's right wing engaged the southernmost, or right, companies of the 47th Alabama and the 15th Alabama's left, the 20th Maine's left wing stood firm against the relentless hammering from the 15th Alabama's center and right.[7]

The timely tactical readjustment of the defensive line by

Colonel Chamberlain combined with the murderous fire from the fast-working Maine veterans in double ranks—except for Colonel Chamberlain's extreme left companies which stood in single ranks—on elevated terrain continued to cull the best and brightest from the onrushing ranks of the 15th Alabama. On a day of many horrors in the bloodstained woodlands of Little Round Top, Colonel Oates described without exaggeration how "the carnage in the ranks was appalling."

Another fine company leader of the 15th Alabama was killed in the determined effort to drive the Yankees from their strong defensive positions. Having recovered from a leg wound at Cross Keys, Captain Henry C. Brainard was "one of the bravest and best officers in the regiment," wrote Colonel Oates. Captain Brainard had won a lieutenant's rank for bravery on the battlefield and a captain's rank in April 1863. He was now leading the "Henry Pioneers" of Company G, after filling the void left after Colonel Oates's promotion to regimental commander. The twenty-one-year-old leader in gray continued to encourage his screaming attackers up the eastern slope of the embattled spur of Little Round Top to meet the enemy face-to-face amid the tangled woodlands now filled with drifting layers of smoke, bodies, and gore. Hand-to-hand combat erupted across the bloody eastern slope. There, soldiers in blue and gray clashed violently, fighting and dying for possession of this obscure hilltop in south-central Pennsylvania.

While shouting encouragement to his Company G soldiers on Colonel Oates's center, Captain Brainard was fatally struck down. An inspiring presence to his men was no more, when the young captain fell heavily while "attempting to lead his company up a large ledge of rock, behind which the enemy were in great numbers." Lying on the body-littered slope, the leader of the "Henry Pioneers" spoke his last wish on this earth: "O God, that I could see my mother!"

As when Lieutenant Guerry took command of Company C after Captain Ellison's death, Company G was now led forward by the colonel's younger brother, Lieutenant John Alva Oates. Not far from his brother–colonel Lieutenant Oates led the Henry County soldiers straight into the raging storm. All the while, the bullets continued to pour down in sheets from the blazing Maine rifles. At the 15th Alabama's center, the Company G Rebels surged up the wooded slope from the east. Lieutenant Oates's soldiers now attacked up the higher elevation of the spur north of, or above, the 20th Maine's color company to the south and at the apex of the horseshoe-shaped defensive line. Much like Colonel Chamberlain's hard-hit color Company F, the ever-dependable Company G on the 15th Alabama's left-center served as a solid anchor on the center of the Alabamians's line which surged up the eastern slope.

Meanwhile, to Company G's right and also charging westward and up the heavily timbered eastern slope of the spur, Companies H, I, J, K, and L, 15th Alabama. These units continued surging uphill in a desperate effort to overrun the high ground. To Company G's left, beyond the advancing ranks of Companies D through F, Colonel Oates's Companies A through C attacked primarily up the southern slope of the spur. The howling Company C soldiers of the "Macon County Commissioners" now struck the angle held by the 20th Maine's color company, dropping more color-guard members with their fire, bayonets, and musket butts.[8]

Many of the best enlisted men in the 15th Alabama's ranks were cut down by the murderous fire from the New Englanders, who continued to rapidly blast away from the high ground. Among those Alabama soldiers hit by the rain of bullets was James R. Woodham, age nineteen. One of his brothers, twenty-year-old Samuel E. Woodham, meanwhile, continued fighting in the increasingly bitter struggle for possession of Little Round Top, as if to avenge his relative's fall. They were only two of the members of the six-man Woodham clan of the Wiregrass country who helped to make Company G perhaps the best company of Colonel Oates's veteran regiment. Like other families across the North and South, the brothers' war had divided the Woodham family from Henry County, with one member now wearing Yankee blue. Other Woodham soldiers in the 15th Alabama included young John A. Woodham, who was fated to die in a Federal prison, thirty-year-old Uriah Woodham, and Edward C. Woodham. Also destined to serve in Company G's ranks was teenage John Woodham, Edward's son.

A number of other father-son teams of the 15th Alabama and familial clans were now battling to secure possession of Little Round Top. Another member of one of these hard-fighting father-son teams of Colonel Oates's regiment was sixteen-year-old Samuel H. Gardner. An admiring Colonel Oates described how "there was no better soldier in the company than Sam Gardner," whose father was Captain Benjamin Franklin Gardner who led the "Quitman Guards" with distinction. The elder Gardner had been the first leader of this Pike County company. And another Gardner of Company I, Samuel D. Gardner, had died of disease at age twenty-four.

In addition, the father-son team of William Gill Sr. and William Gill Jr. served faithfully in the "Glennville Guards" of Company H. These two Gills in gray charged through the trees heavy with summer foliage, surging forward to close-in on the Maine soldiers. Also in the 15th Alabama's ranks was at least one set of twins, the Peters brothers of Company I, who surged up the wooded slope to Company H's right. The two brothers had been inseparable from their earliest days, growing up together on the Alabama frontier. Therefore, they now fought side-by-side amid the storm raging over Little Round Top. Swarming uphill against the high ground covered with well-concealed Maine soldiers, Benton W. and Noah J. Peters continued onward until Benton fell badly wounded. On this day in hell, Noah also would become a casualty and then a prisoner of the 20th Maine.[9]

Despite heavy losses, the grayclads on the right advanced far enough to meet the Maine soldiers face-to-face with clubbed muskets and flashing bayonets. After vicious hand-to-hand fighting, the Alabamians drove the Maine men from their first defensive position, which Colonel Oates described as yet another ledge of rock. Unable to withstand the Alabamians's assault and after having been swept by two volleys, two Maine companies, C and G, retreated up the slope with discipline, fading away through the smoke-laced trees.

With considerable understatement, Major Spear described how "at one time the left [which he commanded] swayed back a few steps . . . " Then, after falling back, Major Spear's soldiers gamely turned and quickly took yet another excellent defensive position higher up the slope and across even more commanding ground. There, the Federals once again found good firing positions among the rocks and trees, hurriedly reloading in preparation for meeting Colonel Oates's next attack.

Strengthening rather than weakening the 20th Maine's defensive stand and ironically now working to Colonel Oates's disadvantage, the retreat of Companies C and G up the slope resulted in the additional bending back of the Maine line. This retrograde movement before the onrushing Alabamians transformed the horseshoe-shaped line of Colonel Chamberlain's hard-pressed regiment into a hairpin shape. Consequently, the two parallel wings of the 20th Maine were now drawn closer together than ever before, strengthening the overall defense of the embattled spur. From this more elevated terrain higher up the spur and along its north-south crest, the sheltered Federals could more easily shoot down Colonel Oates's soldiers who continued to surge up the timbered slope with Rebel Yells and bayonets glistening in the hot afternoon sunlight.

Despite having been driven back, these Maine soldiers continued to demonstrate that they were exceptionally tough amid the battlefield crisis and the Alabamians's most tenacious adversaries to date. By the volume of the return fire it was clear that Colonel Chamberlain's bluecoats were determined to relinquish as little as possible of the precious real estate of Little Round Top, for which so many young men and boys on both sides were dying this afternoon.

Sensing that the moment of victory had arrived when they saw the Maine soldiers falling back to find new shelter behind more rocks, boulders, trees, and fallen timber higher up the slope, Colonel Oates ordered his men to continue attacking to exploit the hard-won success. The Alabama Rebels, stained with dirt, sweat, and black powder, surged farther up the eastern slope of the spur while firing, yelling, and loading as rapidly as possible amid the smoke-laced thickets and rocks. Then all of a sudden, another close-range volley from the leveled line of Maine rifles exploded from this second natural defensive line. Once again, the point-blank volley tore through the gray and butternut ranks with a vengeance, dropping more Alabamians across the slopes of Little Round Top.

Stung by yet another close volley and with more Alabama boys cut down, Colonel Oates's survivors took cover to escape the storm of lead. From sheltered positions, the Rebels now exchanged shot for shot with the Maine defenders. All the while, the contest around the spur continued to intensify to greater levels, roaring to a degree not seen in any other Little Round Top sector. Sergeant William Livermore, 20th Maine, described this stage of the gory struggle: "We found the enemy flanking us, and got behind a row of rocks under our left wing and were making fearful havoc in our ranks as every one who dared raise his head was sure of his man, but many lost their brains in the attempt."[10]

Now for some time a deadly contest at close range ensued, with Maine and Alabama marksmanship vying for supremacy on this obscure hilltop. But the hot exchange of fire was not enough to bring victory and Colonel Oates realized as much. More of his soldiers were falling by the minute, and time was running out. With the heavily pressured Maine line now bent amid the thick woodlands in the shape of a hairpin, Companies A, B, and C on Colonel Oates's left continued to strike northward from the south or the direction of Big Round Top, hitting the westernmost and southernmost sides of both Little Round Top and the 20th Maine's battle line with relentless blows. Meanwhile, to the right, the onrushing soldiers of Companies D, E, F, G, H, I, J, K, and L of Colonel Oates's center and right continued to assault the 20th Maine's left wing from the east in a desperate attempt to force an advantage by applying heavy pressure to overrun the crest of the embattled spur.

The extended right wing of the 20th Maine was under the command of dark-haired and bearded Captain Atherton W. Clark, the regiment's senior captain. The right wing now consisted of Companies D, K, I, and E, from left to right, or south to north, and these units were aligned in natural defensive positions nestled amid the rocky outcroppings and trees. And the refused Companies of A, H, C, and G, of Major Spear's left wing, remained deployed in good cover near the crest of the spur. With an iron determination to stand firm, Company E's soldiers held the right end of Colonel Chamberlain's line, stabilizing this hard-hit sector.

However, the key defensive position of the bent-back Maine line continued to be that held by the embattled Company F at the salient. These crack soldiers of the color guard held their own at the apex of the V-shaped line, despite the pounding and heavy losses. Situated farther south than any other Maine company on the battle line, Company F's flaming salient pointed south like a dagger as if beckoning Colonel Oates to launch yet another attempt to capture this vital point and the solid rock of Colonel Chamberlain's battered line.

Consequently, this advanced position of the Maine regiment's color guard anchored amid the trees and rocks was hit especially hard by repeated blows delivered by the "Macon County Commissioners" of Company C. Meanwhile, in the Maine regiment's left wing, to Company F's left, Companies A and H maintained their defensive positions but Companies C and G had earlier fallen back. Symbolically with Colonel Chamberlain's Company G occupying the extreme left flank and wavering under the punishment, the battle plan of the first commander of Company G, 15th Alabama—Colonel Oates—hinged upon the conquest of Company G, 20th Maine, in order to turn Colonel Chamberlain's left flank and gain the Union army's flank and rear.

Throughout the tenacious struggle for this little rocky hilltop, the Maine soldiers, like the remainder of Colonel Vincent's hard-fighting troops, benefitted from the tactical advantage of interior lines. Both the right and left wings of the 20th Maine were well within easy and mutual supporting distance, and the thick woodlands could conceal movements from one wing to the other from Rebel eyes. In fact, by this time, Colonel Chamberlain's two wings stood almost back-to-back and this front all along the Maine line presented an elevated and solid barrier to the ever-thinning ranks of Colonel Oates's regiment.

Minute after minute, the dead and wounded on both sides piled up ever-higher. Injured Northerners and Southerners were mingled and clumped together amid the sweltering woodlands, as the savage fighting raged up and down the slope of Little Round Top with a murderous fury until Colonel Oates's attackers were outnumbered.

Amid the carnage growing more nightmarish on Colonel Oates's right, Captain William J. Bethune, the teenage leader of Company K, fell critically wounded. There, the 15th Alabama soldiers were doing everything in their power to drive the Maine soldiers from the rocks and fallen trees near the fiery crest, struggling against the odds to force an advantage by any means possible.

Except for Company L to its right, the Barbour County Rebels of Company K were now fighting farthest north of any of Colonel Oates's attackers sweeping up the eastern slope of the spur of Little Round Top. Captain Bethune was before his men when cut down by a bullet which ripped through his face. The minie ball from the Maine rifle permanently disfigured him, leaving both physical and psychological scars. This terrible injury would require almost half a year of recuperation before the hard-fighting Irishman was once again back leading his Sons of Erin into battle. But Captain Bethune's actions this day reaffirmed the faith that Colonel Oates had placed in him.

Captain Prince, 20th Maine, wrote in amazement of the horror of the close-range fighting for "continually the gray lines crept up by squads under protecting trees and boulders, and the firing became at closer and closer range." Besides heavy losses, other factors diminished the momentum of Colonel Oates's attack: the rough and rugged terrain, the rocks and boulders along the wooded spur, tangled underbrush, and the battle smoke which blanketed the spur like a white shroud.

Indeed, by this time, the Alabamians's advancing lines, both regimental and company formations, were fragmented. Heavy casualties, a good many fallen officers, and rough terrain wreaked havoc on alignment. Therefore, isolated knots of screaming Rebels continued onward on their own hook, fighting uphill inch by inch in small groups. Each surge up the slope was met by Maine soldiers who greeted the Alabamians with bayonets, curses, and clubbed muskets. Men on both sides fought as individuals without orders or commanders, dodging from rock to rock or tree to tree to get a better shot, and to close in on their adversaries with bayonet and musket butt.

By this time, the struggle for possession of Little Round Top was turning into a nightmarish contest not unlike the battle to come in the Wilderness, Virginia, in May 1864. Indeed, point-blank fighting raged across Little Round Top and casualties escalated to new heights with groups of men stumbling blindly into adversaries who greeted them with volleys or bayonets. As Colonel Chamberlain described the horror of the hand-to-hand contest, repeatedly "the two lines met and broke and mingled in the shock [and] the crash of musketry gave way to cuts and thrusts, grapplings and wrestlings" across the hillside strewn with the bodies of blue and gray.

Despite the heavy pressure, however, the Maine soldiers on the high ground continued to maintain the advantage of their strong defensive positions, holding their own, despite the earlier faltering of Companies C and G. Buzzing around the smoke-wreathed spur like a swarm of angry bees, the Alabama marksmen on the lower ground could see no neatly silhouetted targets against the skyline, thanks to Colonel Vincent's orders to not align his troops along the crest of Little Round Top. Clouds of smoke hovering over the bloody spur, and the thick underbrush and heavy summer foliage, fallen timber, and rocks, therefore, now concealed Colonel Chamberlain's defenders, providing the Alabamians with relatively few good targets. Colonel Chamberlain explained how at this time "our regiment was mantled in fire and smoke" of battle. Consequently, the Alabama soldiers could now only fire at the yellow and red flashes of flame and puffs of smoke from the Maine rifles. But realizing in this bitter struggle that he could only win the day by hurling his soldiers into the Federals's midst to fight them at close quarters in trying to force an advantage, Colonel Oates repeatedly led his soldiers into the midst of the Yankee line in desperate efforts to turn the tide.

Through the drifting smoke and in between the layers of dense green foliage which covered the slopes of Little Round Top, one keen-eyed Alabamian now utilized the instincts and savvy of a natural woodsman hunting white-tailed deer in the woodlands along the Chattahoochee. He spied the finely uniformed Colonel Chamberlain out in the open. From the vantage point of this 15th Alabama soldier, Colonel Chamberlain stood out as an easy and exposed target on the high ground of Little Round Top. As a strange destiny would have it, Colonel Oates and his soldiers may have been at this crucial moment only one shot away from ensuring the capture of Little Round Top.

Meanwhile, the savage fighting—some of the most bitter of the war—continued its surge back and forth across the wooded hillside now covered with bodies. Dead and wounded men, groaning and splattered in blood, lay thickly scattered among the bullet-scarred trees and jumbles of rocks. Repeatedly, groups of 15th Alabama and 20th Maine soldiers lunged forward with wild shouts and gleaming bayonets to meet in a bloody flurry of hand-to-hand combat. But each Alabama thrust and counterthrust amid the steaming woodlands was driven back down the slope during a confused melee of jabbing bayonets, swinging musket-butts, and slashing sabers.

Continuing to make the plight of the isolated 15th Alabama even more precarious was the 47th Alabama's repulse to Colonel Oates's left. Consequently, some 83rd Pennsylvania and 44th New York defenders, after hurling back Colonel Bulger's men, turned their fire downhill, or southward, to rake the 15th Alabama's left. This plunging flank fire caused considerable destruction among the 15th Alabama's ranks on the lower ground.

To compensate for the collapse of what little support remained to his left, Colonel Oates ordered a change of front to the left to both relieve some of the heavy pressure from the hard-hit 47th

Alabama, and to allow enfilade fire to be delivered upon the 20th Maine. But Colonel Oates now knew beyond all doubt that he and his 15th Alabama were alone in terms of having the best opportunity to capture Little Round Top or fail in the attempt. Then, Colonel Oates returned to the line's right, where he once again focused on the task of flanking the 20th Maine's left.

Despite the disjointed offensive efforts of both General Law's brigade and Hood's Division and the escalating casualties, however, Colonel Oates was beginning to force an advantage by applying this relentless pressure. And each time he led his soldiers forward up the body-covered slope, Colonel Oates hoped to reap the tactical gain that could be decisively exploited—but as yet to no avail.

And now, one opportunity was presented to one of Colonel Oates's sharp-eyed marksmen. Already, a Rebel marksmen, probably an Alabamian, had fatally wounded Colonel Vincent, sending a bullet through his groin. And now the 15th Alabama was perhaps only a single shot away from the fulfillment of a dream as the humble 15th Alabama private settled into an ideal firing position, and took "a safe place between two rocks." He then prepared to sight his rifle upon Colonel Joshua Chamberlain, who remained out in the open and a perfect target. Clearly, to this Alabama sharpshooter's view, the resplendently uniformed officer with the shoulder straps was the leader of the Maine defenders, conspicuously inspiring and encouraging his hard-fighting troops by his presence on the front lines.

From his secure perch among the rocks, the Alabama soldier was safe from the fire of Yankee sharpshooters, who were lining the crest of Little Round Top and even up in trees. Thus the young Alabama Rebel kept his eye trained on the tempting target. With the natural flow of a seasoned veteran, the Alabama marksmen quickly snapped his trusty, well-worn Enfield rifle to his shoulder with the smooth ease of someone who knew how to use it with deadly skill. The Rebel could hardly believe his eyes as Colonel Chamberlain continued to offer a most inviting target "standing in the open behind the center of [the regimental] line, full exposed," commanding one of the most tenacious small unit defensive actions of the war like a master conductor at a symphony.

The young Alabama sniper in dirty gray "drew bead fair and square on" the exposed colonel from Maine. All that this 15th Alabama veteran now had to do was to slowly squeeze the trigger as he had done so many times before. "I knew your rank by your uniform and your actions, and I thought it a mighty good thing to put you out of the way," later wrote the Confederate to Chamberlain of this opportunity of a lifetime. Consequently, with his Enfield rifle resting on a rock to steady his aim, the graycoat marksman was careful when he "took steady aim" on the exposed form of Colonel Chamberlain.

Destined to be wounded five times in the war, Colonel Chamberlain had early expected the worst when leading his regiment for the first time in a major battle. Harboring dark premonitions of bodily harm and death, the colonel had penned to his wife Fanny, "most likely I shall be hit somewhere at sometime." And now Little Round Top seemed to be that time and place.

But incredibly, at this critical moment, the Alabama soldier suddenly hesitated while in the process of slowly pulling the trigger. This inexplicable hesitation was most unexpected because this veteran possessed considerable experience in shooting down blue-clad officers, artillerymen, and color bearers during the fighting of the Valley campaign, Second Manassas, and Antietam. But this unusual and unfamilar sensation that so suddenly came over him was something altogether new.

As the Alabama sniper described his inexplicable hesitation in a postwar letter to Colonel Chamberlain: "I started to pull the trigger, but some queer notion stopped me. Then I got ashamed of my weakness and went through the same motions again. I had you, perfectly certain. But the same queer something shut right down on me. I couldn't pull the trigger, and, gave it up—that is, your life."

At this crucial moment, the sudden reemergence of time-worn romantic concepts of Southern chivalry and honor within the consciousness of this sole sharpshooter came at a most costly time for

Colonel Oates's 15th Alabama. The old concepts of warfare and chivalry from a bygone age, which no longer existed in this first of all modern wars, perhaps now saved Colonel Chamberlain's life. Thanks to a single shot never fired from an Alabamians's .577 Enfield rifle at Little Round Top, Colonel Chamberlain would continue to serve as an inspirational example for the 20th Maine's tenacious defense.

As a result of Colonel Chamberlain remaining in action and serving as the linchpin of the stubborn defensive stand, the 15th Alabama's losses continued to soar and Colonel Oates soon began to realize that he was fighting a losing battle. The young colonel now could count less soldiers with him than could his Maine counterpart. Even worse, Colonel Oates continued to struggle on his own without support, water, reinforcements, or a resupply of ammunition during what was developing into a brutal contest of attrition—and he was on the short end of that struggle.

Colonel Oates understood that the crisis now called for even more drastic action. No more time could be wasted. Only a few rounds remained in the cartridge-boxes of the Alabama soldiers thanks to the fight earlier at the stone wall, while the Maine Yankees resupplied themselves with cartridges from their dead and wounded comrades during lulls in the fighting. He, therefore, ordered yet another assault in a desperate last-ditch effort to turn Colonel Chamberlain's left flank and take the rocky hill at all costs.

This would be the most successful assault up the hill of the day, the fifth attack launched by the never-say-die Alabamians. As Colonel Oates described the final assault up the bloody slopes, "I again ordered the advance, and knowing the officers and men of that gallant old regiment, I felt sure that they would follow their commander anywhere in the line of duty. I passed through the line waving my sword, shouting, 'Forward, men, to the ledge!' and was promptly followed by the command in splendid style."

With a cheer and knowing that everything now depended upon the success of this final attack, the Alabama soldiers unleashed their war-cries from the Chattahoochee Valley, and once again surged forward. The howling Rebels raised up as one from behind the rocks and trees and charged out of the drifting palls of smoke like phantoms.[11]

Bracing for yet another Alabama assault, one Yankee officer never forgot how Colonel Oates's "rebels came on like wolves, with deafening yells," which echoed over the smoke-wreathed inferno of Little Round Top. With chances for success growing dimmer by the minute, the Alabama soldiers swarmed up the slope and through the timber and brush, loading and firing on the move. And the swarm of bullets from the Maine rifles made the air sing, knocking down more and more Alabama Rebels. The torrent of minie balls swept down the slope and through the dark woodlands, causing a rain of debris, branches, leaves, and bark, to cascade over the attackers and fall to the ground.

A larger number of Colonel Oates's followers now littered the ground, lying among the logs and rocks like fallen leaves on a windy October morning. One of Colonel Oates's Rebels who was especially motivated to do or die was Corporal C. N. Mallett, a teenager of Company I. He had been absent without leave during the battle of Fredericksburg and consequently, had been reduced in the ranks, but continued to serve despite the humiliation. Like Colonel Oates, therefore, the young corporal had much to prove to himself and his comrades and not surprisingly was in the forefront of the assault when he fell seriously wounded amid the tempest swirling across Little Round Top like a thunderstorm.

Once again on the bloody hillside, the two lines of young soldiers from New England and the Deep South met in a nightmarish swirl of savage fighting. Amid the twisted tangles of trees and underbrush, soldiers grappled hand-to-hand in the suffocating heat and smoke. Whenever a ragged private in gray was shot, clubbed down, or bayonetted, an Alabama officer would grab the fallen man's Enfield rifle to fight back beside the surviving privates. Thus during this final attack of the day, many of Colonel Oates's officers rapidly loaded and fired muskets amid the deafening noise and confusion.

But the Alabamians once again clashed with an adversary

who was like no other that they had met previously on a battle-field, smashing into a solid wall of blueclad defenders who refused to break under the pressure. As Colonel Oates's men were discovering at such high cost, these hearty New England soldiers consisted of a "strong race of backwoodsmen," and they fought accordingly. Colonel Chamberlain's soldiers struggled with tenac-ity, firing their .577 Enfield rifles with a deadly skill which equaled the sharpshooting Alabamians, natural woodsmen from the Deep South.

The Maine soldiers' combination of natural and artificial breastworks resulted in what was in essence an impregnable line. But despite their defensive advantage, the Maine soldiers had met their match this day in tangling with Colonel Oates's hard-fighting Alabamians. Indeed, the 20th Maine had never previously met a tougher or more resilient Rebel soldiery than the Alabamians. Sergeant Livermore recorded in his diary that he never forgot how the Alabama Rebels "fought like demons."[12]

Private Gerrish, 20th Maine, recorded how at this time, "the air seemed to be alive with lead. The lines at times were so near each other that the hostile gun barrels almost touched. As the contest continued, the rebels grew desperate that so insignificant a force should so long hold them in check. At one time there was a brief lull in the carnage, and our shattered line was closed up, but soon the contest raged again with renewed fierceness [and] the rebels . . . were now determined to sweep our regiment from the crest of Little Round Top."[13]

All the while, additional young men in gray dropped amid the blazing sheets of flame. A frustrated William R. Holloway, age thir-ty-eight, jumped atop a boulder at the regiment's center in an attempt to get a clear shot at a Maine Yankee. However, he contin-ued to see little through the heavy foliage of the trees and under-brush which was laced with layers of sulphurous smoke blanket-ing the hillside. Unable to catch a glimpse of the well-concealed bluecoats, Holloway yelled to Colonel Oates, who was in the fore-most ranks near his old Company G, "Colonel, I can't see them!" Suffering unacceptable losses for continued offensive operations and now commanding what was little more than a skeleton command, Colonel Oates watched Holloway's fall: "I directed him to look under the smoke. He took deliberate aim and fired. As he took his gun down from his shoulder a bullet passed through his head [and] I caught him in my arms, laid him down, took up his gun and fired a few rounds myself . . . Poor Holloway was a good man" and the father of ten. But on this bloody afternoon, many more good men from both Alabama and Maine continued to die on Little Round Top for what they believed was right. The escalating loss of life among his 15th Alabama caused Colonel Oates to lament how "the carnage in the ranks" exceeded anything that he had ever seen before.[14]

Meanwhile, the blueclad defenders were equally shocked by the savage nature of the struggle for possession of Little Round Top, which seemingly had no end. As described in his battle report, Colonel Chamberlain never forgot how "this struggle of an hour & a half, was desperate in the extreme: *four times* did we lose & win that space of ten yards between the contending lines, which was strewn with dying & dead."[15]

Fearing that the 20th Maine was about to be overrun, Captain Prince was amazed by the tenacity of the Alabama Rebels during the final attack up the slope. Hardly believing the Alabamians's fanatical efforts to gain the hill at all costs, Captain Prince wrote how "again and again was this mad rush repeated . . . Colonel Oates himself advanced close to our lines at the head of his men, and at times the hostile forces were actually at hand-to-hand distance. Twice the rebels were followed down the slope so sharply that they were obliged to use the bayonet [as] the front surged backward and forward like a wave."[16]

Never able to forget the surreal horror of the savage fighting on Little Round Top, Private Gerrish described how " . . . our companies have suffered fearfully . . . but there is no relief, and the carnage goes on. Our line is pressed back so far that our dead are within the lines of the enemy. The pressure made by the [hurling forward] of the enemy's line is severely felt." And Colonel Chamberlain, shocked by the surreal carnage, penned in his report how this "struggle [was] fierce and bloody beyond any that I have witnessed . . ."[17]

Meanwhile, Colonel Oates's younger brother, Lieutenant John Alva Oates, was especially conspicuous during the final effort to drive the Maine soldiers off Little Round Top. Near each other during the Alabamians's most determined attempt, he and his colonel–brother spearheaded the assault of the regiment's center. Despite being hardly able to keep on his feet, the weak and sickly Lieutenant Oates led his Henry County attackers of Company G onward to drive the left wing of the Maine regiment off the high ground.

Somehow the young lieutenant from Henry County had managed to keep up with the regiment during the lengthy advance from Warfield Ridge, across the valley of Plum Run, throughout the fight for the stone wall, during the arduous climb up Big Round Top, and then down the steep mountain before ascending Little Round Top to meet the 20th Maine—a lengthy advance against a determined adversary.

But Lieutenant John A. Oates was now leading the "Henry Pioneers" forward so as not to let his older brother and his comrades down during their supreme moment of crisis. Lieutenant Oates's ordeal caused concern for Colonel Oates. Nevertheless, the colonel remained focused on the tactical task of attempting to turn General Meade's left flank and gain the Union army's rear, encouraging his attackers onward into the tumult. Colonel Oates could only hope that Johnny Oates could take care of himself as so often in the past.

And then another Alabama leader was fatally cut down from the fire of the roaring Maine muskets—Lieutenant Barnett Hardeman Cody. He fell near Colonel Oates at the line's center which was surging westward up the eastern slope of Little Round Top. Lieutenant Cody was a hard-fighting teenager whose diminutive size beguiled his leadership qualities and pugnacity. The handsome lieutenant went down with a badly shattered left leg near the hip, a mortal wound. Known to the Henry County Rebels of Company G simply as "Bud," the popular young man had scribbled a final message which was laced with bitter irony in his last letter to his family in April 1863: "You promised to give [me] as many vegetables and chickens as I could eat if I would come home. That is quite an inducement [so] look out for me some time between now and next August. One who loves chicken as well as I do cannot take such a dare. I will try and come in July about vacation time. I think I could see more pleasure then than at any other time of the year." But instead of a happy reunion with his family in southeast Alabama during this third July of the war, Lieutenant Cody lay dying on a wooded hillside in south-central Pennsylvania far from home. At Little Round Top where inspired leadership was especially needed, Lieutenant Cody had risen to the challenge. He always "discharged every duty promptly without a murmur [with] promptness, ability, and faithfulness," wrote Colonel Oates, explaining how the nineteen-year-old leader of the Henry Pioneers "was one of the finest soldiers of his age I ever knew [and] with the same opportunities he would have compared favorably with [Colonel John] Pelham," of Alabama.

Corporal McClendon keenly felt the tragic loss of his good friend. He recalled the long-ago Abbeville "parting between the Misses Codys and their brother Barnett, was very sad to me [for] those girls were so devoted to their brother [because] of his genial, loveable and generous disposition, [and] they could not help but love him, and for those traits of his character he became the idol of the company [and we] realized that in the death of Barnett H. Cody we had lost a friend, and the company one of its most useful members."[18]

But the terrible slaughter among the hard-hit Alabama soldiers continued. Unabated by this time, the 15th Alabama's attack was reaching a zenith. While leading his hard-hitting assault, Colonel Oates continued to extend his line farther north, or to the right, in an attempt to outflank the left of Colonel Chamberlain's line. During this most determined and penetrating attack of the day, "I sustained nearly all my losses," described Colonel Oates of the carnage which was reaching unprecedented levels.

And then before the onrushing ranks of his Company G and

while imploring his boys up the slope, Lieutenant Oates fell backward, pierced by a volley of minie balls. Quite likely, a Maine officer had directed a group of soldiers—perhaps much of an entire
company—to direct their fire on this foremost Rebel officer, who
was leading his men onward into the raging storm. At this point,
ironically, Lieutenant Oates might have been mistaken for his
brother and the regimental commander of the 15th Alabama.

Falling about the same time as Lieutenant Cody near the regiment's center and close to the top of the bloody spur, Lieutenant
Oates dropped to rise no more only five minutes after taking charge
of Company G after Captain Brainard's fall. One 15th Alabama soldier wrote of the horrible affect of the point-blank volley which
raked the lower extremities of Lieutenant Oates, who fell with "7
wounds [in both] hips & legs." Incredibly, he still lived for awhile
despite being ripped apart by bullets.

A childhood friend of Johnny Oates, Sergeant Isaac H. Parks, a
teenager of Company I and destined for an officer's rank and a
future role as the regimental adjutant, dragged the yet breathing
Lieutenant Oates behind a large boulder near the center of Colonel
Oates's attacking line for protection amid the torrent of minie balls.
Before reaching the boulder's safety, however, a Yankee bullet tore
off one of Lieutenant Oates's fingers. But it was already much too
late to save the life of the colonel's younger brother. But now this
distinctive boulder on the eastern slope of the spur of Little Round
Top not only marked the loss of many of the best officers and men
of the 15th Alabama but also was the true "High Water Mark of the
Confederacy."

Lieutenant John Oates's fatal wounding was a severe blow
from which Colonel Oates would never fully recover and it would
haunt him for the remainder of his days. A big part of the heart and
soul of Colonel William Calvin Oates died at Little Round Top
with the fatal wounding of Lieutenant John Alva Oates.[19]

At this bloody point, Colonel Oates described how the slaughter among his soldiers "was appalling." The destruction among
the 15th Alabama was more severe than the young colonel had
ever seen before with the Alabamians's officer corps especially cut

to pieces. But the fighting for the 15th Alabama was far from over as the furious struggle for Little Round Top was intensifying, reaching new heights of savagery. As one Union captain described the slaughter across the body-littered slopes of Little Round Top, Colonel Oates's "officers had freely exposed themselves in leading the successive charges and the mortality among them was great. The Lieut. Co. had lost his leg, two Captains and four Lieutenants had been instantly killed, John Oates, the colonel's brother, struck by eight balls . . ."[20]

Despite the staggering losses, Colonel Oates's veterans continued to stand up well both in the face of the blistering fire at close range and during the vicious hand-to-hand combat. Like the Maine soldiers, these hardened veterans from southeast Alabama were not unnerved by the many horrid sights which continued to swirl around them like a surreal nightmare: comrades, neighbors, and close relatives clubbed, bayoneted, and shot down and mangled by bullets. Colonel Oates's soldiers were long accustomed to the sound and sight of the heavy lead balls of the .577 Enfield rifles tearing into bodies and smashing bone, ripping through large sections of flesh, and blowing off parts of the heads, arms, and legs of their closest comrades and relatives.

However, not even the most jaded or hardened 15th Alabama soldier on this bloody afternoon would be prepared to witness the grisly death of thirty-two-year-old Private John Keels of Company H. "An excellent soldier" of the "Glennville Guards," the young man in gray had survived a bad wound at Second Manassas the past summer. The fatal bullet "cut his throat, and he ran across the mountain breathing at his neck," with an eerie sucking sound and splattering blood. But despite his terrible injury, Private Keels somehow survived July 2. Thankfully, however, he would be finally relieved of his torment, dying on the 4th of July while the Union celebrated its anniversary of independence and the Confederacy had all but lost its own dream of winning its independence at Gettysburg.[21]

Meanwhile, Colonel Oates continued to lead his soldiers forward in a desperate effort to slip around Colonel Chamberlain's left flank, while simultaneously hammering the 20th Maine's center. Indeed, Colonel Oates's surging center and right had advanced to gain much of the eastern slope of the spur of Little Round Top and charged forward to near the top of the spur north of Colonel Chamberlain's color company. With a singleminded purpose of driving the Maine regiment off the hill at all costs, Colonel Oates continued to win more of the advantage by securing additional yards of high ground.

Thanks to Colonel Oates's relentless hammering of the Maine regiment, the refused Companies F, A, H, C, and G, 20th Maine, took such a severe beating that more ground was relinguished during the Alabamians's final attack. Almost three-fourths of Colonel Chamberlain's losses that day came from these five refused companies of the left wing, which the sharpshooting Alabamians simply shot, bayoneted, and clubbed to pieces. But the Maine soldiers fought back tenaciously and "clubbed their muskets, brained a number of their assailants on the spot . . ."

Grim testimony to the accuracy of the Alabamians's fire, the majority of the killed and mortally wounded Maine soldiers fell from head shots and chest wounds. Typical victims to the Alabama rifles were William S. Jordan, Company G, who was shot through the left lung, and the spunky Sergeant George Washington Buck, a twenty-year-old of Company H promoted on the field for gallantry, who took a bullet through the chest.[22]

By this time, the indescribable thirst among Colonel Oates's Rebels, who were fighting with empty canteens hour after hour during one of the hottest days of the summer, was simply unbearable. The soldiers' tongues were swollen, lips broken and bleeding, and mouths parched and dry from the blazing summer heat and biting off dozens of paper cartridges.

The long march across the Plum Run valley, the torturous climb up Big Round Top, the descent down Big Round Top, and then up Little Round Top under the hot summer sun was too much physical exertion for some Alabamians, especially after marching almost twenty-five miles to start. These veteran soldiers had already sweated out so much body fluid that perspiration no longer poured forth from their sore and bruised bodies. Black powder from torn paper cartridges was smeared across the Alabamians's lips and mouths, covering hands and faces like black shoe polish. But Colonel Chamberlain's defenders simply refused to relinguish their hill and flee like so many other Yankees had done during the Valley campaign and Second Manassas under comparable pressure. So in the northernmost sector of the Alabamians's line, Colonel Oates and what little remained of his decimated regiment continued to attempt to coil around and turn the weakening left flank of not only Colonel Chamberlain's regiment but also Colonel Vincent's brigade. And in this fifth assault these howling Rebels came closer to victory than ever before.

The two crack Alabama companies on the right flank, the "Pike Sharpshooters" of Company L and the "Eufaula City Guards" of Company K, were going for broke in attempting to turn the Army of the Potomac's left flank. It was now or never for the 15th Alabama with time rapidly running out for Southern fortunes on the afternoon of July 2.

Despite Captain Bethune' death, the Sons of Erin of Company K continued to fight furiously against the Maine soldiers. Firing and yelling like banshees, the Irishmen in gray inflicted heavy damage on Colonel Chamberlain's bent-back left wing by unleashing an enfilade fire that raked the 20th Maine's left. Amid the underbrush and trees of the eastern slope of Little Round Top, these Celtic warriors now fought with a tenacity reminiscent of their forefathers' struggles against the British in behalf of Ireland's independence. Captain Bethune had earlier ordered Sergeant O'Conner to keep a close eye on a Private John Nelson, age twenty-four. Tough and dependable, Sergeant O'Conner had been instructed to make sure "to hold Nelson to his work" at Little Round Top.

Private Nelson was an unusual and complex soldier, one of the few enigmas among the Celtic warriors of Company K. Private Nelson's "most prominent characteristics was his desire to fight. He would fight any of the men personally, and would go into every battle, and then at the first opportunity would run out of it."

As usual, Private Nelson attempted to sneak rearward as the fighting swelled at Little Round Top, and Sergeant O'Conner, a large, rawboned Irishman, "collared him and held him to his place" on the firing line. However, Private Nelson was soon hit by a fatal bullet. Sergeant O'Conner caught Private Nelson's fall, before the young man touched the ground. As O'Conner let him down, the hardened Irish sergeant shouted in contempt at the dying Nelson in his Irish brogue, "Now I guess you will not run away." Another Irishman of the 15th Alabama had run away though, unnerved by the prospect of more hard fighting. John J. Carter, recently promoted to corporal in May and only seventeen, had deserted before entering the battle. He simply refused to risk his life in another bloody slaughter which were becoming commonplace in the army of the offensive-minded General Lee during this most nightmarish American war.[23]

But by now in terms of manpower, the chances for success on Colonel Oates's far right was much reduced, with Company K having taken a severe beating during this fifth desperate attack uphill. Among the killed of the crack Irish company were Privates James M. Brown and John Ingram, age twenty-three. Meanwhile, among the many wounded Irish Rebels from the "Eufaula Guards" ranks were Privates William T. Bynum, a teenager, Reuben J. Craft, eighteen-year-old Burrell V. McKlevane, who had recently recovered from a bad Antietam wound, and James Rutledge, age thirty-four.

However, the most important member of the hard-fighting Celtic unit who was the heart and soul of Company K and the inspirational leader of the Irish Rebels on this afternoon was Sergeant O'Conner. Leading by example, he continued to fight amid the smoke-laced and humid woodlands blanketing the eastern slope of Little Round Top, conspicuously encouraging his Irish lads forward into the raging storm. At this critical moment during the zenith of the 15th Alabama's offensive strike that afternoon, Sergeant O'Conner provided the inspirational leadership which now helped to make up for the many fallen Celtic soldiers of Company K.[24]

Like the hardened Maine soldiers who somehow yet continued to hold against the Alabamians's fifth attack of the afternoon, never before had the 15th Alabama soldiers fought so tenaciously. These veterans in gray and butternut instinctively seemed to realize that everything was at stake. And by this time, success for Colonel Oates's survivors largely depended upon their own ability to shoot rapidly and accurately, and bayonet and club down the enemy with musket butts with their remaining strength.

While Colonel Oates continued to concentrate his main effort in attempting to turn Colonel Chamberlain's left, and after the 47th Alabama's repulse hard-earned gains were finally achieved during the desperate attempt to turn the 20th Maine's right. Colonel Oates's men began to gradually turn the Maine regiment's right flank to gain an advanced point on the southwestern slope of Little Round Top, after more vicious fighting and more loss in life. These gains caused more bluecoats at various portions of the 20th Maine's line to retire farther uphill, falling back to the summit of the spur. Indeed, Colonel Chamberlain later admitted that the 20th Maine was pushed from its original positions all along the line. He also stated that the relentless Alabamians on his right almost cut him off from the rest of Colonel Vincent's brigade.

Gaining more ground, scores of Alabama attackers surged uphill through the trees while fighting from rock to rock. Achieving significant gains, the Alabamians on the left had advanced so far eastward that some Rebels eased between the left of the 83rd Pennsylvania and the 20th Maine's right. But this success only drew the attention of Colonel Vincent's units to the 20th Maine's right, and more Federal muskets were now turned on the Alabamians's surging ranks. On the verge of success, Colonel Oates described in a letter, " . . . we encountered the left oblique fire of [the] 83rd Pa. and 44th N.Y. . . . before [succeeding in] my turning movement to roll up [Colonel Chamberlain's] left."

However, Colonel Oates's most determined bid for success continued to be applied on the embattled left flank of the 20th Maine. And there, after some of the most vicious fighting of the war, the left flank of the battered Maine regiment was finally successfully turned by the 15th Alabama's right, with the bluecoats being hurled over the crest.

Incredibly, the Alabamians had accomplished the impossible, capturing the top of the body-strewn spur. Going for broke, Colonel Oates was now close to victory. Indeed, the 15th Alabama soldiers, while fighting on their own and without support, had achieved a success which might well have resulted in turning the left flank of the entire Army of the Potomac.

Colonel Chamberlain described the nightmarish fighting which raged over his center and left with new furies. He wrote how the young men in blue and gray were engaged at close quarters, consumed in a bloody melee of "cuts and thrusts [as] the edge of the conflict swayed to and fro, with wild whirlpools and eddies. At times I saw around me more of the enemy than of my own men."

On the far left of his decimated line, the Maine colonel later admitted how close Colonel Oates and his relative handful of Rebels came to victory at this time as the northernmost Alabamians smashed through the Union line with a vicious flurry of jabbing with bayonets, swinging muskets like clubs, and firing of muskets and revolvers at point-blank range. Colonel Chamberlain was shocked to suddenly see entire "squads of [Alabamians] who had cut their way through us."

Meanwhile, the vicious struggle continued on the Alabamians's left with increasing fury. During their desperate bid to capture Little Round Top, the attacking Alabama soldiers of Company B were especially hard-hit. These "Midway Southern Guards" on the regiment's left lost more men killed than all of Colonel Oates's eleven companies except one, Company G. And before the many wounded 15th Alabama Rebels lining the wooded slopes now loomed the grim prospect of Yankee prison camps and epidemics of diseases in bitter winter weather of the North. Illnesses such as smallpox would prove fatal to many of Colonel Oates's captured soldiers in the months after Gettysburg.

Ignoring the blow of witnessing his younger brother's mortal wounding, his regiment's decimation, and the personal danger of leading by example in his repeated attacks up the hill, Colonel Oates continued to encourage his men forward to exploit their gains. He led his howling Alabamians onward to capture the length of the spur's crest from which the Yankees were driven away after so much effort.

Major Spear, the Bowdoin College graduate commanding the five refused Union companies on the left and now second in command of the 20th Maine, described the extent of the panic on Colonel Chamberlain's out-flanked left for he clearly "remember[ed] that [Captain Joseph F.] Land & I were, in the excitement of the moment, holding our swords in both hands, by hilt & top, against the backs of the men to keep them up" and in line. During this crisis in which his hard-hit left wing gave ground and fell back under the pounding, Major Spear explained how " . . . the [rearward] movement was from the color company toward the left [but] the colors [and Company F] did not move." But the wavering of the 20th Maine's left wing continued at the next defensive line as well under the punishment delivered by the Alabama Rebels.

Colonel Oates never forgot the dramatic moment that saw the turning of the left flank of the 20th Maine and gaining the rear of Colonel Vincent's brigade. Captain Judson of the 83rd Pennsylvania described how the Alabama Rebels " . . . still kept pressing to the left and were now in the rear of the brigade [and] this was one of the most critical periods during the whole engagement." But Colonel Oates took no time to celebrate his success. Instead, he continued to encourage his troops onward to secure more of the crest of Little Round Top's spur.

If they gained the commanding point of the crest, Colonel Oates's soldiers could then fire downhill and also launch an attack northward off the spur and up Little Round Top, hitting and enfilading the left flank of the 83rd Pennsylvania on Colonel Chamberlain's right, which stood on the higher ground of Little Round Top to the northwest. Then after smashing through the Pennsylvanians's left flank and driving the Keystone State soldiers rearward, the next regiment of Colonel Vincent's brigade, the 44th New York, would likewise be wrecked by the Alabamians's attack from the left flank—if only the 20th Maine could first be swept aside and off the spur. Colonel Oates could almost envision the complete collapse of Colonel Vincent's brigade and decisive victory now that he and his men were so near capturing the crest of the spur.

More than anyone else, Colonel Chamberlain now feared how "if a strong force should gain our rear, our brigade would be caught as by a mighty shears-blade, and be cut and crushed." Such a dramatic 15th Alabama success as Colonel Chamberlain now feared as imminent would mean that the 47th and 4th Alabama, along with the 4th and 5th Texas to their left, would then resume the attack up the southwestern and western face of Little Round Top to exploit Colonel Oates's success in overrunning the embattled spur, striking the right and center of Colonel Vincent's brigade. Then, once the 15th Alabama and General Hood's other units were united on Little Round Top's crest for one last push to decisive victory, Colonel Vincent's entire brigade would be enfiladed and blasted by musketry and then hurled off Little Round Top. Then, farther northward, additional Federal units of the army's exposed left flank, which dangled in mid-air, would also be crushed by the steamrolling flank assault of the regiments of General Hood's Division. Hood's hard-fighting brigades would then roll-up General Meade's battle lines until the name Gettysburg would be immortalized forever across the South with the decisive success at Yorktown which had won a nation's independence.

But first, the bullet-tattered battle flags of bright red with the St. Andrew's Cross carried by Color Sergeant John G. Archibald would first have to wave from the spur's crest and then from the top of Little Round Top before this dream became reality. However, the 15th Alabama's chances for fully exploiting this success were severely limited. Colonel Oates earlier had been forced out of necessity to keep his left flank connected with the 47th Alabama. Because of this extension combined with ever-increasing losses, the 15th Alabama's available manpower for the tactical requirement that would ensure success by curling completely around the 20th Maine's left flank was not quite enough.

Another offensive tactic, therefore, was urgently needed by Colonel Oates to yet gain the tactical advantage sufficiently to crack the 20th Maine's obstinate line before it was too late. It was around 6:30 P.M., and a blood-red sun of summer now hovered on the western horizon like a great ball. Unfortunately for Southern fortunes, the July 2 sun was dropping rapidly to the Alabamians's left, heralding the end of day and the end of Confederate chances for decisive victory.

The distant glow of the setting sun bestowed an eerie light on the dead and wounded Alabama soldiers who were lying back in the "Valley of Death," and along the bullet-swept slopes of Little Round Top. The large number of fallen Alabamians who lay strewn on the field were now badly needed by Colonel Oates to ensure Little Round Top's capture as no reinforcements were forthcoming.

At this critical time on the far southern end of General Lee's line, the disjointed and uncoordinated assaults of General Law's brigade and Hood's Division likewise continued to all but sabotage Colonel Oates's efforts, limiting his offensive capabilities. The collapse of the 47th Alabama's offensive efforts continued to haunt Colonel Oates at this critical moment. Earlier Colonel Oates had raced over to the left in a futile attempt to get the hard-hit 47th Alabama moving again and rejuventate the attack in this sector. But Major James Campbell had been unable to galvanize his seven companies to win significant gains after Colonel Bulger's fall with a bullet through his lung. After having suffered heavily in attacking the western slope of Little Round Top and taking a vicious fire from the 20th Maine's right and the 83rd Pennsylvania's left, Colonel Bulger's men had been cut down "like grass before the scythe."

The 15th Alabama, therefore, continued to pay a heavy price for the lack of support from the 47th Alabama and other units to its left as well. Clearly, by this time in a disadvantageous situation not of his own making, an increasingly desperate Colonel Oates needed to develop a new tactical plan to somehow secure permanent possession of the crest of the spur. Now though Colonel Oates not only kept his command fighting but, more important, also repeatedly launched the tactical offensive despite facing a long list of disadvantages which normally eroded unit stability and cohesion during the heat of combat in a crisis situation: high losses that sapped offensive strength and momentum; the lack of reinforcements; support units either having been repulsed or providing no assistance; diminished levels of ammunition to dangerous lows; a tenacious adversary under cover and fighting in good defensive positions on high ground; top brigade and division leaders either cut down or absent; and lack of communication, guidance, and instructions from headquarters and commanders.

CHAPTER XII

For Want of a Regiment

"If I had had one more regiment we would have completely turned the [left] flank and have won Little Round Top, which would have forced Meade's whole left wing to retire."

—Colonel Oates

On the afternoon of July 2, nevertheless, the 15th Alabama experienced no moral disintegration in its decimated ranks amid the heat of combat which would have sabotaged Colonel Oates's chances for capturing Little Round Top. And when needed the most during a crisis situation, the ever-reliable Adjutant Waddell brought a tactical solution to resume the offensive with a chance for success. Colonel Oates wrote, Adjutant Waddell "came and asked me to let him take forty or fifty men from the right wing of the regiment and advance to some rocks from which to enfilade the Union line, the Twentieth Maine and Eighty-third Pennsylvania." Thus another opportunity was found which might result in the turning of Colonel Chamberlain's left flank if the tactic worked as planned.

No longer firing the Enfield rifle of the fallen Holloway, Colonel Oates readily consented to Adjutant Waddell's new tactical plan which offered a ray of hope to yet win the day. He now ordered Waddell, "a very fine officer" and his most trusted "right arm" after Lieutenant Colonel Feagin's fall, and around fifty dependable Alabamians to embark on the mission in a last-ditch effort to somehow gain the tactical advantage once and for all. Colonel Oates had complete faith in the abilities of the twenty-seven-year-old Waddell, who he would promote to captain of his old Company G—a high compliment—in September 1863. Without exaggeration, Colonel Oates believed that Adjutant Waddell "would have made a fine colonel of a regiment."

This bold tactical plan proposed by Adjutant Waddell called for Waddell's men to rapidly push farther northward through the woods of the spur's timbered eastern slope and beyond the Alabama regiment's right flank to strike the Maine soldiers from the east and from higher ground up the spur just northeast of the 20th Maine's left flank. Here they planned to inflict havoc by unleashing a flanking fire. After launching repeated frontal assaults up the hill, Colonel Oates now made his last bid to somehow yet reverse the tide and drive the obstinate Maine defenders off the crest.

Clearly, this was a decision made by Colonel Oates out of desperation and due to urgent battlefield necessity in large part because of the lack of support or assistance. So after already dispatching the twenty-two-man water detail and Company A's skirmishers under Captain Shaaff—some fifty to sixty veterans—he now ordered another forty to fifty soldiers from his ever-dwindling regiment. He hoped that despite the odds, the opportunity yet remained for a dramatic 15th Alabama success at Little Round Top and a 20th Maine defeat.

And a golden opportunity yet existed. Indeed Private Gerrish later wrote that at this time "a critical moment has arrived, and we can remain as we are no longer; we must advance or retreat. It must not be the latter, but how can it be the former?" Even Colonel Chamberlain realized that his decimated defensive line "did not seem possible to withstand another shock."

Embarking on their all-important mission with high hopes,

Adjutant Waddell's soldiers now raced northward on the double through the brush and trees clogging the gently sloping ground at the southeastern base of Little Round Top. Minute after minute, this band of Alabamians advanced higher up the spur as it rose toward the rocky crest.

Colonel Oates now possessed less than 250 men to face more than 350 20th Maine defenders. As during his prewar days, nevertheless, Colonel Oates continued to play the role of the daring gambler this afternoon. And now he had raised the stakes, betting everything on yet another desperate bid to win Little Round Top with an all but empty hand.

However, if anyone could do the impossible and reverse the tide at Little Round Top it was Adjutant Waddell. By the time of Gettysburg, Waddell was a promising officer and well respected by his men. With the battle swirling around him and despite the danger, Adjutant Waddell had relinquished his adjutant duties to embark upon his mission, being suddenly thrust into a center stage role in the unfolding drama on Little Round Top.

Like the men he commanded, Colonel Oates placed complete faith in the belief that Adjutant Waddell could succeed in this crucial mission. Private Jordan described Adjutant Waddell as " . . . a good officer, and a brave soldier." Private Jordan explained that in Waddell's younger days the now pious adjutant in gray "was a little wild" before a new spirituality was gained by him from the regimental chaplain and the war's horrors. Colonel Oates called Adjutant Waddell "quite religious." Tactically flexible and single-minded in his purpose, Adjutant Waddell was an ideal choice for this key assignment.[1]

Adjutant Waddell's soldiers now continued to double-quick through the steamy woodlands farther to the right and beyond Colonel Oates's right flank. The graycoats raced northward with the intent of gaining an advantageous position higher up the spur from which to fire into the rear and enfilade the line of "down Maine" men from New England. In addition, from their elevated vantage point, if possessed, Adjutant Waddell's Rebels would also have the opportunity to blast into the 83rd Pennsylvania's left and rear and to wreck havoc on the left and rear of Colonel Vincent's entire brigade.

After gaining their elevated perch higher up the timbered spur and beyond the 20th Maine's left and the 15th Alabama's right, Adjutant Waddell's flankers hurriedly took cover behind the rocks and fallen trees above, or north of, Colonel Oates's main line to the south. From good cover atop the high ground near the crest of the spur, Adjutant Waddell's soldiers immediately opened up a blistering fire on the Maine soldiers of Captain Spear's left wing, catching them by surprise and raking them with a hail of lead.

In tactical terms, Adjutant Waddell had succeeded in the first requirement of his mission by gaining an advanced and dominant position from which to pour a blistering flank fire into Colonel Chamberlain's left flank. In fact, Adjutant Waddell's band of flankers had advanced so far westward up the slope that they were now almost atop the northern neck of the spur's crest, fighting well beyond Colonel Oates's right flank.[2]

Remaining a primary target of Colonel Oates to the south, meanwhile, was Company F because of its advanced position and role in anchoring the 20th Maine's defensive line. The bullet-tattered flag of the 20th Maine was emplaced firmly in the ground around the rocks at the regiment's center at the angle, lying limp in the scorching heat and humidity. Guarded faithfully by Sergeant Andrew Jackson Tozier, who was rapidly loading and firing a musket with cartridges taken from the heaps of dead and wounded around him, this colorful blue banner served as a constant source of irritation to the Alabamians, and especially Colonel Oates.

In contrast, the stirring sight of Color Sergeant Tozier's defiance beside the flag which stood above his fallen comrades inspired the Yankee defenders to new heights of desperation and resistance. Amid the blood and carnage at the embattled angle of Colonel Chamberlain's battered line amongst the bullet-scarred rocks and trees stood what little remained of the determined color-guard of the 20th Maine.

Indeed, after taking the brunt of the Alabamians's wrath, Company F had been shot to pieces. Leaving command of the left wing to a subordinate, Major Spear had earlier checked on the vanishing defensive line of the color guard during a lull between assaults. He described the unforgottable sight when after "their fire slackened a little on the left [and] I walked along to the center it seemed to me most of the color guard were knocked out . . . what I most distinctly remember there . . . was the Color Sergeant Tozier, who had picked up a musket dropped by one of the killed and wounded, and with his left arm about the colors, stood loading and firing, and chewing a bit of cartridge paper."

Despite the heavy losses, this bloodied color company remained under the command of one of Colonel Chamberlain's best officers, Lieutenant Holman S. Melcher. He was a young teacher of only twenty-two, having been well educated at the Maine State Seminary. A fighter and an officer who could be depended upon during a crisis, he was formerly a hardnosed sergeant major who had been promoted for gallantry on the battlefield. And as proven throughout the struggle for possession of Little Round Top, these regimental color guardians were the hardest fighting men of the Maine regiment, and their casualties provided grim testimony to that fact.

Colonel Chamberlain had earlier made an adroit tactical decision by placing Company F in the right spot to anchor his defensive line. And now these blueclad defenders of the regimental banner continued to hold the body-strewn angle with grit against whatever Colonel Oates could throw at them this afternoon. On this bloody day, Company F, 20th Maine, would lose seven killed and another fourteen wounded to the 15th Alabama's marksmen. Despite the punishment, Company F's position at the advanced salient of the line's center continued to pay dividends, stablizing the ragged defensive line which practically no longer existed. The surviving color-guard members held firm around a large boulder, which was surrounded by smaller boulders amid the tangle of trees and underbrush. With the largest boulders anchoring the defensive line of his center, Colonel Chamberlain understood how this "great boulder gave token and support" to Little Round Top's defense.

Against the Alabamians's repeated offensive thrusts in this sector, this boulder perched on the rocky "ledge" at the southernmost end of the Maine line and defended by its color guard stood like the Rock of Gibraltar, resisting Colonel Oates's best efforts to make it crumple throughout the afternoon. Hour after hour, the heroic color guard of the 20th Maine withstood the punishment. In fact, so many color-guard members were shot down that men from other Maine companies were detailed to bolster Company F, including Corporal James A. Knight, who was soon cut down himself when a bullet whistled "right through me." And this punishment was severe, for the Alabama soldiers, when not surging up the slope, blasted away from "a strong position behind the rocks 3 rods in front of us," wrote Color Corporal Coan.[3]

Colonel Oates realized that the 20th Maine's battle flag had to be captured, especially if Little Round Top was to be overrun. Such a stunning psychological blow to the defenders would act like a dagger thrust into the heart of Colonel Chamberlain's defensive line, and might just be enough to turn the tide. Indeed, the capture of the regimental colors might be enough to break the fighting spirit of the Maine warriors.

During the height of the furious struggle, consequently, Colonel Chamberlain was astounded by the near loss of the regimental colors, describing how "in the very deepest of the struggle while our shattered line had pressed the enemy well below their first point of contact, and the struggle to regain it was fierce, I saw through a sudden rift in the thick smoke our colors standing alone. I first thought some optical illusion imposed upon me. But as forms emerged through the drifting smoke, the truth came to view. The cross-fire had cut keenly; the center had been almost shot away . . . [and] the blood of the slain was pooled on the rocks below and around."

For some time, Colonel Oates ordered his Alabamians to concentrate their fire not only on the color company but also on Companies A and D, 20th Maine, on either side of the battered flag of Company F. Protruding south toward the attacking Rebels as if daring them to once again attempt to capture this advanced position, the vulnerable salient became a slaughter pen. The exposed salient was now littered with blue bodies which were clumped together in piles, draped over rocks and logs, and slumped against the stony "ledge."

Even much of the timber covering the slope were devoid of bark at head level and scarred by the intense musketry from both sides. Saplings were cut in two leaning over after being shot in half. But nothing could be gained by the 15th Alabama men in this southernmost sector despite their most determined efforts. Against attack after attack, the Maine soldiers held firm in this advanced point of Colonel Chamberlain's line, and the bullet-tattered battle flag of the 20th Maine yet anchored the defensive line.[4]

In contrast to the stalemate in this southernmost sector near the southern base of Little Round Top, the Alabama soldiers to the north continued to do considerable damage to Colonel Chamberlain's left. From their high-ground perch near the crest of the wooded spur, Adjutant Waddell's Alabamians continued to lay down an effective flank fire, inflicting severe punishment. Captain Judson and other 83rd Pennsylvania soldiers realized that the Alabama Rebels "were now in rear of the brigade" and causing considerable mischief. This was now "the most critical" time during the struggle.

Enfilading the blueclad victims like a hailstorm, Adjutant Waddell's volleys were not only causing havoc in the bent-back left wing of the 20th Maine—which now attempted in vain to protect the rear of Vincent's brigade—but also in the rear and flank of the 83rd Pennsylvania and 44th New York higher up the slope.

After seeing his 83rd Pennsylvania soldiers hit from behind by Adjutant Waddell's fire, a panicked Captain Woodward immediately dispatched his acting adjutant, Lieutenant Martin Van Buren Gifford, over to the 20th Maine to ascertain if Colonel Chamberlain's left was successfully turned by the Alabama Rebels. Knowing that his regiment was barely holding its own, Colonel Chamberlain "assured him that he was holding his ground . . ."

The hail of Alabama bullets raking the Pennylvanians's rear caused Captain Woodward to shift his regiment's center back some ten to fifteen paces and extend his left to cover "a little more ground to the left." This tactical readjustment resulted in a shortening, straightening, and consolidating of the 83rd Pennsylvania's line to better protect the 20th Maine's right even before receiving Colonel Chamberlain's reply. Indeed, Captain Judson of Company E, 83rd Pennsylvania, wrote, " . . . fearing that in case the enemy continued to press back to the left of the Twentieth [Captain Woodward] would close up the only avenue of escape (a small space of ground between his line and the large rock in his rear), he ordered the centre of the Eighty-Third to fall back some ten or fifteen paces. This movement straightened his line and brought him into a position where he could better command the passage, in case the enemy attempted to gain it."

This urgent realignment on the battlefield was conducted while the Pennsylvania boys continued to load and fire. In the words of Captain Judson, Captain Woodward now feared the worst "in case the enemy continued to press back to the left of the Twentieth . . ." Captain Woodward learned upon Lieutenant Gifford's return of the extent of the crisis in the 20th Maine's defensive sector for Colonel Chamberlain relayed the alarming message that "the enemy were pressing his left and had almost doubled it back upon the right . . ."

A desperate Colonel Chamberlain urgently requested an 83rd Pennsylvania company as a reinforcement but the hard-pressed Captain Woodward could send none under the circumstances. However, Captain Woodward informed Colonel Chamberlain by way of messenger that "if Col. Chamberlain would move his right to the left he would move the Eighty-Third also and fill up the gap [and] Chamberlain at once moved his regiment to the left, so that the Twentieth now occupied a line perpendicular to what it had at first, and protected fully the right flank of the brigade. This baffled the attempts of the enemy to turn our left . . ., " explained Captain Judson of the tactical readjustments which played a role in thwarting Colonel Oates's best efforts.

Facing the most severe crisis of his career, Captain Prince, 20th Maine, recorded how in this sector "continually the gray lines crept up by squads under the protecting trees and boulders, and the firing became at closer and closer range. And even the enemy's line essayed to reach around the then front of blue that stretched out in places in single rank and could not go much farther without breaking. So far had they extended, that their bullets passed beyond and into the ranks of the other regiments farther up the hill . . ."

In stirring up a hornets' nest, Adjutant Waddell's flankers, isolated on their high-ground perch beyond and above Colonel Oates's right, paid a high price for taking an advanced position so near the crest and drew an angry response from Colonel Chamberlain's right. Nevertheless, Adjutant Waddell kept his soldiers firing as rapidly as possible, and the flame of musketry erupting from these most-advanced Alabama rifles poured down to tear through the refused Companies H, C, and G along the battered left flank of the 20th Maine. And because the Maine regiment's left flank was bent-back nearly upon its right wing, Adjutant Waddell's fire also struck the rear of Companies D, K, I, and E, 20th Maine, as well as the Pennsylvanians's rear to Colonel Chamberlain's right. This hot fire continued to reconfirm the 83rd Pennsylvania's fears that the 20th Maine's flank had been turned, which were well-founded, as realized by Major Spear and others on the regiment's left. Indeed, at this time and thanks to Adjutant Waddell's initiative, Colonel Chamberlain's left was in the process of being successfully turned by Colonel Oates.

Even though they were no longer attacking up the southwestern slope of Little Round Top, some fire from members of the 47th Alabama Rebels likewise now smashed into the rear of Colonel Chamberlain's left wing. This fire belatedly came to the assistance of the long-isolated 15th Alabama. Applying constant pressure, Colonel Oates's relentless pounding of the 20th Maine's left wing continued to double Colonel Chamberlain's line even more upon itself. To the north, meanwhile, Adjutant Waddell's deadly fire was piling up more casualties among the Maine soldiers until a full third of Colonel Chamberlain's regiment was cut down.

At this time, the crisis for the badly battered 20th Maine was severe. The disheartening news reached them that the brigade commander, Colonel Vincent, had been killed, and a good many other leading officers now lay dead or dying. Many bluecoats were wounded or out-of-action including soldiers who had fired so many times that their rifles had jammed. "The last defense of the last army of the Republic" on the far left seemingly was about to be overwhelmed.

In his report written shortly after the battle Colonel Chamberlain wrote that the day's worst crisis came at this time when the Maine soldiers "met the enemy on their last & most desperate assault. In the midst of this, our ammunition utterly failed, our fire, as it was too terribly evident, had slackened, half my left wing lay on the ground, & although I had brought two companies from the right to strengthen it, the left wing was reduced to a mere skirmish line. Officers came to me, shouting that we were 'annihilated', . . . " And in another report, Colonel Chamberlain described the extent of the crisis, writing how "the heroic energy of my officers could avail us no more [and] our gallant line writhed & shrunk before the fire it could not repel."

Many Maine soldiers had by this time already expended their own rounds. Colonel Chamberlain explained in his report how, "our 'sixty rounds' were rapidly reduced" during this exchange of musketry which roared for about an hour and a half from beginning to end. Lieutenant Holman S. Melcher, commander of what little was left of the 20th Maine's decimated color company, was now convinced that " . . . it was only a question of only a short time when every man must fall before the superior fire of our enemy." And Corporal Coan, one of the few survivors of the decimated color guard of Company F, wrote how " . . . our line was melting away . . ."

Too little, too late, the 15th Alabama boys received a small measure of assistance from the pinned-down Alabama and Texas Rebels, which now ensured that no reinforcements from Colonel

Vincent's brigade would be sent to assist Colonel Chamberlain. These soldiers blasted away from behind the jumbles of rock on the west side of Little Round Top. Streaming in from the west, bullets from these Confederates took a handful of Maine blue-clads from the ever-thinning ranks of Colonel Chamberlain's left wing which fought Colonel Oates's attackers in front, or to the east. Now incredibly, thanks to the combination of Colonel Oates's relentless pounding and Adjutant Waddell's flanking fire, the hard-fighting 15th Alabama was seemingly within an inch of breaking the severely punished left wing of the mauled 20th Maine.[5]

Colonel Chamberlain fully realized the extent of the danger after "the center had been almost shot away" by the Alabamians's frontal and flank fires. By this time, all of the corporals and one sergeant of the color company had been cut down by the Alabamians. Only two color-guard soldiers from Maine would escape the day unscathed, including twenty-five-year-old Color Sergeant Tozier. Against the odds, Sergeant Tozier continued to defy the wrath of the hail of bullets, winning a Congressional Medal of Honor in the process. Colonel Chamberlain later described the crisis at the southernmost point of the line which was held by Color Company F: "only two of the color guard had been left, and they fighting to fill the whole space; and in the center, wreathed in battle smoke, stood the Color-Sergeant, Andrew Tozier [with] his color-staff planted in the ground at his side . . . "

Bolstering the shaky defensive line in Colonel Chamberlain's center were Adjutant Tom Chamberlain and Sergeant Ruel Thomas. Colonel Chamberlain had dispatched these two reliable natural leaders in an effort to somehow patch together a defensive line from what little was left of the other companies around decimated Company F to create an ad hoc center. Shot to pieces and hammered by Colonel Oates's relentless attacks, a distinct defensive line of Maine soldiers was no more by this time. Around the grotesque clumps of dead and wounded Maine warriors, a zigzag, irregular line of bluecoats stood gamely behind their rocks and trees in "groups and gaps, notched like saw-teeth . . ." One officer wrote how the 20th Maine's ranks "had become so thinned by the battle that they had but a little more than a strong skirmish line" in place by this time.

But because he had maximized his offensive effort by stretching his line to turn the 20th Maine's left flank and due to the high losses and the heavy expenditure of rounds, Colonel Oates was yet unable to break the defensive line held by the Maine color guard. By this time, Colonel Oates lacked the offensive capabilities to hit Colonel Chamberlain's collapsed center at the southernmost portion of the Maine line, with a crushing blow to exploit the tactical advantage gained by Adjutant Waddell's flank fire. Knowing how close he came to defeat on July 2, Colonel Chamberlain could never understand for the rest of his life how "it was strange that the enemy did not seize that moment and point of weakness." The answer could be found in the Alabamians's heavy losses and lack of ammunition.[6]

On Colonel Chamberlain's left flank north of the position of the 20th Maine's color guard, Colonel Oates continued to make the most desperate effort of the day to yet complete the task of turning the 20th Maine's left flank. The Alabamians's successive charges up the hill had surged over the many bodies now strewn along the bloody contours of Little Round Top. These men in gray from southeast Alabama had fought today like few other soldiers of the Army of Northern Virginia. During the fifth attack up the slope, the Alabamians were so exhausted and few in number that they now surged forward without unleashing their Rebel Yell.

Appalled by the carnage swirling around him, Colonel Chamberlain never forgot how "the formidable 15th Alabama, repulsed and as we hoped dispersed, [and] in solid and orderly array [had come] rolling through the fringe of chaparral on our left. No dash; no yells; no demonstration for effect; but settled purpose and determination."

Fearing that the 20th Maine's line was about to snap, another worried Union officer wrote how the Alabama attackers repeatedly "came on like wolves" to yet win the day at any cost. In his own words, Colonel Oates recorded the desperation at this time among his soldiers, who would not quit: "knowing the officers and men of that gallant old regiment, I felt sure that they would follow their commander anywhere within line of duty, though he led them to certain destruction."[7]

Most of all, the Maine colonel feared the worst, and that disaster was imminent, if not inevitable, because "our thin line [was now] broken, and the enemy in rear of the whole Round Top defense—infantry, artillery, humanity itself—with the Round Top and the day theirs." And gradually Colonel Oates gained more precious ground of the spur despite the devastating losses, encouraging his boys onward for one final supreme effort.

At his center near the boulder where his brother had been fatally wounded, Colonel Oates continued to implore his surviving officers and men to keep moving forward and to fight on as the day was nearly won. Reflecting the gravity of the situation and believing that the end was near, Colonel Chamberlain ordered his soldiers "to sell out as dearly as possible . . ." Surrounded by the many dead and wounded comrades of the 20th Maine's color guard, Sergeant Livermore later scribbled in his diary that the 15th Alabama Rebels "fought like demons."[8]

Knowing that it was now or never, the 15th Alabama made its deepest penetration up the body-littered slopes of Little Round Top at the line's center. Striking hard at the 20th Maine's left, Colonel Oates never forgot the dramatic moment when he "sprang upon the ledge of rock, using my pistol within musket length, when the rush of my men drove the Maine men from the ledge." Throughout this attack as during the previous four assaults, Colonel Oates lived a charmed life, somehow escaping the hail of bullets but not detection.

Firing his revolver until every chamber was emptied and encouraging his soldiers onward to yet win the day, Colonel Oates never before witnessed such savage fighting. Captain Prince recalled how "not a man in that devoted band but knew that the safety of the brigade, and perhaps of the army, depended on the steadfastness with which that point was held, and so fought on and on [even though] already nearly half of the little force is prostrate [and now] the dead and the wounded clog the footsteps of the living."

Despite Colonel Oates's most determined effort that resulted in the deepest penetration of Colonel Chamberlain's line, however, the Maine defenders advanced to reclaim the crest of the spur and continued to hold it, after regrouping once again. By any measure, the Maine soldiers were proving to be as hard fighting and resilient as the Alabamians. Colonel Oates possessed the advantage of the high-ground perch for only a short time, and lacked the strength to exploit his success.

Maintaining the tactical advantage despite the fire from Adjutant Waddell's flankers, Colonel Chamberlain's soldiers continued to blast away from the higher ground farther up the spur near the crest and above the large boulder. Hundreds of bluecoats continued to fire from behind the safety of fallen logs, trees, and the rocks raking the Alabama Rebels with a scorching fire.

Describing the key tactical advantage gained by his success in briefly overrunning the spur during the fifth attack and the successful turning, if only briefly, of the 20th Maine's left flank, Colonel Oates later emphasized in a letter to Colonel Chamberlain how, "as your left was driven back, my right was advanced, swung around until the rear, or greater part of my regiment was northward and which faced nearly south or southwest." In the same letter, Colonel Oates described that Colonel Chamberlain himself had "concede[d] that my regiment turned your left flank and swung that back some distance . . . " Indeed, Colonel Chamberlain explained that the Alabama attackers had "enveloped us completely" during the most determined assault of the day. And, in his diary, Major Spear wrote that Colonel Oates's soldiers succeeded in doing the impossible and "flanked us . . ." And most significant, Colonel Chamberlain also "acknowledged the Alabamians pushed his men back almost to Hazlett's guns" on the crest of Little Round Top.

Meanwhile, the soldiers on Colonel Oates's left continued to fight from the low ground of the wooded saddle between the Round Tops. It now seemed to the Alabamians that they could count almost as many dead and wounded of Colonel Chamberlain's refused left behind them as the number of defenders who were fighting before them.

The large numbers of these fallen bluecoats indicated the extent of the 15th Alabama's success in both gaining ground and turning the 20th Maine's left. More than one-third of the Maine regiment was cut down, including around forty men killed or mortally wounded. But the most extensive damage was inflicted on the Maine regiment's left wing under Major Spear. One-half of Colonel Chamberlain's left wing was knocked out of action by Alabama bullets, sabers, musket butts, and bayonet thrusts by this time.

Immeasurably providing support—both moral and in terms of firepower—to assist the 20th Maine were the steadfast veterans of the 83rd Pennsylvania. They were the forgotten heroes of Little Round Top in this sector. As historian John Pullen explained, "had the [83rd Pennsylvania] not held fast . . . the affair [on Little Round Top] might have had a very different outcome." Unfortunately for Confederate fortunes, Colonel Oates could count on no such close and supportive counterpart to exploit his gains.

All the while, a savage flurry of hand-to-hand fighting continued to flow up and down the wooded slope of death. During the most successful assault of the day, Colonel Oates described how at this crucial moment a portion of "the Maine regiment charged my line, coming right up in a hand-to-hand encounter. My regimental colors were just a step or two to the right of that boulder, and I was within ten feet."

A bold Maine soldier made a desperate attempt to wrestle the 15th Alabama's flag from the hands of Color Sergeant Archibald. Protecting the colors with his life as throughout the day, Sergeant Archibald stepped back to dodge the Yankee. The tough Irishman Sergeant O'Conner immediately drove his bayonet through the Federal's head with terrific force. So savage was his thrust with the bayonet that Sergeant O'Conner had difficulty removing it from the skull of the unfortunate Maine soldier, before turning to meet the next Yankee in hand-to-hand combat along the bloody hillside.

Color Sergeant Archibald would live to carry and rescue the 15th Alabama's colors in future battles. And after promotion to regimental ensign, on a beautiful Palm Sunday in April 1865 which the Irishman in gray would never forget, he would tear the battle flag from its staff and hide it in his shirt to smuggle the cherished emblem out of the Yankees's midst during the surrender at Appomattox. He would eventually take the precious banner back to southeast Alabama, fulfilling his promise to his people and regiment.[9]

Against the odds, Colonel Oates had doubled up the 20th Maine even more so than in any previous attack, relentlessly pushing the Maine regiment's left even farther upon its right. In addition, the 15th Alabama's success in turning Colonel Chamberlain's left made the 20th Maine's right more vulnerable, especially if the 47th Alabama Rebels and other troops on Colonel Oates's left resumed the attack to exploit the 15th Alabama's gains. Unfortunately for Southern fortunes this day, Colonel Bulger's hard-hit soldiers would not strike such a knock-out blow.

In contrast to the role played by the 83rd Pennsylvania in bolstering the 20th Maine's defense, this critical lack of assistance was a wasted opportunity to exploit Colonel Oates's gains at the critical moment of success. A simultaneous Confederate attack from both east and west at this time promised much. Such a combined, one-two punch delivered by the 15th and the 47th Alabama—as both Colonel Oates and Bulger fully realized—would have probably cut the Maine regiment off from the remainder of Colonel Vincent's brigade to the north.

Meanwhile, Colonel Oates, Color Sergeant Archibald, Sergeant O'Conner, and other surviving Alabamians remained at the regiment's farthest and deepest point of penetration around the large boulder, while the tattered Alabama battle flag waved in triumph over the bodies of those who paid the price of these gains. And Colonel Oates and his 15th Alabama believed that the day was theirs.

Meanwhile, Adjutant Waddell's veterans continued to fire from their high-ground perch, sending a hail of bullets into the rear of Colonel Vincent's brigade and delivering punishment from behind. All the while, more savage fighting raged across the wooded and brush-covered slope of Little Round Top. Maine and Alabama soldiers continued punching, yelling, lunging with bayonets, swinging musket butts, and dying in the intense heat of early July.

But the Alabamians's effort to capture Little Round Top was a task which was becoming increasingly impossible with each passing minute. At last, the raging gray tide finally receded as a result of exhaustion, high losses, and the lack of water, ammunition, and support. Nevertheless, Colonel Oates and his surviving officers were far from finished fighting the 20th Maine that day. Colonel Oates gathered as many men as he could find in the smoky woodlands along the eastern slope of the spur. Incredibly, he was planning to launch the sixth attack of the day up the body-covered slope of Little Round Top.[10]

With his fighting blood up, Colonel Oates never forgot the intoxicating mixture of the sweet taste of success mingled with surreal nightmare of the hand-to-hand combat. Smeared with black powder and the grime and dirt of battle, Adjutant Waddell's men, meanwhile, continued to busily fire from the "rocks from which to enfilade the Union line, the 20th Maine and Eighty-third Pennsylvania," fighting their own private war against the Maine Yankees.[11]

Rapidly loading and firing, these Alabamians shot down additional Maine soldiers from the tier of rocks and boulders. Adjutant Waddell's elevated position almost at the top of the spur was so high that it was well within sight of Little Round Top's crest to the right, or northwestward. A slight rounded ridge ran north-south along the midpoint of the spur, which extended southeastward from, or below, Little Round Top proper. From this rocky perch near the spur's crest, Adjutant Waddell's Alabamians possessed a commanding view and wide field of fire. These northernmost 15th Alabama Rebels could now see the southern end of Little Round Top. In addition, Adjutant Waddell's butternuts could also see the long bluish-colored range of South Mountain on the western horizon beyond the intervening valley of Plum Run and Devil's Den, which lay immediately to their front but hidden from view.

The rocks on this elevated point held by Adjutant Waddell's men made ideal firing positions. Waddell's marksmen were partially screened by the thick foliage and underbrush, while firing as rapidly as possible. This protective green shroud of cover hid these busy Rebels from the bluecoats of Captain Walter G. Morrell's Company B behind the stone wall, even though Colonel Chamberlain's skirmishers were only a short distance to Adjutant Waddell's rear to the southeast. And, despite the dense timber and thick underbrush covering the spur, Colonel Oates could coordinate his offensive efforts because the flashes of gunfire erupting from Adjutant Waddell's elevated position on the far right were just within sight of Colonel Oates's center around the boulder farther down the spur, allowing for an united effort to turn Colonel Chamberlain's left. Below Adjutant Waddell's position, meanwhile, a steady rain of minie balls from the rapidly firing Alabamians continued to unmercifully sweep Company F and other 20th Maine companies from left to right, or east to west.

All the while, the Maine defenders continued to cling onto the elevated and exposed position at the jumble of rocks and boulders above the timbered saddle between the Round Tops—where the present-day 20th Maine monument now stands. In his diary, Sergeant Livermore, one of the last remaining color guardsmen left fighting besides Color Corporal Coan and Sergeant Trozier, explained the terrible destructiveness of both a vicious frontal and flank fire of the "enemy [who were] flanking us, [and] had got behind a row of rocks under our left wing and were making fearful havoc in our ranks as every one who dared raise his head was sure of his man, and many lost their brains in the attempt. We stood until our center had lost half our men, and we knew we could not stand longer."

Now, consequently, Colonel Chamberlain's "two companies at the colors, receiving a fire from three sides, are swept like trees by a whirlwind," described Captain Prince of the slaughter in this sector. Consequently, Major Spear described how "the center suffered most [and Company F] lost in killed and wounded about 50 percent . . ."[12]

Like Colonel Oates who was busily making preparations for the sixth attack of the afternoon, Adjutant Waddell was gambling to yet win the day and his flanking movement brought an unexpected dividend as well. The boulder-studded terrain sloping gradually east from the eastern base of Little Round Top west of the stone wall provided an avenue for additional gains. Some of Adjutant Waddell's soldiers eased stealthily through the smoke and trees to get between Company B and the 20th Maine. This movement effectively isolated the entire company of Maine skirmishers, along with Berdan's Sharpshooters and Colonel Vincent's skirmishers, who remained idle behind the stone wall at the edge of the field which spanned eastward to the Taneytown Road.

In fact, some of Adjutant Waddell's men managed to slip all the way behind Captain Morrell's bluecoats of Company B. Captain Morrell, who was destined for a lieutenant colonel's rank and regimental command by the war's end, recorded "the first he knew of the [immediate] proximity of the rebels was the firing in his rear when they struck" Colonel Chamberlain's line. However, because of the heavy foliage, Colonel Oates and his top officers were unable to detect the Maine bluecoats lying low to their rear behind the stone wall—which itself was nestled amid the woodlands of the lower terrain of the gradually descending slope. And despite only a short distance away, Captain Morrell's Maine soldiers could not see their own regiment to the west now that it had been driven back upon itself, except for the flashes of fire exploding out of the summer greenery.

From their concealed position and yet undetected, Captain Morrell's Yankees, Berdan's Sharpshooters, and the Michigan skirmishers now unleashed a fire at close range through the trees to hit the Alabamians from behind. These hidden Federals now did "some excellent service in awakening uneasiness in the Confederate ranks." Ironically, Captain Morrell's Yankees behind the stone wall had already played a role in sabotaging Colonel

Oates's efforts to win the day by serving as an effective barrier between the Russell County Rebels of Captain Shaaff's Company A and the ordnance train of the Army of the Potomac.

While going for broke in attempting to overrun the 20th Maine's position, Colonel Oates's men were now being cut down from behind by the unexpected fire pouring in from the east. As they continued to hurriedly load and fire at the Maine soldiers in their front, these Alabama boys never knew what hit them from behind. With so many bullets flying in every direction amid the brushy woodlands, Colonel Oates's soldiers initially did not realize the direction of Captain Morrell's steady fire from the east which dropped more soldiers from their ranks. In addition, the deafening noise of battle, and the thick layers of whitish smoke of battle obscured the direction of the fire which was now tearing into the Alabamians's rear.[13]

Drenched in sweat, a breathless Captain Frank Park, who led the "Quitman Guards" of Pike County, and twenty-four-year-old Captain Blanton Abram Hill, a capable officer known as Blant who commanded the "Fort Browder Roughs" of Barbour County, came running over to Colonel Oates from the right, where their boys were being cut down from behind. These two young captains of promise, who were both destined for battlefield deaths later in this war, brought the astounding news that an unknown number of Yankees were firing in their rear. Alarmed but not panicked by the startling report of Federals threating his rear, the colonel immediately dispatched thirty-year-old Sergeant Major Robert Cicero Norris on the double to the left to secure reinforcements from the 4th Alabama before it was too late.

Sergeant Major Norris was a finely educated lawyer and physician who made "an excellent soldier [of Company F who had been recently captured at Antietam and exchanged] and a good man every way," wrote Colonel Oates. But like so many of Colonel Oates's efforts that day, the last-minute effort to round up reinforcements would be in vain. Sergeant Major Norris would be unable to locate the 4th Alabama.

As in the past, the poised Colonel Oates remained cool amid

the crisis, despite having no choice but to face some tough choices during this most severe crisis of the day. Colonel Oates feared that the Federals in his rear indicated the arrival of reinforcements from the Taneytown Road. Attempting to ascertain the exact tactical situation, Oates immediately sent Captain Park, who was "a fine officer, splendid disciplinarian, and commanded the respect and confidence of his men," back to the right to determine, if possible, the strength of the Yankees now firing into the 15th Alabama's rear. The trusted Captain Park who "had as much cool bravery as any officer in the regiment," panting and wet with sweat, quickly returned with the dreaded news which Colonel Oates feared most of all.

Captain Park estimated that two Union regiments were behind the stone fence only a short distance to the east, after spying two unit battle flags about 150 yards beyond the 20th Maine's left flank. These two distinct banners ascertained by Captain Park were evidently those of the 2nd United States Sharpshooters and the forty-three soldiers of Company B, 20th Maine.

In place to protect the 20th Maine's left at the western edge of Jacob Weikert's green hayfields immediately east of Little Round Top, these bluecoats beyond the 20th Maine's line had been suddenly transformed into a strategic reserve by circumstance and fate. Morrell's and Berdan's soldiers had not only protected the Army of the Potomac's wagons but now, most important, played a key role in saving the 20th Maine's left flank and the left of Colonel Vincent's brigade.

As Colonel Oates explained the no-win situation for the 15th Alabama with this new threat in his rear: "By this time, the Federal reinforcements has completely enveloped my right . . . at this moment the 15th Alabama had infantry to the right of them, dismounted cavalry to the left of them, infantry in front of them, and infantry in rear of them."[14]

With no hope remaining for victory and little for survival, Captains Park and Hill suggested to Oates what was unthinkable to the irrepressible young colonel from Abbeville: an immediate withdrawal in the face of the enemy. However, even by this time, the die-hard Colonel Oates was not the type of man to readily give up on anything, despite the odds. Even when now facing this new threat to the rear, he was not about to forsake his bid to capture Little Round Top. Colonel Oates, therefore, remained determined to fight it out despite the fact that "my dead and wounded were then greater in number than those still on duty [around 225]. Of 644 men and 42 officers I had lost 343 men and 19 officers. The dead literally covered the ground. The blood stood in puddles on the rocks [but] I still hoped for reinforcements."[15]

Meanwhile, the crisis became even more severe for the isolated and hard-hit 15th Alabama, which had already fought far beyond what had been expected of it on this day. Believing that "it seemed impossible to retreat," Colonel Oates told Captains Park and Hill to "return to your Companies [and] we will sell out as dearly as possible." After just receiving a virtual death sentence from his colonel, Captain Hill made no reply to the order, but like a good soldier he simply obeyed it in silence. He headed off through the trees eastward to rejoin his Company D and his Barbour County soldiers who were heavily engaged.

But Captain Park took the grim news of the suicidal order a bit differently. Captain Park's instantaneous response sent a sense of pride surging through Colonel Oates, who never forgot the moment. Despite knowing that such an order all but ensured his death, Captain Park, the fiery "Quitman Guards" leader, instantly smiled. The broad grin which highlighted Captain Park's dirt and powder-stained features said more than words could ever communicate. While whizzing minie balls poured across the eastern slope of Little Round Top's spur, young and handsome Captain Park then snapped to attention and presented Colonel Oates with a firm salute. This final gesture demonstrated the amount of respect that Captain Park felt for Colonel Oates and his determination to fight to the bitter end. Before dashing off to rejoin his Company I on the right, Captain Park responded to the crisis with an enthusiasm which impressed even the battle-hardened Oates, saying with a smile in response to the colonel's directive, "All right, sir!"[16]

With Colonel Oates's order to keep fighting to the end, and to sell their lives "as dearly as possible," the slaughter on Little Round Top continued unabated. And the ever-lengthening casualty lists continued to grow, with more Alabama soldiers falling to the blistering fire spitting from the angry Maine rifles. Finally, watching more good soldiers fall to rise no more for no gain and with success now out of reach, Colonel Oates reconsidered the wisdom of his decision to fight to the end. So far, the stubborn Colonel Oates had maintained not only his advanced position on the Army of the Potomac's left flank but also the initiative because "I still hoped for reinforcements or for the tide of success to turn my way." But that tide had now turned, going against the 15th Alabama for good, and reinforcements were nowhere in sight.

As additional minutes passed more of Oates's men fell and some soldiers were cut down with multiple wounds, after being hit by bullets from different directions. Colonel Oates, therefore, became more convinced that his regiment would be wiped out for neither gain nor glory if he remained in the fight. In addition, the threat to Colonel Oates's rear seemed to be growing. Perfecting a ruse, Captain Morrell yelled out frantic orders that seemed to indicate the advance of a much larger command, while their 20th Maine soldiers and the green-coated sharpshooters continued to maintain a heavy fire into the 15th Alabama's rear.

Oates later explained the no-win situation by writing how "with no one upon the right or left of me, my regiment exposed, while the enemy was still under cover, to stand there and die was sheer folly." Doing what previously was unthinkable, Colonel Oates was forced to finally call it quits, forsaking his dream of capturing Little Round Top and turning the left flank of the Army of the Potomac. But he did so only because a number of valid reasons could no longer be ignored or overlooked: the battered 15th Alabama was now seemingly all but surrounded by Yankees; they had launched five desperate assaults up the rocky hill against a strong defensive position on high ground and the resulting devastating losses now made his combat unit ineffective, especially in regard to launching the sixth attack of the day; an unknown number of Federals now hovered in his rear, apparently about to advance; he had lost many of his top officers, including his younger brother, and many of his best soldiers from the enlisted ranks; the lack of assistance from either headquarters or support troops; half of the Alabama soldiers were now without ammunition, after fighting not one but two battles this hellish afternoon; the Alabamians were also without food, rest, or water during one of the hottest days of the year; the long, exhausting march to Gettysburg had worn down the 15th Alabama men before they even fired their first shot; they lacked the presence of higher ranking officers to assist or advise him; and far too many 15th Alabama soldiers had been dispatched away from the regiment on detached assignments on this ill-fated afternoon in Adams County.

Consequently, Colonel Oates had no choice but to try to save as many of his remaining men as possible. He, therefore, was forced to cancel his ambitious plans for the sixth consecutive attack up Little Round Top. A frustrated Oates now ordered a withdrawal, after concluding with bitter resignation a simple reality which could no longer be denied: "I found the undertaking to capture Little Round Top too great for my regiment unsupported." He now dispatched Sergeant Major Norris, who had returned after having been unable to locate the 4th Alabama, to inform company commanders to retire upon the colonel's signal.

As Colonel Oates explained the disadvantageous tactical situation for which there was simply no solution, "with a withering and deadly fire poured in upon us from every direction, it seemed that the entire command was doomed to destruction. While one man was shot in the face, his right hand or left hand comrade was shot in the side or back. Some were struck simultaneously with two or three balls from different directions." Indeed, Major Spear described how " . . . Morrell had been keeping up a fire on the enemy, from the rear, during the fight [and] gave them the impression that they were surrounded, an impression the more easily entertained for the reason that they knew they had no support on their right, & must also have known that they were in rear of our main line."

In his battle report, Colonel Oates described what forced him out of a fight for the first time in his life: "Finally, I discovered that the enemy had flanked me on the right, and two regiments were moving rapidly upon my rear and not 200 yards distant, when, to save my regiment from capture or destruction, I ordered a retreat." Colonel Oates's dream of capturing Little Round Top and winning a decisive success was no more.[17]

Ironically, Colonel Chamberlain was nearly on the verge of making a comparable decision to retreat in part because his troops, like the 15th Alabama, also were being hit by a fire streaming from the opposite side of Little Round Top, where Texas and Alabama Rebels blasted into the 16th Michigan and the 44th New York from the rear. Most of all, however, Colonel Chamberlain feared that Colonel Oates was about to launch his sixth assault of the day, and realized that his 20th Maine would certainly break under the strain. He apparently saw the 15th Alabama forming in column for a withdrawal, and reasoned that yet another assault was pending. Consequently, and almost as if hoping to scare off Colonel Oates and his band of Alabama Rebels by a final show of bravado and defiance, a final volley poured from a beaten 20th Maine. With ammunition low, high casualties, and his position seemingly compromised, Colonel Chamberlain was fearing the worst, knowing that "it would be impossible to fight off another assault." The day seemed lost for the Union.

But Colonel Oates had no choice under the circumstances but to retire. For the rest of his life, one thought would remain to forever haunt Colonel Oates as a painful obsession and haunting memory of days gone by: "If I had had one more regiment we would have completely turned the flank and have won Little Round Top, which would have forced General Meade's whole left wing to retire."

CHAPTER XIII

Advance of the 20th Maine

"With no one upon the right or left of me, my regiment exposed, while the enemy was still under cover, to stand there and die was sheer folly."

—Colonel William C. Oates

In being forced to withdraw, Colonel Oates left behind much more than simply the cherished dreams of decisive Confederate victory at Gettysburg. Behind the boulder near the top of the spur a blood-soaked Lieutenant Oates lay writhing in pain, too badly hurt to be taken rearward. Amid the tangled brush and hot woodlands of bloody Little Round Top, this granite boulder on the bloody eastern slope of the spur near the top was not high enough to protect Lieutenant Oates from the fire pouring from the highest point of the spur. Like most of the 15th Alabama's badly wounded, Lieutenant Oates would have to be abandoned to the Federals's mercy.[1]

Like the Alabama Rebels, the hard-pressed bluecoats were now also greatly concerned about the welfare of their many wounded friends, comrades, and relatives. Dozens of wounded Maine sol-

287

diers lay farther down the wooded and body-strewn slope before the Alabamians's main line. As demonstrated that afternoon, these hard-fighting Alabama Rebels were known for their ferocity in combat. Colonel Chamberlain's survivors might now have incorrectly equated this combat reputation with a desire to kill wounded Yankees. This fear of an Alabama no-quarter policy caused some Maine soldiers to think the worst of their adversary.

Therefore, young Lieutenant Melcher, Company F's commander, raced from the center and over to Colonel Chamberlain. He now suggested "an advance of his company [F], in order to cover the line of wounded, exposed by the retirement of the left wing . . .," wrote Captain Prince. Indeed, Major Spear explained the existing situation that had developed "immediately on the left of the colors [Company F], the line thinned by the fire had readjusted itself amongst the boulders, and this left wounded men in front of the line and still exposed to the fire [and] these were calling on their comrades to take them to the rear . . ."

During the lull, Colonel Chamberlain agreed to the suggestion and granted permission for Lieutenant Melcher, a most promising "officer who had worked his way up from the ranks," to advance down the eastern slope of the body-littered spur. Then Lieutenant Melcher returned to what little remained of his decimated Company F.

The advance by the regiment's center downhill was to occupy the first "ledge" position which had been earlier captured by the 15th Alabama. This was where so many Maine soldiers now lay wounded and dying. Lieutenant Melcher and his color guard and other Maine soldiers in the center were eager to make the advance to secure this lost ground and their wounded comrades. By advancing only a short distance downhill, the Yankees could take possession of the many wounded comrades who were strewn across the hillside.

But more than simply humanitarian considerations called for a Maine advance eastward. The cartridge-boxes of the wounded, both blue and gray, yet contained rounds, and the Maine soldiers—like the Alabamians—had by this time expended most of their ammunition. With no resupplies forthcoming to either Oates's or Chamberlain's regiments fighting to the death on the far southern end of their respective armies, only the cartridge-boxes of the fallen could now provide additional rounds to both the Alabama and Maine men.

In preparation for Lieutenant Melcher's and Company F's advance, Colonel Chamberlain bellowed, "Bayonets!" Then Lieutenant Melcher dashed some ten paces before his Company F, which was "more than half the distance between the hostile lines," wrote Private Gerrish. Melcher's bold example was destined to work like magic to the worn and battle-weary Maine troops, encouraging other 20th Maine soldiers along the line to also consider moving forward and down the slope.

Lieutenant Melcher surged downhill with the remaining survivors of the color guard, Color Sergeant Livermore, Color Corporal Coan, and Color Sergeant Andrew Tozier, who carried the 20th Maine's battle flag. "With a cheer, and a flash of his sword, that sent an inspiration along the line," wrote Private Gerrish, Lieutenant Melcher served as the catalyst for the launching of the general spontaneous advance not only by the 20th Maine but also by a heavy skirmish line from the 83rd Pennsylvania.

While Colonel Chamberlain watched in silence, the lieutenant "sprang ahead of the line, the colors [also] advancing" as Melcher led the way down the wooded slope covered with bodies. The sight of the advancing colors—more than any of Colonel Chamberlain's orders or actions—was the spark which inspired the general advance of the 20th Maine.

On the regiment's left, Major Spear, ironically much like Colonel Chamberlain, had no idea that a general advance had been sparked. In his own words of shocked disbelief: "Suddenly, in the midst of the noise of musketry, I heard a shout on the center, of 'Forward,' & saw the line & colors begin to move. I had received no orders, other than to hold the left and guard the flank and did not understand the meaning of the movement." It is not known but perhaps a noncommissioned officer or even an enlisted man of Company F had shouted, "Forward."

Following Lieutenant Melcher's inspiring example, Major Spear then led the 150 men of the left wing forward and down the hill with fixed bayonets. As Major Spear described the confusing situation in the absence of Colonel Chamberlain's orders to advance and his own decision to likewise move forward, ". . . there was no time to seek explanation [as] the center was going ahead, apparently charging the enemy, if any, then all of course, and we all joined in the shouts and movement, and went in a rush down the slope and over the boulders."

The 20th Maine's bayonet "attack" little resembled today's highly romanticized and popularized versions of a glorious charge which swept aside all resistance and achieved decisive victory. Major Spear described how the spontaneous, if not accidental in terms of a general advance, forward movement hardly resembled what has been immortalized by generations of historians in realistic terms: "This, as was said of the [British cavalry] charge of Balaklaver [sic], was 'fine but not war' [as] it could not be done as [Lieutenant Melcher] meant it; but as it turned out, better than he meant it. For the cry once started, went along the line with the movement which accompanied the cry. A few files away from the point where the cry and movement started, the men heard only [the word "advance"] and took it for a charge, and acted accordingly." Thus Major Spear and his soldiers of the five refused companies surged down the slope and were surprised to meet few Rebels, and these quickly gave up because they were out of ammunition.

The explanation for the lack of resistance was simple. Colonel Oates had already ordered his survivors to depart. Consequently, the advance of the 20th Maine met little, if any, resistance. In Major Spear's words, "behind one boulder, on the slope, over which I went, were two Confederates, who rose up, evidently with empty muskets . . . but there was no contest with them."

A knee-jerk, instinctive and spontaneous response not based upon either a well-developed plan or tactical decision, Colonel Chamberlain merely followed Lieutenant Melcher's and then Major Spear's example as events beyond the college professor's control now dictated the outcome of the course and sequence of events on Little Round Top. Therefore, Colonel Chamberlain and his right wing also now surged forward, belatedly joining in the advance of the regiment's center and left after both had already advanced a good distance down the slope. As discussed in countless lectures at military schools and military leadership seminars and as carefully explained in popular military textbooks, the idea that the 20th Maine's counterattack was a well-planned, premeditated right wheel of the left half of the 20th Maine which united with the right wing for a general advance in a well-coordinated feat of tactical brilliance that led to victory is popular fiction.

In addition, the forward movement of the entire 20th Maine down the wooded slope was more in an easterly direction than the commonly believed southerly direction as later claimed by Colonel Chamberlain. After Chamberlain decided to join the advance of the unit he commanded, the entire Maine regiment surged down both the wooded eastern and southern slope of the spur.

But clearly, the 20th Maine's advance was most opportune. By this time, the Maine soldiers knew that they could not withstand another assault as fierce as the last one. If launched by Colonel Oates, this would have been the sixth attack of the day by the 15th Alabama. It seems almost as if the Alabamians's repeated assaults had resulted in the Maine soldiers launching their own general advance in more of a preemptive strike than an effort to win victory.

But the 20th Maine's advance a short distance down the slope had unexpectedly and suddenly turned into a general attack without Colonel Chamberlain having ever given the order to "Charge!" Major Spear explained how "some men in Co. K suggested that they 'advance & cover them' & therefore started the shout to advance. The shout & corresponding movement immediately spread to the left, (and I suppose to the right also.) But the cause & nature of the movement was not also transmitted with the shout, it was understood to be an order to charge—I repeated the order, which came 'in the air,' though I had received none directly, as it seemed to be the only thing to be done [and] fortunately it result-ed well."

Clearly, this first Maine advance of the day was as much an effort from the enlisted ranks as from its officers. Rather than the 20th Maine's romanticized commander, the average common sol-dier from Maine more correctly deserved credit for turning an advance to secure wounded and regain lost ground into a general attack. Indeed, it was these men in the ranks who instinctively advanced on their own without orders from Colonel Chamberlain, following Lieutenant Melcher's example and a legend was born. This unplanned and unexpected forward movement by the Maine regiment now pushed down the wooded slope of Little Round Top with a will of its own. As Captain Prince described: " . . . with one wild rush the devoted regiment hurls down the ledge into the midst of the gray lines, not thirty paces distant."[2]

With plenty of fight remaining and while retiring by the way they had come, some Alabama soldiers turned to face the sudden surge of the 20th Maine's center and right off the high ground. Making stands behind trees, those Alabamians with a few car-tridges remaining snapped off quick shots, bracing for the impact of the Union advance before they could retire all the way down the slope as ordered by Colonel Oates. Captain Prince described the meeting of blue and gray for the last time in this sector, as it erupt-ed into another savage clash and hand-to-hand struggle: "For one instant the battle wavers in the balance. Pistols are leveled, swords flash in the air and bayonets clash." But no one was more sur-prised by the Alabamians's continued defiance than Colonel Chamberlain, who led the regiment's right wing forward. In his battle report, he described with amazement how at this point "the enemy's first line scarcely tried to run—they stood" their ground. The Alabama soldiers stood so firm that Captain Prince doubted the outcome of this final hand-to-hand struggle even after the 20th Maine's counterattack had struck home. Captain Prince was yet very much concerned as to "which [side] wins the day, Union or rebel? Will our little line be swallowed up in the gray ranks?" And a few remaining shots, thrusting bayonets, and swinging musket butts of the Alabama Rebels did momentarily check the counter-stroke of the right and center of the 20th Maine.[3]

Indeed, in this hotly contested sector the struggle for Little Round Top was yet to be decided. This final defiance now cost a few Maine soldiers their lives and again almost cost Colonel Chamberlain his life. Standing with Company L's survivors of the "Pike County Sharpshooters" was Lieutenant Robert Wicker, who had fought on the Alabama regiment's right just to the left of Adjutant Waddell's band on the north but had retired as ordered by Colonel Oates. Confronted while withdrawing, he turned to now face the 20th Maine's advancing center. The twenty-one-year-old Lieutenant Wicker was "a fine soldier" and capable leader of the Pike County Rebels. Promoted to an officer's rank in October 1862, young Wicker "was as brave a man as any in that regiment."

Lieutenant Wicker now stood his ground before the 20th Maine's center as the attack swept southward down the timbered slope of the embattled spur. Colonel Chamberlain described how "at the first dash the commanding officer I happened to confront, coming on fiercely, sword in one hand, and big navy revolver on the other, fires one barrel almost in my face; but seeing the quick saber-point at his throat, reverses arms, gives sword and pistol into my hands and yields himself prisoner."

Impressed by Lieutenant Wicker's defiance in a hopeless situation and against the odds, Colonel Chamberlain assigned "a brave sergeant" to protect the captured lieutenant who was destined for imprisonment at Fort Delaware, while the combat swirled viciously around them. The Alabamians fought back to repel the counterattack with a spirit which marked their five assaults up the hill.[4]

However, what most of all had determined the final outcome of the struggle for Little Round Top in this sector was not as much the 20th Maine's charge downhill from the west and south as the combination of the enfilade and fires from the east. Indeed, Captain Morrell and his forty-two men of Company B and at least twenty of Colonel Berdan's 2nd United States Sharpshooters under the command of a noncommissioned officer, and perhaps as many as fifty detached 16th Michigan skirmishers of Colonel Vincent's brigade most of all effectively had ended Colonel Oates's offensive efforts that day. More than one hundred men in blue, evidently under the overall command of Captain Morrell, continued to pour a vicious flanking fire from the east to punish the Alabamians from the rear while they faced the 20th Maine's advance in front. This threat from the east was significant, representing almost one-third as many men who stood in the 20th Maine's ranks before the battle. "For some time [these Rebels to the north were] experiencing the effects of a fitful and mysterious fire, which came apparently from his rear, and at times his men had been struck by bullets from front and rear at the same time," described one survivor of Little Round Top's horror. Because the effects of this hot fire tearing into the Alabamians's rear from the stone wall was yet "unknown and unsuspected" by Colonel Chamberlain's attackers, these men, and especially the colonel, incorrectly believed that their advance alone had been decisive in defeating the 15th Alabama.

However, it was this threat from the east and not the counterattack from the south and west which was most decisive in convincing Colonel Oates to withdraw. The most reliable and accurate chronicler of the struggle for Little Round Top, Major Spear realized as much, describing how the Alabama Rebels were swept rearward not so much by the 20th Maine's spontaneous attack but by Captain Morrell's strike upon the Alabamians's rear: "Then we discovered that Morrill and Company B had been behind a stone wall at the edge of the field behind the line of the enemy, and had been firing upon them [the Alabamians] from the rear. This probably accounts for the readiness with which they yielded to our charge."[5]

Colonel Oates and his men knew the truth of what had played the most important role in determining the day at Little Round Top more clearly than the boys in blue. Colonel Oates later explained how "the historian of [the 20th Maine] claims that its charge drove us from the field [but] this is not true; *I ordered the retreat.*" As Private Jordan, Alabama Company B, explained the proper sequence of events which largely determined the outcome of the struggle for Little Round Top: "While the duel [with the 20th Maine] was in progress, Colonel Oates saw the situation, and ordered a retreat, as the enemy would have soon been in our rear . . ."

It is clear that Colonel Oates had ordered his withdrawal *before* the 20th Maine surged down the southern and eastern slope of Little Round Top because of this perceived serious and potential threat from the flank and rear. Colonel Oates described the situation when he "did order a retreat, but did not undertake to retire in order. I sent Sergeant-Major Norris and had the officers and men advised the best I could that when the signal was given that we would not try to retreat in order, but every one should run in the direction from whence we came, and halt on the top of the Big Round Top Mountain."

The withdrawal down the eastern slope resulted in the Alabamians retiring southeastward to the low ground along the eastern base of Little Round Top. As fate would have it, this angle of withdrawal meant that the Rebels were moving in the direction that they had come with such high hopes after capturing Big Round Top. However, this retrograde movement took the Alabama soldiers on the right and center toward the stone wall held by the Yankees at the western edge of farmer Weikert's hayfield. Consequently, the Alabamians's withdrawal led them into a collision course with the Union counterattack that had smashed into their rear. Combined with the high losses and with half his soldiers being out of ammunition, this attack and punishing fire was too much for the battle-weary troops to stand.

In summarizing the devastating effect of Captain Morrell's flank and rear attack from the east, Colonel Oates wrote in a postwar letter to Lieutenant Colonel Stoughton, the commander of Berdan's Sharpshooters who struck the exposed right flank and rear of the 15th Alabama only minutes before the 20th Maine's advance downhill. In this letter, Colonel Oates accurately described the tactical situation, which was not distorted by the romanticized postwar writings of Colonel Chamberlain and other 20th Maine soldiers: ". . . you appeared directly in my rear and opened fire on me. I then occupied a ledge of rocks from which I had driven the 20th Maine [but] you in the rear, forced my thinned ranks to face and fire in both directions, which we could not long endure." Revealing the truth of the story of Little Round Top, Colonel Oates concluded in his letter with no exaggeration how "you and your command deserve a monument for turning the tide in favor of the Union cause." Captain Judson, 83rd Pennsylvania, also realized as much, writing how Captain Morrell's soldiers and the other men from the stone wall "contributed importantly" to Union success on the far left of the Army of the Potomac.[6]

Thereafter, the bloody struggle for Little Round Top came to an anticlimactic end, with the Maine regiment sweeping off the high ground and over the Alabamians to overpower some of the last remaining resistance. Major Spear's men on the left wing rounded up prisoners, while "down the slope we plunged, in not [a] very orderly line, but with a good deal of momentum, & with no small noise [and] the enemy did not seem to resist much [and] it seemed as if we must go over them. We did run over some, the men scattered & lying behind the low boulders." Yet the battle continued in some sectors as a few Alabama soldiers continued to simultaneously either surrender, run, or stand firm to fight back against the blue tide pouring down the slope.

Meanwhile, Captain Morrell's backwoods soldiers from Piscataquis County, the 16th Michigan skirmishers, and Colonel Berdan's Sharpshooters continued sweeping westward up the gradually sloping ground of the wooded saddle between Big and Little Round Top. But with most of the 15th Alabama men without ammunition, water, or hope for success, surrender became the only escape for many Alabamians. A good many of Colonel Oates's battle-weary men, caught while withdrawing, simply raised their hands, surrendering without a fight. Private Jordan described the quandary faced by the 15th Alabama's survivors:

> . . . it seemed impossible to avoid capture. I had determined never to be a prisoner, as I preferred death, without

hesitation, I made the attempt . . . I escaped a volley, there was not a thread cut on me . . . but expected to be riddled with bullets. When I had gone about one hundred yards, I heard a man hallowing. I looked back and saw Elisha Lane, of my company, a stout young man, who had been behind a rock to my right, in attempting to escape, was shot through the flesh of his thigh, was limping and bleeding . . . when I heard Lane and stopped to assist him, I saw six men at the rock that was with me surrender, five of whom were unhurt, one was wounded in the foot. This was a place that required more courage and determination to get out than to get in. So out of eight of us that were together, two made their escape from capture, six surrendered . . . out of forty-two of my company that went into the charge, there was only eight who escaped [but] where the 15th Alabama Regiment went [was] the high water mark of the Confederacy.[7]

Other surviving Alabama soldiers made one last stand. These Rebels hurriedly formed behind trees and boulders on the northern slope of Big Round Top, after escaping Little Round Top by running "like a herd of wild cattle," wrote Colonel Oates of his men responding to his specific order and upon his "signal" as opposed to a reaction to the 20th Maine's advance. Some soldiers could not run, however. In the words of Major Spear, "the wounded and dead of the enemy lay scattered along our front on the ground we had passed over in charging. One little fellow [of the 15th Alabama] I remember called to me for water. His arm was broken above the elbow." Certainly, this unfortunate soldier was about to endure the agony of his arm's amputation in a Federal field hospital, if he survived long enough after receiving water from the Yankees. Captain Judson, 83rd Pennsylvania, described the surreal carnage, writing, "Some idea of the slaughter made of the enemy may be formed from the fact that over fifty of their dead were counted in front of the 20th Maine alone, and judging from the usual proportions of five wounded to one killed, that regiment had probably inflicted a loss upon the enemy of over three hundred men [for] they laid in every conceivable position among the rocks [with] some crouched behind the rocks as if about to fire, some lying upon their faces, and some stretched upon their backs, like corpses laid out for a funeral . . ."

Then bolstered at the last minute by the timely return of Captain Shaaff and his Russell County Rebels of the "Cantry Rifles" [Company A] who rejoined the withdrawing regiment at the base of Little Round Top, a last defiant volley by the 15th Alabama, which had been rallied on Big Round Top by Colonel Oates and Adjutant Waddell, finally thwarted the Maine advance. And later that night, the killing of Yankees continued. One 15th Alabama soldier near the northern crest of Big Round Top, wrote a Northerner, " . . . killed or wounded 17 of our men during the night [of July 2 after] he had rolled a rock as big as a bushel basket ahead of him, while he crawled behind it."

At last the nightmarish fighting around Little and Big Round Top finally faded away like a summer thunderstorm rolling beyond the horizon. Only the scores of dead and wounded men now remained of the Confederate presence on Little Round Top. And in a letter to his wife, Captain Keene wrote of Gettysburg's horror describing the "blackened and mangled corpses" that covered the field. After surveying the carnage, he began to understand how "the Confederacy had received its death blow" in losing Little Round Top and the bid to win it all on July 2.

Retreating with his men Colonel Oates passed out from heat exhaustion and sunstroke near the summit of Big Round Top. The command of what little remained of the decimated 15th Alabama now went to the dependable Captain "Blant" Hill, the commander of the "Fort Browder Roughs" of Barbour County. For the first time all day, Colonel Oates was out-of-action—the fourth regimental commander of Law's Alabama Brigade to suffer such a fate that afternoon—after leading the 15th Alabama with skill and initiative during the most decisive small-unit action of the war. Thanks to Colonel Oates's efforts, a handful of the 15th Alabama soldiers had survived to fight another day. Captain Hill now commanded what little was left of the 15th Alabama in defensive positions near the crest of Big Round Top.

As a cruel fate would have it, however, Adjutant Waddell's soldiers never reached the safety of Big Round Top. Because they were the farthest north of any of Colonel Oates's men, Adjutant Waddell's soldiers had little chance for escape. After being dispatched by Colonel Oates to spread the withdrawal order, Sergeant Major Norris for whatever reason had not reached Adjutant Waddell's Rebels, who were fighting on their own hook when "enfilad[ing] the Union line, the 20th Maine and Eighty-third Pennsylvania [from] behind a ledge of rocks or ridge of ground, and doing effective work when I ordered a retreat," described Colonel Oates.

Though Adjutant Waddell eventually spied Colonel Oates's withdrawal to his left, and ordered his flankers rearward it was already too late for Waddell's forty to fifty soldiers who faced the onslaught of the extreme left wing of the 20th Maine. Colonel Oates described the fate of these hard-fighting Alabamians after Adjutant Waddell "gave the order and broke to run. He saw two of his men fall. He escaped, but his men were captured."

But in fact most of Adjutant Waddell's soldiers were actually cut down, never having had a chance of escape. Major Spear, commanding Colonel Chamberlain's five refused companies on the left, wrote how his soldiers chased Adjutant Waddell's unfortunate men off Little Round Top through a narrow lane, which led from the spur, at the north end of the stone wall. This dusty lane bordered by a rail fence became a death-trap for Adjutant Waddell's exposed soldiers who were cut-off from the main body: " . . . they did try to get out, some of them, and these got upon the fence and, painful as the necessity was, we were obliged to shoot them" during the hot pursuit. Major Spear also described how " . . . those in front ran, not so many towards the [Big] Round Top as to the rear [toward the Taneytown Road], and many ran and corralled themselves in a worm fence lane [and there] some of these, attempting to escape, were shot down, as they climbed the fence, and the others surrendered."

Only one officer of this band of Rebels escaped, after running a gauntlet of fire, Adjutant Waddell himself. And with the exception of the enterprising adjutant and one enlisted man, all of Waddell's soldiers were either captured, killed, or wounded. After escaping to the saddle between the Round Tops, Adjutant Waddell met and then rallied Captain Shaaff's long-lost Company A, which returned from the east side of Big Round Top, after their failure to capture the Army of the Potomac's trains.[8]

That night, the band of survivors of the 15th Alabama finally rested and slept in the patter of cool rain, trying to erase the haunting memories of the defeat and horror of Little Round Top from their tortured minds. Evidently under Colonel Oates's orders, a handful of Company H soldiers of the "Glennville Guards" ventured down Big Round Top, crossed the saddle, and entered the killing ground of Little Round Top on a mission to reclaim the bodies of Lieutenants Cody and Oates. The pitch blackness and the dense woodlands provided cover for the stealthy Rebels of Company H but the two mortally wounded Company G officers could not be found.

For their determined bid to capture Little Round Top, the bloody price paid by the 15th Alabama was frightfully high on July 2. Colonel Oates's regiment lost a higher percentage, 34.3 percent, of men than any other regiment of General Law's Alabama Brigade—more than one in every three soldiers that Colonel Oates took into battle became a casualty in only a few short hours. Oates calculated the number culled from his ranks, thirty-three men were killed, seventy-six soldiers wounded, and another eighty-four Alabama Rebels were captured from the barely four hundred men who went into the battle with such high hopes on July 2. However, Colonel Oates underestimated the total number of killed, which was higher than the thirty-three soldiers indicated.

In the savage fighting for possession of both Big and Little Round Top, Colonel Oates lost his most reliable officers, Lieutenant Colonel Feagin, Captain Ellison, and Lieutenants Oates, Brainard, and Cody, all of whom—except Feagin—fell to rise no more. Without exaggeration, one surviving Alabamian concluded how " . . . it was nothing short of a miracle that any escaped."[9]

The large number of captured 15th Alabama soldiers resulted for a number of reasons, including the expenditure of ammunition and sheer exhaustion and especially the 20th Maine's advance while the regiment was in the process of withdrawing from the field. In the words of Private Jordan, "the enemy had the drop on us and it seemed impossible to avoid capture [therefore] some of the men said they would not attempt to escape as it would be death to undertake to escape."[10]

The killed and mortally wounded men of the 15th Alabama included Captain Ellison, Lieutenants Oates, Brainard, and Cody, Sergeants Bailey L. Bibby, C. A. Parker, Lewis Spence, Leven Vinson, Corporal Samuel H. Gardner, Privates James Andrew Jackson Bagwell and James M. Brown, Major Edward Byrd, Privates Jasper Cureton, Daniel Hartzog, William R. Holloway, John Ingram, William F. Jones, John C. Jordan, John Keels, Benjamin E. Kendrick, A. Kennedy, William Lindsey, Amos Mansel, "Sandy" A. P. McMillan, John Nelson, Hardy R. Norris, Whitson Pugh, James M. Purdue, James Nicholas Shephard or "Nick," Lewis Spence, Henry D. Stone and William Trimner.

The Henry County boys of Company G suffered the greatest loss in the 15th Alabama with nine killed or mortally wounded. Colonel Oates had led the "Henry Pioneers" of Company G, his old company from Henry County, during the deepest penetration of the day when he nearly turned the left flank of the 20th Maine, Colonel Vincent's brigade, and the Army of the Potomac.

In 1896, then Governor Oates in Montgomery, Alabama, would receive a letter from a former Union soldier who described the tragic fates—like so many other forgotten 15th Alabama soldiers at Gettysburg—of Colonel Oates's younger brother and Lieutenant Cody:

> "Your brother, Lieutenant John A. Oates, after being wounded, was brought to the hospital of the Second Division, Fifth Army Corps. I found him to be severely

wounded, and expressed a doubt regarding his ultimate recovery. Lieutenant Cody was brought in about the same time, and I had them placed upon separate cots in one of our hospital tents . . . My sister-in-law remembers that your brother died on a Friday evening [July 25] as the sun was about setting [while Lieutenant Cody died three days previous on July 22 and] your brother's remains, as well as Lieutenant Cody's, were buried in a field very near to our hospital, along with many others who died at this hospital [and] at your brother's burial we marked his grave with a board head-piece, placing his name and rank upon it. But I fear time has removed all this."[11]

A complete list of 15th Alabama fatalities resulting from the decisive showdown at Gettysburg would eventually soar even higher. The arduous campaign and hard fighting during the ill-fated Northern invasion had weakened the 15th Alabama's captured survivors, playing a part in making them both early and easy victims of fatal disease once in prison. Two sets of brothers, E. A. and William P. Sellers, Company K, were captured at Gettysburg. William would soon die in the wintry hell of prison before the year's end. Both Joseph and George R. Henderson were also captured at Gettysburg but survived, while twenty-four-year-old Joe Henderson fell victim to a fatal disease in a filthy Northern prison.

As in having the largest number of both killed and mortally wounded, Company G also lost the regiment's highest number of captured at Gettysburg. Fourteen "Henry Pioneers" were taken prisoner by the Maine soldiers. The Dale and Barbour County soldiers of Company H, the "Glennville Guards," also suffered a high loss of captured personnel. John C. Beasley, age twenty-six, was "in poor health" at the battle's beginning. Therefore, Beasley's prison death came before the end of 1863. In total, fifteen 15th Alabama soldiers who were captured at Gettysburg would die in prisons across the North.[12]

The 20th Maine likewise took a severe beating in saving Little

Round Top and the day for the Union. More than one hundred Maine soldiers were cut down by the Alabamians and half a dozen captured. A total of thirty-two lifeless Maine soldiers were now sprawled across the southern spur of Little Round Top. Just over 33 percent of the 20th Maine's strength fell to Alabama bayonets, sabers, clubbed muskets, and bullets on the afternoon of July 2. This was a testament to the accuracy of the Alabamians's fire and the ferocity of their five assaults.

Colonel Vincent's other regiments also suffered severely. Shocked by the high casualties of Colonel Vincent's brigade, one 16th Michigan survivor, described how "when darkness covered us we held the same ground . . . that Warren had entrusted us with, and with what sacrifice! . . . Although unable to describe the fight, the memory of what I saw, the bravery, heroism and fearful grandeur of it all, I never shall forget [and] we who had survived the battle thanked God that we had been spared, whilst so many of our comrades had fallen" to save the vital high ground of Little Round Top.

In a July 4, 1863, letter to his wife, Colonel Chamberlain savored his success—which surprised him as much as Colonel Oates—and boasted with pride, and with what would become a Chamberlain trademark, no small amount of exaggeration and embellishment: "The 20th has immortalized itself. We had the post of honor in the severe fight of the 2d, on the extreme left where the enemy made a fierce attempt to turn the flank. My Regt was the extreme left & was attacked by a *whole Brigade*." A much more truthful and accurate witness to the factual realities of Little Round Top than Chamberlain, Major Spear scribbled in his diary on this bloody Thursday in hell: "we fought at close quarters more than 2 hours. They flanked us & hurt us severely [and] our men fell rapidly [but the] Regiment behaved nobly."

Clearly, even evident in this letter to his wife, Colonel Chamberlain had a self-serving dramatic flair and propensity for exaggeration, if not hyperbole, which dominated his extensive postwar writings and speeches. But on at least one important point, Colonel Chamberlain certainly did not exaggerate in a July

11, 1863, letter, when he maintained that "we held the extreme left of our line when the most furious attack was made." And he was also correct in describing Colonel Oates's hard-fighting soldiers in a July 17 letter with a rare hint of respect as "fierce fellows from Alabama [who had] never before been *stopped*."[13]

Besides Colonel Chamberlain, probably no one was more surprised by the success of the 20th Maine's spontaneous advance than Major Spear. He knew that the Maine regiment had been most fortunate, if not lucky, because "it was an extraordinary act, to charge as we did [and especially by] leaving our place in the line of battle without orders from the brigade commander or some higher officer [including Colonel Chamberlain, because] I heard no orders, & did not see Chamberlain during the fight."

Another factor played a role in the 20th Maine's success and that was the tenacious defense of the remainder of the brigade and the actions of Colonel Vincent. In fact, Colonel Vincent probably deserved more recognition as the real Union hero at Little Round Top. However, Colonel Vincent's death on Little Round Top only ensured obscurity for him while Chamberlain's own legacy was only beginning. In addition, the 83rd Pennsylvania was a forgotten player in the success story of Little Round Top for the regiment's defense helped to set the stage, "allowing the charging 20th Maine to" surge down the slopes of Little Round Top.

While Colonel Chamberlain would be presented the Medal of Honor and garner widespread recognition and ever-lasting fame for his role at Little Round Top, Colonel Oates would be forgotten because of his losing effort in failing to capture Little Round Top. In part because of this negligence and absence of recognition, he never forgave the failures of Southern leadership for the lack of support that led to the decimation of his proud old regiment on July 2 in yet another losing effort.

More than the performance of either Colonel Chamberlain or the 20th Maine, Colonel Oates blamed his losses and lost opportunities squarely on the failure of Confederate leadership, fate, and bad luck. Indeed, even when Confederate leadership knew what had to be accomplished on Lee's far right, General Longstreet largely sabotaged the offensive effort by taking too much time in getting his I Corps into position for the attack, and General Hood wasted much precious time in filing a protest instead of taking decisive action before it was too late. Both General Longstreet and Hood played roles in squandering the opportunity and wasting the precious time that allowed the Federals to occupy Little Round Top at the last minute.

To his dying day Colonel Oates firmly believed and swore that a fatal combination of factors conspired to decisively turn the tide against the 15th Alabama at Little Round Top. Indeed, when General Longstreet's troops finally struck after doing no fighting in the morning, midday, early afternoon, or midafternoon, only five Confederate infantry regiments attacked Little Round Top, and these offensive thrusts were disjointed, isolated, and uncoordinated. Neverthless, Colonel Oates, the most junior regimental commander in General Law's Alabama Brigade and with the least command experience, almost succeeded in doing the impossible task of driving the 20th Maine off Little Round Top and turning the Union left.

Never able to forget how close he had come to decisive success on Little Round Top which might have changed the course of the battle of Gettysburg and the Civil War, Colonel Oates could hardly believe the extent of the carnage on the second bloody day at Gettysburg. He described how "when the battle commenced, four hours previously, mine was the strongest and finest regiment in Hood's division. Its effectives numbered about five hundred officers and men. Now two hundred and twenty-three enlisted men answered the roll-call, and more than one-half of the officers had been left on the field—only nineteen answered to their names . . ."[14]

Worst of all, Colonel Oates realized beyond a doubt that he would have to live the remainder of his life with the haunting realization that on a hot afternoon at Little Round Top and not during Pickett's Charge "the high-tide of the Confederacy had reached its flood stage. This day [July 2, 1863] began its ebb, which reached low-water mark at Appomattox nearly two years thereafter." After the slaughter of three bloody days at Gettysburg, that "high-tide" of the Confederacy would never come again for the fledgling Southern nation, and would continue to recede. The Confederate experiment in nationhood slowly died an agonizing death after July 1863, and especially after the failure to capture an obscure rocky hill in south-central Pennsylvania called Little Round Top.[15]

CHAPTER XIV

The Death of a Dream

"The brave sons of the South never displayed more gallant courage than on that fatal afternoon of July 2d."

—Private Theodore Gerrish

When it mattered the most to Southern fortunes and as believed by Colonel Oates and his Alabama soldiers, a fatal combination of fate, circumstance, and luck had played a significant role in the final outcome of the struggle for Little Round Top.

Ironically, in attempting to hasten the death of the primary eastern army of one nation, Colonel Oates's failed attempt to capture Little Round Top and turn the Army of the Potomac's left flank on July 2, 1863, only paved the way to the eventual death of another nation, the Confederacy. In the words of one modern historian, what had been at stake during the struggle for possession of Little Round Top was an all-important and dramatic contest "to decide the fate of the Union," and "the fight for Little Round Top is almost universally viewed as the single most important struggle of the battle" of Gettysburg. Even though exaggerating the amount of opposition, Captain Judson, 83rd Pennsylvania, realized as much, writing how "a small brigade of four regiments, scarcely numbering eleven hundred and fifty men, had resisted and hurled back the best part of a division of the enemy's chosen troops, and had saved the army from rout and perhaps the nation from disgrace."

After their success at Little Round Top, Colonel Chamberlain and his 20th Maine soldiers began to slowly realize the full significance of their victory. The 20th Maine's success at Little Round Top had played a key role in placing the Army of the Potomac on the one-way "road to Richmond" which led to decisive victory and a future meeting between Generals Lee and Grant at Appomattox Court House. Colonel Oates's desperate effort to capture Little Round Top and turn the Union army's left flank to open the "road to Washington, D.C." for the Army of Northern Virginia was in vain, hastening the end of Confederate dreams of nationhood.

Only five days after the bloodbath at Gettysburg and partly explaining what had happened at Little Round Top to decide the destiny of two republics, a thankful General Meade wrote in a short letter to his wife that he was only too well aware "of knowing as I do that battles are often decided by accidents" and not grand strategy. Even while basking in the glow of winning the most decisive battle in American history, not even General Meade could yet fully comprehend how an obscure Alabama colonel and only a few hundred 15th Alabama soldiers had been cheated out of success at the last minute by the narrowest of margins, preventing them from capturing Little Round Top and perhaps turning his army's left flank, if their significant gains could have been exploited.

In overall terms, the 15th Alabama had failed because of a lengthy list of factors which determined victor from loser at Little Round Top; but that they came as close as they did to victory that day was an amazing feat when these factors are considered. By any measure, these disadvantages were simply too much to overcome: the long, exhausting march of more than twenty-five miles to Gettysburg; the many delays in reaching the field and the precious time wasted in finally getting into action; a missing water detail and fighting for hours with empty canteens during one of the hottest days of the year; the lengthy advance of more than a mile over rough terrain even before reaching Little Round Top; the hot fight that resulted in the attack and capture of the stone wall at the base of Big Round Top; the sheer height of imposing Big Round Top and rough terrain of both Round Tops; thickly wooded slopes clogged with boulders, woodlands, and underbrush to impede the advance; the order to immediately evacuate the commanding perch of Big Round Top and launch the futile effort to drive a Union brigade off the high ground; the soaring casualties which sabotaged the overall offensive effort, especially without the arrival of reinforcements or support of any kind; the dispatching of too many soldiers on independent assignments from the 15th Alabama; the lack of maps and guides or intelligence of the topography that could have enhanced the effectiveness of the Alabamians's movements and assaults; the overall confusion among the highest levels of Confederate leadership in terms of tactics and the mismanagement and misunderstanding of orders; the Yankees's timely observations of the Alabamians's approach which resulted in the last-minute arrival of a Union brigade to defend Little Round Top; the overall lack of support and assistance for the 15th Alabama for the entire day; the Alabama soldiers running out of ammunition during the long bloody showdown with the 20th Maine; and, of course, the fighting prowess of the 20th Maine and Colonel Chamberlain's leadership.

With bitterness and regret over what he believed was the greatest lost opportunity of the war, Oates vented his anger not at the Yankees but at his superior by writing with some emotion:

"Had General Longstreet been where the attack [on Lee's right] began, he would have seen the necessity of protecting my flank from the assault of United States sharpshooters. Had that been done, I would, with the six hundred veterans I had, have reached Little Round Top before Vincent's brigade did and would easily have captured that place, which would have won the battle. Or had he seen the Fifteenth and Forty-seventh [Alabama] regiments when they reached the top of Great Round Top, and ordered a battery and another regiment to aid me in holding that mountain, it would have been held, which Meade admitted, in his testimony on the conduct of the war, was the key to his position. With that in our possession he could not have held any of the ground which he subsequently held to the last, for it was the key-point of his position."

But perhaps most of all, an odd fate and destiny helped to determine which side won permanent possession of the rock-strewn hilltop called Little Round Top. Colonel Chamberlain was correct in believing that only a mere five minutes had separated winner from loser at Little Round Top, and hence at Gettysburg, on July 2. More than anyone else, Colonel Chamberlain fully understood how "it was certainly a narrow chance for us [and] this 'give and take' would soon have finished us . . . had the 15th Alabama continued their [attacks then] they would have walked over our bodies to their victory. Or, still again, if one more Confederate regiment had come upon our flank, we must have been rolled into a zero figure and swallowed up in the envelopment [by] those brave Alabama fellows [for] none braver or better in either army . . ." In addition, Private Gerrish described how "the brave sons of the South never displayed more gallant courage than on that fatal afternoon of July 2d" but this was not enough to ensure Colonel Oates's victory on General Lee's far right.

Colonel Oates also understood what an important role that fate, luck, and circumstance played on the second day at Gettysburg. Therefore, for the rest of his life, he would be obsessed with and haunted by the lost opportunities of July 2. Most of all, he would long lament "the absence of Company A from the assault on Little Round Top, the capture of the water detail, and the number overcome by heat who had fallen out on scaling the rugged mountain, reduced my regiment to less than four hundred officers and men who made that assault."

And, of course, Colonel Oates also regretted the loss of the five Alabama skirmish companies, explaining how "had these five companies joined my column on the north side of Great Round

Top, I could have captured the ordnance train, and it would have enabled me, in all probability, to have captured Little Round Top."[1]

But the 20th Maine's "obstinate hold of that important position baffled the plans of General Lee and made the battle of Gettysburg a Union victory." In overall tactical terms, Gettysburg was the worst performance during the four years of war for General Lee, his top lieutenants, and the Army of Northern Virginia, while the Army of the Potomac orchestrated its finest battlefield performance. The 20th Maine could make the same claim to having its finest day. However, Gettysburg also witnessed the best three days of fighting by the common soldiers of the Army of Northern Virginia. But the hard fighting and determination of the average fighting man in General Lee's ranks had not been enough to overcome the many mistakes and miscalculations of a fumbling Southern leadership at almost every level but especially at the top. Though in General Longstreet's corps, besides the brilliant success of the Mississippi Brigade's General Barksdale and Colonel Humphreys in overrunning the Peach Orchard and almost splitting the Union army in half and nearly reaching Cemetery Ridge, the dynamic leadership team of General Law and Colonel Oates was the shining exception to the rule on the afternoon of July 2. These two fine Alabama commanders demonstrated an inordinate amount of skill, aggressiveness, tactical flexibility, and initiative exactly when and where it was needed the most. After some of the hardest fighting on the bloody second day at Gettysburg and making significant gains on Little Round Top in turning the 20th Maine's left flank, the efforts of Colonel Oates's Alabamians should have won them fame as those soldiers who in reality achieved the "High Water Mark of the Confederacy," because they possessed a better opportunity to achieve decisive success then Pickett's Charge.

At Little Round Top, Colonel Oates's 15th Alabama had the golden opportunity to win it all, if they had only been able to push the 20th Maine off the high ground and turn Colonel Vincent's and the Union army's left flank, if sufficiently supported by their superiors to capitalize upon their success and to fully exploit those gains. Ironically, the Alabamians had come ever so close to accomplishing that feat despite the slim chances for success and their struggle against the odds. Unfortunately for the Confederacy, such an opportunity to win it all for the Confederacy during a battle on Northern soil would never come again in the short lifetime of the infant Southern nation.[2]

This lost opportunity at Gettysburg was most galling for Colonel Oates who realized the bitter irony on July 2, 1863: "There was no better regiment in the Confederate Army than the 15th Alabama, and when properly commanded, if it failed to carry any point against which it was thrown no other single regiment need try it. The long and rapid march, the climb of Great Round Top's rugged front without water impaired its power of endurance, but it fought hard and persistently until ordered to retreat. The other regiments of the brigade did their duty at Gettysburg, but the Fifteenth struck the hardest knot." But after some of the hardest fighting during the three days of Gettysburg, the shattered remains of the 15th Alabama left the battlefield with nothing left but their bullet-shredded battle flag and pride in their unsung role at Little Round Top, when they possessed the opportunity to forever alter the future destiny of the American nation for only a few hours on a hot afternoon in July.[3]

End Notes

Chapter I

1. Wilbur Sturtevant Nye, *Here Come The Rebels!* (Dayton: Morningside Bookshop, 1988), pp. 3–20.
2. Richard M. McMurry, *John Bell Hood and The War for Southern Independence* (Lexington: University of Kentucky Press, 1982), p. 74; William C. Oates, *The War Between the Union and the Confederacy and Its Lost Opportunities with a History of the 15th Alabama Regiment and the Forty-Eight Battles in Which It was Engaged* (Dayton: Morningside Press, 1985), pp. 198, 598; William C. Jordan, *Some Events and Incidents During the Civil War* (Montgomery: Paragon Press, 1909), pp. 39–40; J. Gary Laine and Morris M. Penny, *Law's Alabama Brigade in the War Between the Union and the Confederacy* (Shippensburg: White Mane Publishing Company, 1996), pp. 66–68; Robert T. Coles, "History of the 4th Regiment Alabama Volunteer Infantry, C.S.A., Army of Northern Virginia," Alabama Department of Archives and History, Montgomery, Alabama; Mark Perry, *Conceived in Liberty: Joshua Chamberlain, William Oates, and the American Civil War* (New York: Viking, 1997) pp. 1–2, 154–156, 319.
3. Jordan, *Events and Incidents During the Civil War*, p. 41; Noah B. Feagin to family, January 30, 1863, Fifteenth Alabama Regimental File, Alabama Department of Archives and History, Montgomery, Alabama; Laine and Penny, *Law's Alabama Brigade*, p. 65; Oates, *The War Between the Union and the Confederacy*, pp. 595, 598; Perry, *Conceived in Liberty*, pp. 1–2.
4. E. P. Alexander, *Fighting for the Confederacy: The Personal Recollections of General Edward Porter Alexander* (Chapel Hill: University of North Carolina Press, 1989) p. 229; Perry, *Conceived in Liberty*, pp. 1–3l; Nye, *Here Come The Rebels!*, pp. 3–6.

313

5. Jordan, *Some Events And Incidents During The Civil War*, pp. 38–39; Reid Mitchell, *Civil War Soldiers, Their Expectations And Their Experiences* (New York: Viking Press, 1988), p. 150; Perry, *Conceived in Liberty*, p. 3; Nye, *Here Come The Rebels!*, pp. 3–6.

6. Henry Figures to Parents, July 18, 1863, Figures Letters, Huntsville-Madison County Public Library, Zeitler Room, Huntsville, Alabama; Nye, *Here Come The Rebels!*, pp. 3–20.

7. Emory M. Thomas, *Robert E. Lee: A Biography* (New York: W. W. Norton, 1995) pp. 304–305; Jordan, *Some Events And Incidents During The Civil War*, p. 40; Perry, *Conceived in Liberty*, pp. 1–3.

8. Jordan, *Some Events and Incidents During The Civil War*, p. 40.

9. Laine and Penny, *Law's Alabama Brigade*, pp. 71–75; Perry, *Conceived in Liberty*, pp. 1–3; Nye, *Here Come The Rebels!*, pp. 3–20.

10. Oates, *The War Between the Union and the Confederacy*, p. 677; Noah B. Feagin to Family, January 30, 1863, ADAH; Perry, *Conceived in Liberty*, pp. 1–3, 120–136.

11. William A. McClendon, *Recollections of War Times* (Montgomery, AL: The Paragon Press, 1909), pp. 13, 16.

12. James M. McPherson, *What They Fought For 1861-1865*, (New York: Doubleday, 1994), p. 9–10; McClendon, *Recollections of War Times*, p. 162; Goodloe, *Confederate Echoes*, pp. 30–31; Wright, ed., "Sam Lary's 'Scraps From My Knapsack'," *AHQ*, pp. 502–504.

13. McPherson, *What They Fought For*, p. 25; Thomas Fleming, *Liberty, The American Revolution*, (New York: Viking Penguin, 1997), pp. 51–52, 93–94.

14. McClendon, *Recollections of War Times*, pp. 7–9, 48; Jordan, *Some Events And Incidents During The Civil War*, p. 14; Albert T. Goodloe, *Confederate Echoes, A Soldier's Personal Story of Life in the Confederate Army From the Mississippi to the Carolinas*, (Washington, D.C.: Zenger Publishing Company, 1893), pp. 10–11, 32; "Casper W. Boyd, Company I, 15th Alabama Infantry, C.S.A., A Casualty of the Battle of Cross Keys, Virginia, His Last Letters Written Home," *Alabama Historical Quarterly*, Volume 23, No. 4, (Winter 1961), pp. 295, 297; W. E. Wright, ed., "Sam Lary's 'Scraps From My Knapsack'," *Alabama Historical Quarterly*, Volume XVIII, No. 4, (Winter 1956), p. 505; William C. Oates, *A Short History of the Fifteenth Alabama Regiment*, Alabama Department of History and Archives, Montgomery, AL; William C. Davis, *"A Government of Our Own," The Making of the Confederacy*, (Baton Rouge: Louisiana State University Press, 1994),

pp. 20–25, 42; Laine and Penny, *Law's Alabama Brigade*, pp. 1–2; Perry, *Conceived in Liberty*, pp. 16–18, 319.

15. William C. Oates, *The War Between The Union and The Confederacy*, (1905), pp. 28–29, 68; McClendon, *Recollections of War Times*, pp. 21, 23; Davis, "*A Government of Our Own*," pp. 39–43.

16. Boyd, "His Last Letters Home," pp. 296–297; Wright, ed., "Sam Lary's 'Scraps From His Knapsack'," *AHQ*, p. 503; Perry, *Conceived in Liberty*, pp. 180–182.

17. Wright, ed., "Sam Lary's 'Scraps From My Knapsack'," *AHQ*, pp. 510, 512; Perry, *Conceived in Liberty*, pp. 180–182.

18. McClendon, *Recollections of War Times*, p. 9; Davis, "*A Government of Our Own*," pp. 20–23.

19. Wright, ed., "Sam Lary's 'Scraps From My Knapsack'," *AHQ*, p. 503; Davis, "*A Government of Our Own*," pp. 148–341.

20. McClendon, *Recollections of War Times*, pp. 11–14, 16–17, 19–20; Wright, ed., "Sam Lary's 'Scraps From My Knapsack'," *AHQ*, p. 508; Laine and Penny, *Law's Alabama Brigade*, pp. 20–21; Perry, *Conceived in Liberty*, pp. 114–115.

21. McClendon, *Recollections of War Times*, pp. 34, 47; Wright, ed., "Sam Lary's 'Scraps From My Knapsack'," *AHQ*, p. 505.

22. Oates, *The War Between the Union and the Confederacy*, pp. 70–73; Laine and Penny, *Law's Alabama Brigade*, pp. 20–21, 349; Perry, *Conceived in Liberty*, pp. 109–110.

23. Henry's Heritage, *Another History of Patrick Henry County, Alabama*, Vol. V, (Abbeville, Alabama: The Henry County Historical Society, 1993), pp. 1–2, 76.

24. Oates, *The War Between the Union and the Confederacy*, pp. 71–73; CASR (Compiled Service Records of Confederate Soldiers who served in Organizations from the State of Alabama, National Archives, Washington D.C.); Grady McWhiney, *Cracker Culture, Celtic Ways in the Old South*, (Tuscaloosa: University of Alabama Press, 1988), pp. xiii–50.

25. Oates, *The War Between the Union and the Confederacy*, pp. 262–263, 590–591.

26. Ibid., p. 337.

27. Perry, *Conceived in Liberty*, pp. 111–112; CASR, NA.

28. McClendon, *Recollections of War Times*, p. 19; Oates, *The War Between the Union and the Confederacy*, p. 68; Henry's Heritage, Vol. V, p. 112; Wright, ed., "Sam Lary's 'Scraps From My Knapsack'," *AHQ*, p. 505; Perry, *Conceived in Liberty*, p. 78.

Chapter II

1. Extended Edition, *Confederate Military History*, Alabama, p. 769; Oates, *The War Between the Union and the Confederacy*, p. 284.
2. "Robert Cicero Norris," *Confederate Veteran*, Vol. XXI (November 1913), p. 547; "Dr. R. C. Norris," *Confederate Veteran*, XXI (August 1913), p. 401.
3. "Dr. Harvey Oliver Milton," *Confederate Veteran*, Vol. XV, (July 1907), p. 320; CASR; Oates, *The War Between the Union and the Confederacy*, p. 589; Davis, *"A Government of Our Own,"* pp. 20–23.
4. Oates, *The War Between the Union and the Confederacy*, pp. 283–285, 709.
5. Billman, ed., *Joseph M. Ellison: War Letters* (1862), *GHQ*, p. 237; Donald B. Dodd, *Alabama, Now & Then*, (Montgomery, AL: The Advertiser Company, 1994), p. 13.
6. Oates, *The War between the Union and the Confederacy*, pp. 72–73, 200, 743, 735, 743, 748, 755–756; Henry's Heritage, Vol. V, p. 95; CASR.
7. Oates, *The War Between the Union and the Confederacy*, pp. 743–744.
8. Ibid., p. 744; CASR.
9. Ibid.
10. Ibid., p. 745; CASR.
11. Ibid.
12. Ibid., pp. 754–756; McClendon, *Recollections of War Times*, p. 210.
13. Oates, *The War Between the Union and the Confederacy*, p. 752, 755; Billman, ed., *Joseph M. Ellison: War Letters* (1862), *GHQ*, p. 235; Laine and Penny, *Law's Alabama Brigade*, p. 46.
14. Oates, *The War Between the Union and the Confederacy*, p. 583.
15. Oates, *The War Between the Union and the Confederacy*, pp. 583, 634–635, 673; McClendon, *Recollections of War Times*, pp. 22, 40, 225; Burnett, ed., *Letters of Barnett Hardeman Cody and Others, 1861-1864*, Vol. XXIII, No 3., p. 292.
16. Oates, *The War Between the Union And the Confederacy*, pp. 277, 666, 735; CASR, NA; Perry, *Conceived n Liberty*, p. 110.

Chapter III

1. CASR; McClendon, *Recollections of War Times*, pp. 29, 55, 63, 160; Oates, *The War Between the Union and the Confederacy*, p. 168; Edmund

Cody Burnett, editor, *Letters of Barnett Hardeman Cody and Others, 1861-1864, Georgia Historical Quarterly*, Vol. XXIII, No. 3, (September 1939), pp. 286, 292; Oates, *A Short History of the Fifteenth Alabama Regiment*, ADHA; Laine and Penny, *Law's Alabama Brigade*, pp. 19–20, 67; Perry, *Conceived in Liberty*, pp. 114–115, 146, 148, 319.

2.   Oates, *The War Between the Union and the Confederacy*, pp. 671–673.

3.   William C. Oates Papers, Sterne Library, Special Collections, University of Alabama, Tuscaloosa, Alabama; Oates Family Genealogy, Mrs. C. Frederick Pingel Family Papers, Enon, Ohio; Extended Edition, *Confederate Military History, Alabama*, (Wilmington, North Carolina: Broadfoot Publishing Company, 1987), p. 724; *Henry's Heritage*, Vol. V, pp. 4–5, 9, 69; Charlton Oates Pingel, Enon, Ohio, to author, November 3, 1994; CASR; Perry, *Conceived In Liberty*, pp. 13–37, 75–105, 406–408.

4.   William Calvin Oates File, Collection of Bruce S. Allardice, Des Plaines, Illinois; Mark Nesbitt, *Through Blood & Fire, Selected Civil War Papers of Major General Joshua Chamberlain* (Mechanicsburg, Pennsylvania: Stackpole Books, 1996), pp. 6–7, 27, 29; Laine and Penny, *Law's Alabama Brigade*, pp. xv, 24, 63; Perry, *Conceived In Liberty*, pp. 39–42, 44, 48, 52, 109–110.

5.   William C. Oates Papers, Sterne Library, Special Collections, University of Alabama, Tuscaloosa, Alabama; William C. Oates Files, Alabama Department of Archives and History, Montgomery, Alabama; *Henry's Heritage*, Vol. V, pp. 4–5; Perry, *Conceived in Liberty*, pp. 16–17.

Chapter IV

1.   R. Lockwood Tower, ed., *Lee's Adjutant, The Wartime Letters of Colonel Walter Herron Taylor, 1862-1865*, (Columbia, South Carolina: University of South Carolina Press, 1995), p. 53; Oates, *The War Between the Union and the Confederacy*, p. 327; Nye, *Here Come The Rebels!*, pp. 11–12.

2.   Douglas Southall Freeman, *Lee's Lieutenants: A Study in Command*, 3 vols. (New York: Charles Scribner Sons, 1934–35) Vol. 2, pp. 648–651; Jordan, *Events And Incidents During The Civil War*, p. 76; Nye, *Here Comes The Rebels!*, pp. 9–10.

3.   Tower, ed., *Lee's Adjutant*, p. 58; Clifford Dowdey, *Death Of A Nation: The Story of Lee and his Men at Gettysburg* (New York: Knopf, 1958) p. 46; Nye, *Here Come The Rebels!*, pp. 9–10.

4. Tower, ed., *Lee's Adjutant*, p. 45; William W. Hassler, ed., *The General To His Lady: The Civil War Letters of William Dorsey Pender* (Chapel Hill: University of North Carolina Press, 1989) p. 176; Nye, *Here Come The Rebels!*, pp. 9–10.

5. Dowdey, *Death Of A Nation*, pp. 3–13; Burnett, ed., "Some Confederate Letters," *GHQ*, p. 192; Edmund Cody Burnett, "Letters of Barnett Hardeman Cody and Others," *Georgia Historical Quarterly*, Vol. XXIII, No. 4, (December 1939), Pt. II, p. 362; Nye, *Here Come The Rebels!*, pp. 3–6.

6. Grady McWhiney and Perry D. Jamieson, *Attack And Die, Civil War Military Tactics and the Southern Heritage* (Tuscaloosa, Alabama: University of Alabama Press, 1982), p. 8; Nye, *Here Come The Rebels!*, pp. 9–10.

7. McClendon, *Recollections of War Times*, p. 141; Laine and Penny, *Law's Alabama Brigade*, p. xvi; CASR, NA; Nye, *Here Come The Rebels!*, pp. 9–10.

8. Extended Edition, Confederate Military History, Alabama, pp. 622–623; Oates, *The War Between the Union and the Confederacy*, p. 712; Henry County Historical Society Papers, Henry County Historical Society, Abbeville, Alabama; Billman, ed., "Joseph M. Ellison: War Letters (1862)," *GHQ*, p. 234; Burnett, editor, "Letters of Barnett Hardeman Cody and Others, 1861-1864," *Georgia Historical Quarterly*, Vol. XXIII, Pt. II, p. 365; Nye, *Here Come The Rebels!*, pp. 14–15.

9. Wright, ed., "Sam Lary's 'Scraps From My Knapsack'," *AHQ*, pp. 511–513, 518.

10. Oates, *The War Between the Union and the Confederacy*, p. 234; Noah B. Feagin to Family, January 30, 1863, ADAH; CASR, NA; Laine and Penny, *Law's Alabama Brigade in the War Between the Union and the Confederacy*, pp. 20–25, 365.

Chapter V

1. Alexander, *Fighting for the Confederacy*, p. 230; Ney, *Here Comes The Rebels!*, pp. 343–348.

2. Jordan, *Events And Incidents During The Civil War*, p. 40; Oates, *The War Between the Union and the Confederacy*, p. 206; McMurry, *Hood*, p. 74; Perry, *Conceived in Liberty*, pp. 1, 209; Emory M. Thomas, *Bold Dragoon, The Life of J.E.B. Stuart*, (New York: Vintage Books, 1988), pp. 241–256; Nye, *Here Come The Rebels!*, pp. 357–366.

3. Oates, *The War Between the Union and the Confederacy*, pp. 206, 631–632; Harry W. Pfanz, *Gettysburg, the Second Day* (Chapel Hill: University of North Carolina Press, 1987) p. 115; Edward G. Longacre, *Pickett, Leader of the Charge, A Biography of General George E. Pickett, C.S.A.*, (Shippensburg, PA: White Mane Publishing Company, 1995), pp. 112–113; 15th Alabama Infantry Regiment, C.S.A. File, Alabama Department of Archives and History, Mongtomery, Alabama; CASR, NA; Laine and Penny, *Law's Alabama Brigade*, p. 76; Perry, *Conceived in Liberty*, pp. 1, 3–4.

4. Oates, *War Between the Union and the Confederacy*, p. 206; Pfanz, *Gettysburg*, p. 113; Dowdey, *Death Of A Nation*, pp. 49–50; Laine and Penny, *Law's Alabama Brigade*, p. 76; Perry, *Conceived in Liberty*, pp. 6–7.

5. John H. Worsham, *One of Jackson's Foot Cavalry*, (Wilmington, NC: Broadfoot Publishing, 1987), p. 60; Perry, *Conceived in Liberty*, pp. 6–8; Oates, *The War Between the Union and the Confederacy*, pp. 206, 678–679, 684–685, 704; Thomas A. Desjardin, *Stand Firm Ye Boys From Maine*, (Gettysburg, PA; Thomas Publications, 1995), p. 39; Laine and Penny, *Law's Alabama Brigade*, pp. 76–77.

6. Oates, *The War Between The Union and the Confederacy*, p. 206; Laine and Penny, *Law's Alabama Brigade*, pp. xiv, 76–77; Perry, *Conceived in Liberty*, pp. 6–8.

7. Jordan, *Events And Incidents During The Civil War*, p. 42; Oates, *The War between the Union and the Confederacy*, p. 206; McMurry, *Hood*, p. 74; Edward Stackpole, *They Met At Gettysburg*, (Mechanicsburg: Stackpole Books, 1960) p. 182; James Longstreet, *From Manassas to Appomattox: Memoirs of the Civil War in America* (Secaucus, New Jersey: The Blue and Grey Press, 1985) p. 365; Burke Davis, *Gray Fox, Robert E. Lee and the Civil War*, (NY: The Fairfax Press, n.d.), p. 143; Extended Edition, *Confederate Military History, Alabama*, p. 725; Laine and Penny, *Law's Alabama Brigade*, pp. 76–77; Perry, *Conceived in Liberty*, pp. 6–8.

8. Stackpole, *They Met At Gettysburg*, pp. 179, 200; Pfanz, *Gettysburg*, pp. 118–119; Account of Colonel William C. Oates, Unpublished Manuscript, Bowdoin College Library; Glenn Tucker, *Lee And Longstreet At Gettysburg*, (Dayton, OH: Morningside Bookshop, 1982) pp. 5–6, 57; Laine and Penny, *Law's Alabama Brigade*, p. 77; Perry, *Conceived in Liberty*, pp. 8–9.

9. Tucker, *Lee and Longstreet at Gettysburg*, p. 14; O.R., XXVII, Pt. 2, pp. 317–319; Perry, *Conceived in Liberty*, pp. 8–9.

10. McMurry, *Hood*, p. 73; Robert M. Powell, *Recollections of a Texas Colonel*

at Gettysburg (New York: Nicole Publishing Company, 1910) p. 11; Perry, *Conceived in Liberty*, pp. 8–9.

11. Pfanz, *Gettysburg*, pp. 115, 119–121; Dowdey, *Death Of A Nation*, pp. 168–171, 198; Oates Account, BC; Jay Luvass and Harold W. Nelson, eds., *Guide to the Battle of Gettysburg*, (Lawrence, KS: University Press of Kansas, 1994), pp. 59–61; Laine and Penny, *Law's Alabama Brigade*, pp. 80–81; Perry, *Conceived in Liberty*, p. 9.

12. Robert U. Johnson and Clarence C. Buel, eds., *Battles and Leaders of the Civil War* (New York: Civil War Press, 1967) p. 320; Oates Account, BC; Perry, *Conceived in Liberty*, p. 9.

13. Pfanz, *Gettysburg*, pp. 121–122, 158–159; Oates Account, BC; Laine and Penny, *Law's Alabama Brigade*, pp. 78–81; Johnson and Buel, eds., *Battles and Leaders of the Civil War*, vol. 3, p. 320; Perry, *Conceived in Liberty*, p. 9.

14. *Recollections of a Texas Colonel at Gettysburg*, pp. 11–14; Pfanz, *Gettysburg*, p. 123.

15. McMurry, *Hood*, p. 75; Johnson and Buel, eds., *Battles and Leaders*, 3: p. 319; Laine and Penny, *Law's Alabama Brigade*, p. 371.

16. Robert K. Krick, *Lee's Colonels, A Biographical Register of the Field Officers of the Army of Northern Virginia*, (Dayton, OH: Morningside Bookshop, 1992), p. 136; Luvass and Nelson, *Guide to the Battle of Gettysburg*, p. 67; CASR; Laine and Penny, *Law's Alabama Brigade*, pp. 24, 39; Perry, *Conceived in Liberty*, pp. 173–174.

17. Jordan, *Some Events And Incidents During The Civil War*, p. 42; Oates, *The War Between the Union and the Confederacy*, p. 586; Wright, ed., "Sam Lary's 'Scraps From My Knapsack'," *AHQ*, p. 522; Laine and Penny, *Law's Alabama Brigade*, pp. 78–79; Perry, *Conceived in Liberty*, p. 9.

18. Wright, ed., "Sam Lary's 'Scraps From My Knapsack'," *AHQ*, p. 522.

19. Johnson and Buel, eds., *Battles and Leaders*, vol. 3, p. 320; Laine and Penny, *Law's Alabama Brigade*, pp. 78–79; Perry, *Conceived in Liberty*, pp. 8–9.

20. Oates Account, BC; Johnson and Buel, eds., *Battles and Leaders of the Civil War*, vol. 3, p. 320; Perry, *Conceived in Liberty*, p. 9.

21. Johnson and Buel, eds., *Battles and Leaders*, vol. 3, pp. 320–321; Laine and Penny, *Law's Alabama Brigade*, pp. 78–79.

22. Oates, *The War Between the Union and the Confederacy*, pp. 206–211; Laine and Penny, *Law's Alabama Brigade*, pp. 76–79; Johnson and Buel, eds., *Battles and Leaders of the Civil War*, p. 320; Perry, *Conceived in Liberty*, p. 9; CASR, NA.

23. Glenn Tucker, *High Tide At Gettysburg*, (Dayton, OH: Morningside Bookshop, 1983), p. 250; Oates, *The War Between the Union and the Confederacy*, p. 212; Laine and Penny, *Law's Alabama Brigade*, p. 79; Perry, *Conceived in Liberty*, pp. 9–10.

24. A. B. Bryant Skipper to family, March 6, 1864, HSHS; McClendon, *Recollections of War Times*, p. 224.

25. Oates, *The War Between the Union and the Confederacy*, pp. 601–602, 608.

26. Ibid., p. 212.

27. Oates Account, BC; Johnson and Buel, eds., *Battles and Leaders*, vol. 3, p. 323; Luvass and Nelson, eds., *Guide to the Battle of Gettysburg*, p. 70; Perry, *Conceived in Liberty*, pp. 200, 215.

28. Johnson and Buel, eds., *Battles and Leaders*, vol. 3, p. 320; Oates, *The War Between the Union and the Confederacy*, p. 622.

29. Oates Account, BC; Johnson and Buel, eds., *Battles and Leaders*, vol. 3, p. 321; Oates, *The War Between the Union and the Confederacy*, pp. 206–207, 676–677; Charles E. Boyd, *Devil's Den, A History of the 44th Alabama Infantry Regiment Confederate States Army (1862-1865)* (private printing, n.d.), pp. 98–100; Jordan, *Some Events And Incidents During The Civil War*, p. 43; CASR, NA; O.R., vol. 27, series I, pt. II, pp. 393–395; Bruce S. Allardice, *More Generals In Gray*, (Baton Rouge, LA: Louisiana State University Press, 1995), p. 46; Richard Wheeler, *Witness To Gettysburg*, (NY: Meridian Books, 1987), p. 187; Tucker, *High Tide At Gettysburg*, pp. 249, 261; McClendon, *Recollections of War Times*, pp. 209, 215, 227, 234; Extended Edition, *Confederate Military History, Alabama*, pp. 622–623; Desjardin, *Stand Firm*, pp. 39–41; Luvass and Nelson, eds., *Guide to the Battle of Gettysburg*, p. 70; Burnett, ed., "Letters of Barnett Hardeman Cody and Others," *GHQ*, Vol. XXIII, Pt. II, p. 368; Pfanz, *Gettysburg*, pp. 158–159; Laine and Penny, *Law's Alabama Brigade*, pp. xv, 2–3, 25–37, 40, 48, 63, 82; James J. Baldwin, III, *The Struck Eagle, A Biography of Brigaider General Micah Jenkins*, (Shippensburg: White Mane Publishing Company, 1996), pp. 10–11, 13–14, 16–18, 224–225, 253, 246–248; Perry, *Conceived in Liberty*, p. 191; *The Daily Picayune*, New Orleans, Louisiana, September 18, 1898.

Chapter VI

1. Johnson and Buel, eds., *Battles and Leaders*, vol. 3, p. 321; William B. Styple, ed., *With a Flash of His Sword: The Writings of Major Holman S. Melcher, 20th Maine Infantry* (Kearny, NJ: Belle Grove Publishing

Company, 1994) p. 101; John B. Hood, *Advance And Retreat, Personal Experiences In The United States & Confederate States Armies*, (NY: Da Capo Press, 1993), p. 57; CASR, NA; Laine and Penny, *Law's Alabama Brigade*, pp. 81–83, 392; Tucker, *High Tide At Gettysburg*, pp. 245, 421; McClendon, *Recollections of War Times*, pp. 188–189.

2. Johnson and Buel, eds., *Battles and Leaders*, vol. III, p. 321; Tucker, *Lee And Longstreet At Gettysburg*, p. 61; Laine and Penny, *Law's Alabama Brigade*, p. 83.

3. Johnson and Buel, eds., *Battles and Leaders*, vol. III, p. 321; Oliver W. Norton, *The Attack And Defense of Little Round Top* (Dayton, Ohio: Press of Morningside Bookshop, 1983) p. 254; Laine and Penny, *Law's Alabama Brigade*, pp. 81, 84.

4. Johnson and Buel, eds., *Battles and Leaders*, vol. III, pp. 321–322; Tucker, *Lee And Longstreet At Gettysburg*, p. 35; Shelby Foote, *The Civil War, A Narrative, Fredericksburg to Meridan*, (3 vols., NY: Random House, 1963), Vol. II, p. 501; Laine and Penny, *Law's Alabama Brigade*, p. 81.

5. Johnson and Buel, eds., *Battles and Leaders*, vol. III, p. 319; Dowdey, *Death Of A Nation*, pp. 208–209; Tucker, *Lee And Longstreet At Gettysburg*, pp. 61–62; Oates, *The War Between the Union and the Confederacy*, p. 261; Laine and Penny, *Law's Alabama Brigade*, p. 84.

6. Dowdey, *Death Of A Nation*, pp. 182–183, 186–187, 204–206; Freeman, *Lee's Lieutenants*, vol. III, p. 98–99; Johnson and Buel, eds., *Battles and Leaders of the Civil War*, vol. II, p. 341; Tucker, *Lee And Longstreet At Gettysburg*, pp. 27–28, 35; H. J. Eckenrode and Bryan Conrad, *James Longstreet, Lee's War Horse*, (Chapel Hill, NC: University of North Carolina Press, 1986), p. 197; William Youngblood, "Unwritten History of the Gettysburg Campaign," *Southern Historical Society Papers*, Vol. XXXVIII, (1910), pp. 314–315; Pfanz, *Gettysburg*, pp. 103–112; Laine and Penny, *Law's Alabama Brigade*, pp. 70, 81, 84; CASR, NA; Perry, *Conceived in Liberty*, p. 214.

7. Tucker, *Lee and Longstreet At Gettysburg*, pp. 14, 32–35; Pfanz, *Gettysburg*, pp. 120–123, 151–152.

8. Dowdey, *Death Of A Nation*, pp. 208–209; Freeman, *Lee's Lieutenants*, vol. III, p. 98; Laine and Penny, *Law's Alabama Brigade*, p. 84.

9. Dowdey, *Death Of A Nation*, pp. 209–210; Freeman, *Lee's Lieutenants*, vol. III, p. 99; McClendon, *Recollections of War Times*, pp. 68–69; CASR; J. B. Polley, *Hood's Texas Brigade* (Dayton: Morningside Bookshop, 1988), p. 157; Laine and Penny, *Law's Alabama Brigade*, p. 84.

10. Johnson and Buel, eds., *Battles and Leaders*, vol. III, pp. 322–323;

McMurry, *Hood*, p. 75; Dowdey, *Death Of A Nation*, pp. 198–199, 201; Tucker, *Lee And Longstreet At Gettysburg*, p. 35; Laine and Penny, *Law's Alabama Brigade*, p. 84.

11. Polley, *Hood's Texas Brigade*, p. 162; Laine and Penny, *Law's Alabama Brigade*, p. 85.

Chapter VII

1. Oates Account, BC; Johnson and Buel, eds., *Battles and Leaders*, vol. III, pp. 321–324; Oates, *The War Between the Union and the Confederacy*, pp. 207, 210, 787; Wheeler, *Witness To Gettysburg*, p. 183; McClendon, *Recollections of War Times*, p. 82; Tucker, *High Tide At Gettysburg*, p. 252; Oates, "*Gettysburg—The Battle on the Right,*" SHSP, p. 181; Russell C. White, ed., *The Civil War Diary of Wyman S. White, First Sergeant, Company F, 2nd United States Sharpshooters*, (Baltimore, MD: Butternut and Blue, 1993), p. 164; Luvass and Nelson, eds., *Guide to the Battle of Gettysburg*, p. 67; Polley, *Hood's Texas Brigade*, p. 174; Laine and Penny, *Law's Alabama Brigade*, pp. 82–83.

2. Oates Account, BC; Oates, *The War Between the Union and the Confederacy*, pp. 207–208, 210; Laine and Penny, *Law's Alabama Brigade*, pp. 83, 87, 90.

Chapter VIII

1. Wiley Sword, *Sharpshooter: Hiram Berdan, his famous Sharpshooters and their Sharps Rifles*, (Lincoln, RI: Andrew Mowbray Publishers, 1988), pp. 8–11, 15–16, 57–58; C. A. Stevens, *Berdan's United States Sharpshooters in the Army of the Potomac, 1861-1865*, (St. Paul, MN: The Price McGill Company, 1892), p. 526; Norton, *The Attack And Defense of Little Round Top*, p. 256; Henry I. Kurtz, "Berdan's Sharpshooters Most Effective Union Brigade?," *Civil War Times Illustrated*, Vol. I, No. X, (February 1963), pp. 15–16, 18; Laine and Penny, *Law's Alabama Brigade*, pp. 83, 87.

2. White, ed., *The Civil War Diary of Wyman S. White*, p. 164; Laine and Penny, *Law's Alabama Brigade*, pp. 83, 87.

3. Krick, *Lee's Colonels*, p. 136; Oates, *The War between the Union and the Confederacy*, pp. 589–590; Perry, *Conceived in Liberty*, pp. 192–193.

4. Krick, *Lee's Colonels*, p. 136; O.R., vol. XIX, ser. l, pt. l, pp. 973, 977, 813; Perry, *Conceived in Liberty*, pp. 192–193.

5. Sword, *Sharpshooter*, pp. 33, 35, 46, 54, 56, 63–95; Kurtz, "Berdan's Sharpshooters Most Effective Union Brigade?," *CWTI*, pp 16–17; Laine and Penny, *Law's Alabama Brigade*, pp. 83, 87.
6. Francis A. Lord, *Civil War Collector's Encyclopedia*, (NY: Castle Books, 1965), p. 253; Oates Account, BC; Sword, *Sharpshooter*, pp. 41–42, 61, 82; McClendon, *Recollections of War Times*, pp. 155–156; Norton, *The Attack And Defense Of Little Round Top*, p. 235; Laine and Penny, *Law's Alabama Brigade*, pp. 83, 87.
7. Oates, *The War Between the Union and the Confederacy*, pp. 639–640.
8. CASR, NA; Oates Account, BC; Oates, *The War between the Union and the Confederacy*, pp. 226, 239; Norton, *The Attack And Defense Of Little Round Top*, p. 235; White, ed., *The Civil War Diary of Wyman S. White*, p. 164; Krick, *Lee's Colonels*, p. 136; Laine and Penny, *Law's Alabama Brigade*, pp. 83, 87; Perry, *Conceived in Liberty*, p. 216.
9. Oates, *The War Between the Union and the Confederacy*, pp. 207–208; Laine and Penny, *Law's Alabama Brigade*, pp. 87–88.
10. Boyd, *Devil's Den*, p. 52.
11. Jordan, *Some Events And Incidents During The Civil War*, pp. 47–48.
12. Jordon, *Some Events And Incidents During The Civil War*, p. 42; Johnson and Buel, eds., *Battles and Leaders of the Civil War*, vol. II, p. 341; Oates, *The War Between the Union and the Confederacy*, p. 211; Oates Account, BC; Norton, *The Attack And Defense Of Little Round Top*, pp. 235, 256–257; White, ed., *The Civil War Diary of Wyman S. White*, pp. 164–165; John Pullen, *The Twentieth Maine, A Volunteer Regiment In The Civil War*, (NY: J. B. Lippincott Company, 1957), p. 113; Gregory A. Coco, *Killed in Action, Eyewitness Accounts of the Last Moments of 100 Union Soldiers Who Died at Gettysburg* (Gettysburg: Thomas Publications, 1992), pp. 36–37.

Chapter IX

1. Wright, ed., "Sam Lary's 'Scraps From My Knapsack'," *AHQ*, p. 522.
2. Powell, *Recollections of a Texas Colonel at Gettysburg*, p. 15; Dowdey, *Death Of A Nation*, p. 212; Tucker, *Lee And Longstreet At Gettysburg*, p. 156; Wheeler, *Witness To Gettysburg*, p. 191; William A. Frassanito, *Gettysburg, A Journey In Time*, (NY: Charles Scribner's Sons, 1975), p. 154; Foote, *The Civil War*, Vol. II, pp. 501–502; Norton, *The Attack And Defense of Little Round Top*, pp. 17, 107, 298–299; William A. Fletcher, *Rebel Private: Front and Rear, Memoirs of a Confederate Soldier*, (NY: Penguin Books, 1995), pp. 79–80; Emil and Ruth Rosenblatt, ed., *Hard

Marching, The Civil War Letters of Private Wilbur Fisk, Every Day, 1861-1865 (Lawrence, KS: University of Kansas, 1992), p. 89; Nesbitt, *Through Blood & Fire,* pp. 67, 83; Laine and Penny, *Law's Alabama Brigade,* p. 29; Polley, *Hood's Texas Brigade,* pp. 173, 177.

3. Oates, "Gettysburg—The Battle on the Right," *SHSP,* p. 179; Frassanito, *Gettysburg,* p. 157; Theodore Gerrish, *Army Life, A Private's Reminiscences of the Civil War,* (Gettysburg, PA; Stan Clark Books, 1995), pp. 104–105.

4. Oates, "Gettysburg—The Battle on the Right," *SHSP,* p. 172; Oates, *The War Between the Union and the Confederacy,* p. 210; Krick, *Lee's Colonels,* p. 292.

5. Oates, "Gettysburg—The Battle on the Right," *SHSP,* p. 178; McClendon, *Recollections of War Times,* pp. 66–67, 94, 109–113, 155, 160; Tucker, *High Tide At Gettysburg,* p. 249; Desjardin, *Stand Firm,* p. 39; Pfanz, *Gettysburg,* p. 217.

6. Jordan, *Some Events And Incidents During The Civil War,* p. 43; Tucker, *High Tide At Gettysburg,* p. 252; Norton, *The Attack And Defense of Little Round Top,* pp. 256–257; Pfanz, *Gettysburg,* p. 217.

7. Oates, *The War Between the Union and the Confederacy,* pp. 673–674; McClendon, *Recollections of War Times,* p. 112; Tucker, *High Tide At Gettysburg,* p. 252; *Henry's Heritage,* Vol. V, p. 5; Oates Genealogy; *CASR*; Perry, *Conceived in Liberty,* p. 18.

8. *Henry's Heritage,* Vol. V, p. 5; Perry, *Conceived in Liberty,* pp. 18–19, 35–36.

9. Oates, *The War Between the Union and the Confederacy,* p. 674.

10. CASR; Oates, *The War Between the Union and the Confederacy,* p. 674; Burnett, ed., "Letters of Barnett Hardeman Cody and Others," *GHQ,* Vol. XXIII, Pt. II, p. 370; Pullen, *The Twentieth Maine,* pp. 3, 13.

11. O.R., vol. 27, ser. I, pt. II, p. 392; Oates, *The War Between the Union and the Confederacy,* pp. 599, 705–706.

12. O.R., vol. 27, series I, part I, p. 392; Edwin B. Coddington, *The Gettysburg Campaign: A Study in Command* (New York: Charles Scribner's Sons, 1968) pp. 392; Norton, *The Attack And Defense of Little Round Top,* pp. 148–149.

13. Oates, *The War Between the Union and the Confederacy,* pp. 690–691; Met to Ned, July 29, 1861, Henry County Historical Society, Abbeville, Alabama; McClendon, *Recollections of War Times,* pp. 16, 116, 122, 177, 233; *Henry's Heritage,* Vol. V, p. 135; Styple, ed., *With a Flash of His Sword,* p. 132.

14. Oates, *The War Between the Union and the Confederacy*, p. 210; McClendon, *Recollections of War Times*, pp. 32, 34.

15. Edmund Cody Burnett, ed., "Letters of Three Lightfoot Brothers, 1861-1864," *Georgia Historical Quarterly*, Vol. XXV, No. 4, (December 1941), pp. 371–378.

16. CASR; Burnett, ed., "Letters of Barnett Hardeman Cody and Others, 1861-1864," *GHQ*, Vol. XXIII, Pt. II, pp. 284, 289, 371–372.

17. Burnett, ed., "Letters of Barnett Hardeman Cody and Others, 1861-1864," *GHQ*, Vol. XXIII, No. 3, pp. 293–294, 296, 375.

18. Ibid., pp. 211–212; William C. Oates to Homer R. Stoughton, November 22, 1888, Sterne Library, Special Collections, University of Alabama, Tuscaloosa, Alabama; Oates Account, BCL.

19. Margaret Pace Farmer, Records of Confederate Soldiers 1861-65, Pike County, Alabama, Papers Of The Pike County Historical And Genealogical Society, Troy, Alabama, (Troy, AL: The Pike County Civil War Centennial Commission, 1962), p. 211; Norton, *The Attack And Defense of Little Round Top*, pp. 235, 256–257; Laine and Penny, *Law's Alabama Brigade*, p. 24.

20. Farmer, "Records of Confederate Soldiers," pp. 211–212; Tucker, *High Tide At Gettysburg*, pp. 252–253; Norton, *The Attack And Defense of Little Round Top*, pp. 235, 299; Pullen, *The Twentieth Maine*, p. 114; Pfanz, *Gettysburg*, p. 217; Oates Account, *BCL*; Laine and Penny, *Law's Alabama Brigade*, pp. 99–100.

21. Oates, *The War Between the Union and the Confederacy*, p. 212; Desjardin, *Stand Firm*, p. 46; Laine and Penny, *Law's Alabama Brigade*, p. 100.

22. Tucker, *Lee And Longstreet At Gettysburg*, pp. 54–55, 63, 70; Stackpole, *They Met At Gettysburg*, pp. 187–188, 190–194, 204–205, 212, 219–223; McClendon, *Recollections of War Times*, pp. 142–143; Tucker, *High Tide At Gettysburg*, p. 253; Desjardin, *Stand Firm*, p. 46; A. T. Cowell, *Tactics At Gettysburg* (Gettysburg, PA: Gettysburg Compiler Print, 1910), p. 52; Mark Nesbitt, *Through Blood & Fire* (Mechanicsburg, PA: Stackpole Books, 1996) pp. 67–68; Abbott Spear, Andrea C. Hawkes, Marie H. McCosh, Craig L. Symonds, and Michael H. Alpert, eds., *The Civil War Recollections of General Ellis Spear* (Orono: The University of Maine Press, 1997), p. 311; Laine and Penny, *Law's Alabama Brigade*, pp. 95–100.

23. O.R., vol. 27, series I, pt. II, pp. 317–319, 392; Stackpole, *They Met At Gettysburg*, pp. 193–194; Tucker, *Lee And Longstreet At Gettysburg*, p.

55; Tucker, *High Tide At Gettysburg*, pp. 253–256; Coddington, *The Gettysburg Campaign*, pp. 391–392; Mitchell B. Houghton and William R. Houghton, *Two Boys in the Civil War and After* (Montgomery, AL: The Paragon Press, 1912), pp. 33, 54; Oates, *The War Between the Union and the Confederacy*, pp. 210, 212–214, 221, 585–586, 775; D. H. Russell, "Had Jackson Been At Gettysburg," *Confederate Veteran*, Vol. XXI, (October 1913), p. 494; Jordan, *Events And Incidents During The Civil War*, p. 91; Foote, *The Civil War*, Vol. II, p. 502; Norton, *The Attack And Defense of Little Round Top*, pp. 13, 21, 135–136, 297–298; Pfanz, *Gettysburg*, pp. 205–206, 217–218; Pullen, *The Twentieth Maine*, pp. 114–115; Joshua Lawrence Chamberlain, *Through Blood & Fire At Gettysburg, General Joshua Lawrence Chamberlain*, (Gettysburg, PA: Stan Clark Military Books, 1994), pp. 5–6; Fitzhugh Lee, *General Lee, A Biography of Robert E. Lee*, (NY: Da Capo Press, 1994), p. 280; Oates Account, *BCL*; Alexander, *Fighting For The Confederacy*, p. 241; Cowell, *Tactics At Gettysburg*, pp. 48, 51; Nesbitt, *Through Blood & Fire*, p. 68; W. C. Ward, "Incidents and Personal Experiences on the Battlefield at Gettysburg," *Confederate Veteran*, vol. 8, (August, 1900), p. 347; Laine and Penny, *Law's Alabama Brigade*, pp. 1–2, 30–31, 60–61, 85, 93–100, 133; Polley, *Hood's Texas Brigade*, p. 170; Spear, Hawkes, Symonds, McCosh, and Alpert, eds., *The Civil War Recollections of General Ellis Spear*, pp. 311–315; Perry, *Conceived in Liberty*, pp. 218–219.

Chapter X

1. Tucker, *High Tide At Gettysburg*, p. 256; Coddington, *The Gettysburg Campaign*, pp. 389–390; Norton, *The Attack And Defense of Little Round Top*, p. 27; Chamberlain, *Through Blood & Fire At Gettysburg*, pp. 7–9; Oates, *The War Between the Union and the Confederacy*, p. 222; Gerrish, *Army Life*, p. 107; Polley, *Hood's Texas Brigade*, p. 173; Compiled Service Records of Union Soldiers Who Served in Organizations from the State of Maine, National Archives, Washington, D.C.; Spear, Hawkes, Symonds, McCosh, and Alpert, eds., *The Civil War Recollections of General Ellis Spear*, pp. 314–315; Laine and Penny, *Law's Alabama Brigade*, pp. 90–96; *New Orleans Picayune*, September 18, 1898; Earl Schenck Miers and Richard A. Brown, *Gettysburg* (Armonk: M.E. Sharpe, 1996), pp. 119–120.

2. Nesbitt, *Through Blood & Fire*, pp. 19, 28, 31, 34; Miers and Brown, *Gettysburg*, p. 119.

3. Amos M. Judson, *History of the Eighty-Third Regiment Pennsylvania Volunteers*, (Dayton: Morningside Bookshop, 1986), pp. xi–xiv, 8–11, 17–26, 125; Norton, *The Attack and Defense of Little Round Top*, pp. 221–222.

4. Judson, *History of the Eighty-Third*, pp. xii, 55–79, 86–90, 100–109, 123–124.

5. Ibid., p. 125.

6. Coddington, *The Gettysburg Campaign*, pp. 389–390; Foote, *The Civil War*, Vol. II, p. 505; Norton, *The Attack And Defense of Little Round Top*, p. 71; Gerrish, *Army Life*, p. 106; Judson, *History of the Eighty-Third*, p. 116, 125.

7. A. H. Belo, "The Battle of Gettysburg," *Confederate Veteran*, Vol. VIII, (April 1900), p. 168; Oates, *The War Between the Union and the Confederacy*, p. 775; Pullen, *The Twentieth Maine*, p. 116; Laine and Penny, *Law's Alabama Brigade*, pp. 4–8, 97–99; Polley, *Hood's Texas Brigade*, p. 177; *New Orleans Picayune*, September 18, 1898; Judson, *History of the Eighty-Third*, pp. 125–127; Jeffrey D. Stocker, *From Huntsville to Appomattox, R. T. Coles's History of 4th Regiment, Alabama Volunteer Infantry, C.S.A., Army of Northern Virginia* (Knoxville: University of Tennessee Press, 1996) pp. 9–109.

8. Oates, *The War Between the Union and the Confederacy*, pp. 214–217; Desjardin, *Stand Firm*, pp. 50–51; Gerrish, *Army Life*, p. 106; Nesbitt, *Through Blood & Fire*, pp. 6–7, 31; CASR, NA; Laine and Penny, *Law's Alabama Brigade*, pp. 20–21, 99–101; Perry, *Conceived In Liberty*, pp. 381–383; CMSR; Spear, Hawkes, McCosh, Symonds, and Alpert, eds., *The Civil War Recollections of General Ellis Spear*, pp. 4, 7, 32–33; *New Orleans Picayune*, September 18, 1898; Miers and Brown, *Gettysburg*, p. 120; Judson, *History of the Eighty-Third*, p. 127; Perry, *Conceived in Liberty*, pp. 208–209.

9. Norton, *The Attack And Defense of Little Round Top*, p. 47; Judson, *History of the Eighty-third*, pp. 126–127.

10. Oates, *The War Between the Union and the Confederacy*, pp. 212, 214; Norton, *The Attack And Defense of Little Round Top*, p. 47; Styple, ed., *With a Flash of His Sword*, pp. 77, 82; Gerrish, *Army Life*, p. 108; Laine and Penny, *Law's Alabama Brigade*, pp. 101–102; *New Orleans Picayune*, September 18, 1898; Judson, *History of the Eighty-Third*, pp. 126–127.

11. Oates, *The War Between the Union and the Confederacy*, p. 586; Desjardin, *Stand Firm*, p. 42; Norton, *The Attack And Defense Of Little Round Top*, p. 111; Oates Account, BCL; Brian C. Pohanka, *Don*

Troiani's Civil War, (Mechanicsburg, PA: Stackpole Books, 1995), p. 106; Spear, Hawkes, McCosh, Symonds, and Alpert, eds., *The Civil War Recollections of General Ellis Spear,* p. 6; Laine and Penny, *Law's Alabama Brigade,* pp. 101–102.

12. Oates, *The War Between the Union and the Confederacy,* p. 214; Foote, *The Civil War,* Vol. II, p. 503; Laine and Penny, *Law's Alabama Brigade,* pp. 101–103.
13. Oates, *The War Between the Union and the Confederacy,* pp. 677–678; Laine and Penny, *Law's Alabama Brigade,* pp. 101–103.
14. O.R., vol. XXVII, series I, pt. II, p. 392; Laine and Penny, *Law's Alabama Brigade,* pp. 101–103.
15. Jordon, *Some Events And Incidents During The Civil War,* pp. 42–44, 53; Oates, *The War Between the Union and the Confederacy,* pp. 214, 600–602; Pohanka, *Don Troiani's Civil War,* p. 107; Laine and Penny, *Law's Alabama Brigade,* pp. 101–103.
16. Elisha Coan Manuscript, Coan Papers, Hawthorne-Longfellow Library Special Collections, Bowdoin College, Brunswick, Maine.
17. Oates, *The War Between the Union and the Confederacy,* p. 214; Desjardin, *Stand Firm,* p. 52; O.R., vol. XXVII, ser. I, pt. II, pp. 392–393; Laine and Penny, *Law's Alabama Brigade,* pp. 101–103.
18. Pullen, *The Twentieth Maine,* p. 115; Desjardin, *Stand Firm,* pp. 54–55; Oates, *The War Between the Union and the Confederacy,* p. 214; Norton, *The Attack And Defense of Little Round Top,* p. 39; Laine and Penny, *Law's Alabama Brigade,* pp. 101–103.
19. Desjardin, *Stand Firm,* pp. 52–54; Pullen, *The Twentieth Maine,* p. 117; Chamberlain, *Through Blood & Fire At Gettysburg,* pp. 14–15; Gerrish, *Army Life,* pp. 105–107; Nesbitt, *Through Blood & Fire,* pp. 52, 70, 112. Spear, Hawkes, McCosh, Symonds, and Alpert, eds., *The Civil War Recollections of General Ellis Spear,* pp. 33–34; Laine and Penny, *Law's Alabama Brigade,* p. 103.

Chapter XI

1. Oates, *The War Between the Union and the Confederacy,* pp. 214, 218; *New Orleans Picayune,* September 18, 1898; CASR, NA; Laine and Penny, *Law's Alabama Brigade,* p. 101; Judson, *History of the Eighty-Third,* p. 127.
2. Coddington, *The Gettysburg Campaign,* p. 393; Oates, *The War Between The Union and The Confederacy,* pp. 52–54, 216; Pullen, *The Twentieth*

Maine, pp. 117–118; Styple, *With a Flash of His Sword,* pp. 77, 82–83; Gerrish, *Army Life,* p. 107; Nesbitt, *Through Blood & Fire,* pp. 70–71, 74–75, 80–81; Spear, Hawkes, McCosh, Symonds, and Alpert, eds., *The Civil War Recollections of General Ellis Spear,* pp. 33–34; Laine and Penny, *Law's Alabama Brigade,* p. 103; Judson, *History of the Eighty-Third,* pp. xii, 128–129.

3. Desjardin, *Stand Firm,* p. 54; Norton, *The Attack And Defense of Little Round Top,* p. 29; CASR; Pullen, *The Twentieth Maine,* pp. 118–119; Styple, ed., *With a Flash of His Sword,* p. 82; O.R., vol. XXVII, series I, pt. II, p. 393; Nesbitt, *Through Blood & Fire,* pp. 80–81; Spear, Hawkes, McCosh, Symonds, and Alpert, eds., *The Civil War Recollections of General Ellis Spear,* pp. 33–34.

4. Styple, ed., *With a Flash of His Sword,* p. 77; Nesbitt, *Through Blood & Fire,* p. 75; Spear, Hawkes, McCosh, Symonds, and Alpert, eds., *The Civil War Recollections of General Ellis Spear,* p. 34.

5. CASR; Oates, *The War Between The Union and The Confederacy,* pp. 612–613; Billman, ed., "Joseph M. Ellison: War Letters (1862)," *GHQ,* p. 229.

6. Oates, *The War Between the Union and the Confederacy,* pp. 71, 613–614.

7. Gerrish, *Army Life,* p. 108; Nesbitt, *Through Blood and Fire,* p. 75; Spear, Hawkes, McCosh, Symonds, and Alpert, eds., *The Civil War Recollections of General Ellis Spear,* pp. 34–35; *New Orleans Picayune,* September 18, 1898; Laine and Penny, *Law's Alabama Brigade,* p. 103.

8. Oates, *The War Between the Union and the Confederacy,* pp. 673–674, 218; CASR.

9. Oates, *The War Between The Union and The Confederacy,* pp. 707–708, 714, 732–733, 738; Laine and Penny, *Law's Alabama Brigade,* pp. 101–103; CASR, NA.

10. Oates, *The War Between the Union and the Confederacy,* p. 54; Spear, Hawkes, McCosh, Symonds, and Alpert, eds., *The Civil War Recollections of General Ellis Spear,* pp. 34–35; Laine and Penny, *Law's Alabama Brigade,* p. 103.

11. Oates, *The War Between the Union and the Confederacy,* pp. 218, 744–745; CASR; Chamberlain, *Through Blood & Fire At Gettysburg,* p. 21; CASR; Pullen, *The Twentieth Maine,* pp. 117–118; Styple, ed., *With a Flash of His Sword,* p. 111; Desjardin, *Stand Firm,* p. 55; Pohanka, *Don Troiani's Civil War,* p. 106; Nesbitt, *Through Blood & Fire,* pp. 19, 28, 36; Spear, Hawkes, McCosh, Symonds, and Alpert, eds., *The Civil War Recollections of General Ellis Spear,* pp. 28, 34–35; Polley, *Hood's Texas*

Brigade, p. 177; *New Orleans Picayune*, September 18, 1898; Laine and Penny, *Law's Alabama Brigade*, p. 103; Judson, *History of the Eighty-third*, p. 128.

12. Norton, *The Attack And Defense of Little Round Top*, pp. 17, 22, 29, 52; Desjardin, *Stand Firm*, p. 55; Styple, ed., *With a Flash of His Sword*, pp. 76–81; Oates, *The War Between the Union and The Confederacy*, p. 727.

13. Gerrish, *Army Life*, pp. 108–109.

14. Oates, *The War Between the Union and the Confederacy*, pp. 218, 688; Desjardin, *Stand Firm*, p. 65; Laine and Penny, *Law's Alabama Brigade*, pp. 103–104.

15. Nesbitt, *Through Blood & Fire*, p. 81.

16. Oates, *The War Between The Union and the Confederacy*, p. 215.

17. Gerrish, *Army Life*, p. 109; Nesbitt, *Through Blood & Fire*, p. 84.

18. Oates, *The War Between the Union and the Confederacy*, pp. 218, 226, 675–676; McClendon, *Recollections of War Times*, p. 15; Burnett, ed., "Letters of Barnett Hardeman Cody and Others, 1861-1864," *GHQ*, Vol. XXIII, Pt. II, p. 370; Laine and Penny, *Law's Alabama Brigade*, pp. 103–104; CASR, NA.

19. CASR, NA; Oates, *The War Between the Union and the Confederacy*, pp. 674, 727; Desjardin, *Stand Firm*, p. 67; Nesbitt, *Through Blood & Fire*, p. 74; Laine and Penny, *Law's Alabama Brigade*, pp. 103–104.

20. Oates, *The War Between the Union and the Confederacy*, p. 218; Styple, ed., *With a Flash of His Sword*, p. 113; Laine and Penny, *Law's Alabama Brigade*, pp. 103–104; CASR, NA.

21. CASR; Oates, *The War Between The Union and The Confederacy*, p. 717; Spear, Spear, Hawkes, McCosh, Symonds, and Alpert, eds., *The Civil War Recollections of General Ellis Spear*, pp. 34–35; Laine and Penny, *Law's Alabama Brigade*, p. 107.

22. Styple, ed., *With a Flash of His Sword*, p. 77; Nesbitt, *Through Blood & Fire*, pp. 72–73; Coco, *Killed In Action*, pp. 41–42, 53–54; Laine and Penny, *Law's Alabama Brigade*, pp. 103–104; Judson, *History of the Eighty-Third*, p. 128.

23. Oates, *The War Between The Union and the Confederacy*, pp. 749–750, 753, 755; Joseph G. Bilby, *Remember Fontenoy! The 69th New York And The Irish Brigade In The Civil War*, (Hightstown, NJ: Longstreet House, 1995), pp. 97, 249; Styple, *With a Flash of His Sword*, p. 133; Desjardin, *Stand Firm*, p. 65; Laine and Penny, *Law's Alabama Brigade*, pp. 103–104.

24. Oates, *The War Between the Union and the Confederacy*, pp. 745, 749,

753, 755–757; "Casualties of the Alabama Regiments, Figures From The 15th and 47th Alabama, Archives, Gettysburg National Military Park," Gettysburg, Pennsylvania; CASR, NA; Laine and Penny, *Law's Alabama Brigade*, pp. 103–104.

Chapter XII

1. Jordan, *Some Events And Incidents During The Civil War*, pp. 63, 89; CASR; Norton, *The Attack And Defense of Little Round Top*, pp. 261, 266; Oates, *The War Between the Union and the Confederacy*, pp. 219, 227, 600, 606, 676, 688; Pfanz, *Gettysburg*, p. 233; Chamberlain, *Through Blood & Fire At Gettysburg*, pp. 14–17; Desjardin, *Stand Firm*, pp. 57–58; Oates to Chamberlain, April 14, 1905, *Pejepscot Historical Society*, Brunswick, Maine; Gerrish, *Army Life*, pp. 109–110; Francis Trevelyan Miller, *The Photographic History of the Civil War, Two Years of Grim War*, (10 vols., NY: Castle Books, 1957), p. 253; Spear, Hawkes, Symonds, McCosh, and Alpert, eds., *The Civil War Recollections of General Ellis Spear*, pp. 313–314; Laine and Penny, *Law's Alabama Brigade*, pp. 103–104; *New Orleans Picayune*, September 18, 1898; Judson, *History of the Eighty-third*, pp. 128–129.
2. Norton, *The Attack And Defense of Little Round Top*, p. 261; Coddington, *The Gettysburg Campaign*, p. 393; Pfanz, *Gettysburg*, p. 233; CASR, NA; Laine and Penny, *Law's Alabama Brigade*, p. 104.
3. Willard M. Wallace, *Soul Of The Lion, A Biography Of General Joshua L. Chamberlain* (Gettysburg, PA: Stan Clark Military Books, 1991), pp. 94, 102; Joshua Lawrence Chamberlain, *"Bayonet! Forward," My Civil War Reminiscences*, (Gettysburg, PA: Stan Clark Military Books, 1994), p. 27; "Maine At Gettysburg," Report of Maine Commissioners, Prepared by The Executive Committee, (Gettysburg, PA; Stan Clark Military Books, 1994), p. 255; Styple, ed., *With a Flash of His Sword*, pp. viii, ix, 78, 83; Nesbitt, *Through Blood & Fire*, pp. 6, 75; Pullen, *The Twentieth Maine*, p. 120; Spear, Hawkes, McCosh, Symonds, and Alpert, eds., *The Civil War Recollections of General Ellis Spear*, pp. 34, 314; CASR, NA; Laine and Penny, *Law's Alabama Brigade*, pp. 103–104.
4. Chamberlain, *Through Blood & Fire At Gettysburg*, pp. 17–18; Desjardin, *Stand Firm*, p. 61; Laine and Penny, *Law's Alabama Brigade*, pp. 103–104; Perry, *Conceived in Liberty*, p. 223.
5. Wallace, *Soul of the Lion*, pp. 99–101; *Lincoln County News*, March 13, 1885; Styple, ed., *With a Flash of His Sword*, p. 83; *The Orleans Picayune*,

September 18, 1898; Laine and Penny, *Law's Alabama Brigade in the War Between the Union and the Confederacy*, pp. 101–106; Judson, *History of the Eighty-Third*, pp. 128–129.

6. Chamberlain, *Through Blood & Fire At Gettysburg*, pp. 18–19; *Maine at Gettysburg*, p. 261; Spear, Hawkes, Symonds, McCosh, and Alpert, eds., *The Civil War Recollections of General Ellis Spear*, p. 34; Laine and Penny, *Law's Alabama Brigade*, pp. 104–106; Judson, *History of the Eighty-third*, p. 129.

7. Chamberlain, *Through Blood & Fire*, p. 21; Abner Doubleday, *Chancellorsville And Gettysburg*, (NY: Da Capo Press, 1994), p. 170; Oates Account, BCL; Laine and Penny, *Law's Alabama Brigade*, pp. 104–106; Judson, *History of the Eighty-Third*, pp. 128–129.

8. Chamberlain, *Through Blood & Fire*, pp. 21–22; Styple, ed., *With a Flash of His Sword*, pp. 78, 114; Laine and Penny, *Law's Alabama Brigade*, p. 104.

9. Oates, *The War Between The Union and the Confederacy*, pp. 215, 219–221; Oates to Chamberlain, April 14, 1905, *Pejepscot Historical Society*, Brunswick, Maine; Pullen, *The Twentieth Maine*, pp. 126–127; Spear, Hawkes, Symonds, McCosh, and Alpert, eds., *The Civil War Recollections of General Ellis Spear*, pp. 33–34, 215; Laine and Penny, *Law's Alabama Brigade*, pp. 104–106, 343; CASR, NA; Miers and Brown, *Gettysburg*, pp. 127–128; Judson, *History of the Eighty-Third*, p. xi–xii.

10. Desjardin, *Stand Firm*, pp. 65–67, 143; Spear, Hawkes, Symonds, McCosh, and Alpert, eds. *The Civil War Recollections of General Ellis Spear*, p. 215; *The Daily Picayune*, September 18, 1898; Judson, *History of the Eighty-third*, pp. xi–xii.

11. Oates Account, BCL; Gerrish, *Army Life*, p. 110; Spear, Hawkes, Symonds, McCosh, and Alpert, eds., *The Civil War Recollections of General Ellis Spear*, p. 215.

12. Oates, *The War Between the Union and the Confederacy*, 221; Laine and Penny, *Law's Alabama Brigade*, p. 104.

13. Styple, ed., *With a Flash of His Sword*, pp. 77, 112; Oates, *The War Between the Union and the Confederacy*, p. 221; Spear, Hawkes, Symonds, McCosh, and Alpert, eds., *The Civil War Recollections of General Ellis Spear*, pp. 37, 127; Pullen, *The Twentieth Maine*, p. 213.

14. Styple, ed., *With a Flash of His Sword*, pp. 83, 114; Desjardin, *Stand Firm*, pp. 74–75; Pullen, *The Twentieth Maine*, p. 289; Laine and Penny, *Law's Alabama Brigade*, p. 106.

15. Oates Account, *BCL*; Oates, *The War Between the Union and the Confederacy*, pp. 219, 221, 620, 725; Laine and Penny, *Law's Alabama Brigade*, pp. 46, 106; CASR, NA; Spear, Hawkes, Symonds, McCosh, and Alpert, eds., *The Civil War Recollections of General Ellis Spear*, p. 35.
16. Oates Account, *BCL*; Laine and Penny, *Law's Alabama Brigade*, p. 106.
17. Oates Account, *BCL*, pp. 620, 725; CASR, NA; Laine and Penny, *Law's Alabama Brigade*, p. 106.
18. Oates Account, *BCL*; O.R., Vol. XXVII, ser. I, pt. II, p. 393; Oates, *The War Between the Union and the Confederacy*, p. 220; Spear, Hawkes, Symonds, McCosh, and Alpert, eds., *The Civil War Recollections of General Ellis Spear*, pp. 35, 315; Laine and Penny, *Law's Alabama Brigade*, pp. 106–107.

Chapter XIII

1. Oates, *The War Between the Union and the Confederacy*, pp. 216, 219; Spear, Hawkes, Symonds, McCosh, and Alpert, eds., *The Civil War Recollections of General Ellis Spear*, p. 35; Laine and Penny, *Law's Alabama Brigade*, p. 106.
2. Styple, ed., *With a Flash of His Sword*, pp. 115, 133, 139; Gerrish, *Army Life*, pp. 109–111; Spear, Hawkes, Symonds, McCosh, and Alpert, eds., *The Civil War Recollections of General Ellis Spear*, pp. 34–36, 315–316; Laine and Penny, *Law's Alabama Brigade*, p. 107.
3. Styple, ed., *With a Flash of His Sword*, pp. 115–116, 143; Nesbitt, *Through Blood & Fire*, pp. 77, 85; Laine and Penny, *Law's Alabama Brigade*, p. 107.
4. Oates, *The War Between the Union and the Confederacy*, pp. 771–772; Chamberlain, *Through Blood & Fire At Gettysburg*, pp. 23–24; Laine and Penny, *Law's Alabama Brigade*, p. 107.
5. Oates, *The War Between the Union and the Confederacy*, pp. 113–114, 143; Sword, *Sharpshooter*, p. 57; Spear, Hawkes, Symonds, McCosh, Alpert, eds., *The Civil War Recollections of General Ellis Spear*, pp. 34–35; Laine and Penny, *Law's Alabama Brigade*, p. 107.
6. Sword, *Sharpshooter*, p. 57; Jordan, *Some Events And Incidents During The Civil War*, p. 43; Desjardin, *Stand Firm*, p. 64; Oates, *The War Between the Union and the Confederacy*, p. 220; Spear, Hawkes, Symonds, McCosh, and Alpert, eds., *The Civil War Recollections of General Ellis Spear*, pp. 35–36; Laine and Penny, *Law's Alabama Brigade*, p. 107; Judson, *History of the Eighty-third*, p. 126.
7. Jordan, *Some Events And Incidents During The Civil War*, pp. 44–45;

Pullen, *The Twentieth Maine*, pp. 13, 125–126; Spear, Hawkes, Symonds, McCosh, and Alpert, eds., *The Civil War Recollections of General Ellis Spear*, pp. 34–36, 314–315; Laine and Penny, *Law's Alabama Brigade*, p. 107.

8. Styple, ed., *With a Flash of His Sword*, p. 301; Desjardin, *Stand Firm*, pp. 71–75; CASR; O.R., Vol. XXVII, ser. I, pt. II, p. 393; Oates, *The War Between The Union and the Confederacy*, pp. 216, 220; Gerrish, *Army Life*, pp. 111, 119; Gregory A. Coco, *Wasted Valor, The Confederate Dead at Gettysburg*, (Gettysburg, PA: Thomas Publications, 1990), p. 32; Spear, Hawkes, Symonds, McCosh, and Alpert, eds., *The Civil War Recollections of General Ellis Spear*, pp. 35, 316, 361; Laine and Penny, *Law's Alabama Brigade*, pp. 107–108; Judson, *History of the Eighty-third*, pp. 133–134.

9. CASR; John W. Busey and David G. Martin, *Regimental Strengths and Losses at Gettysburg*, (Hightstown, NJ: Longstreet House, 1994), pp. 248, 280; McClendon, *Recollections of War Times*, p. 180; Desjardin, *Stand Firm*, p. 196; Laine and Penny, *Law's Alabama Brigade*, pp. 111, 119, 121; Perry, *Conceived in Liberty*, 231.

10. Jordan, *Some Events And Incidents During The Civil War*, p. 44; CASR, NA.

11. Casualties of the Alabama Regiments, Figures from the 15th and 47th Alabama, Gettysburg National Military Park Archives, Gettysburg, Pennsylvania; CASR, NA; Styple, ed., *With A Flash of His Sword*, p. 118; Oates, *The War Between the Union and the Confederacy*, p. 675; Laine and Penny, *Law's Alabama Brigade*, p. 119.

12. Casualties of the Alabama Regiments, Figures from the 15th and 47th Alabama, Gettysburg National Military Park Archives; Oates, *The War Between The Union and the Confederacy*, pp. 592, 765–766, 770; CASR, NA.

13. Nesbitt, *Through Blood & Fire*, pp. 78–79, 95, 97–98; Spear, Hawkes, Symonds, McCosh, and Alpert, eds., *The Civil War Recollections of General Ellis Spear*, pp. 215, 317, 361; CASR, NA; Miers and Brown, *Gettysburg*, pp. 132–133.

14. Oates, *The War Between the Union and the Confederacy*, p. 225; Spear, Hawkes, Symonds, McCosh, and Alpert, eds., *The Civil War Recollections of Ellis Spear*, pp. 312–317; Laine and Penny, *Law's Alabama Brigade*, pp. 119–121; Judson, *History of the Eighty-Third*, pp. xi–xii.

15. Oates, *The War Between the Union and the Confederacy*, p. 239; Laine and Penny, *Law's Alabama Brigade*, pp. 119–121.

Chapter XIV

1. Luvass and Nelson, eds., *Guide to the Battle of Gettysburg*, p. 196; Wallace, *Soul Of The Lion*, p. 104; Chamberlain, *Through Blood & Fire At Gettysburg*, pp. 22–26; Oates, *The War Between the Union and the Confederacy*, pp. 207–208, 222; Gerrish, *Army Life*, p. 105; Laine and Penny, *Law's Alabama Brigade*, pp. 119–121; Miers and Brown, *Gettysburg*, p. 119; Judson, *History of the Eighty-Third*, pp. 131–132; Perry, *Conceived in Liberty*, p. 226.
2. Styple, ed., *With a Flash of His Sword*, p. 248; Laine and Penny, *Law's Alabama Brigade*, pp. 119–121.
3. Oates, *The War Between the Union and the Confederacy*, p. 227.

Index